Puppets and Puppetry

Position of manipulators at the leaning bar

Puppets and Puppetry

Peter Fraser

STEIN AND DAY/*Publishers*/New York

First published in the United States of America in 1982

Printed in the United States of America

STEIN AND DAY/*Publishers*
Scarborough House
Briarcliff Manor, New York 10510

Library of Congress Cataloging in Publication Data

Fraser, Peter 1932–
Puppets and puppetry

Bibliography: p.
Includes index.
1. Puppet making. 2. Puppets and puppet-plays. I. Title.
TT174.7.F72 1981 745.592′ 24 81-40328
ISBN 0-8128-2830-5 AACR2

Contents

American readers please note the following equivalent terms or alternative materials

glove puppets = hand puppets
card = thin white cardboard
celluloid = acetate
craft knife = mat knife
fuse wire = any fairly pliable wire
sugar paper = construction paper
G-clamp = C-clamp
timber = lumber

The metric and imperial measurements are not exact equivalents but are convenient sizes in each system.

Figure 1 A Victorian children's theatre print

Introduction

Puppets may be classified in many different ways: by the country of their origin; whether they are manipulated from above, below or from the side; or whether they are flat or solid. Until recently the puppets most often seen in European countries have been Glove puppets and Marionettes. In this book I have given more space to these types than to others. All puppets however have their own nature and potential, well worth exploring using the same principles of construction and leverage.

When choosing puppets for a performance, the advantages and limitations of each type should be considered:

1 *The flat cut-out figures* of the traditional Victorian children's theatre may not strictly speaking be termed puppets. I have included them because in a contemporary form they can introduce young children to the theatre itself, and to more advanced puppetry.

2 *Shadow puppets*, being flat, are very quickly made. Many performers can work together behind a wide screen presenting scenes of spectacle and procession. Shadow puppets are principally a visual art. Probably the most beautiful puppets ever made belong to this group.

3 *Rod puppets* are being shown increasingly often, sometimes in performance with live actors. Their great advantage is that they can successfully be made to any size, suitable for performance in quite large theatres. Glove puppets are limited in scale to the manipulator's hand, and there are weight-bearing considerations in the use of marionettes.

4 *Glove puppets* provide a very close link between performer and puppet, and are particularly good in lively action with strong characterisation. Puppets are sometimes used as a mask or *persona* from behind which the performer can feel safe to reveal aspects of himself. Glove puppets are most often chosen for such projection techniques because of their directness of control unimpeded by rods or strings.

5 *Marionettes* are the most difficult of all puppets to make and manipulate, but they offer an extra range of expression through complete body movement, and all the extra opportunities for design in depth of grouping, scenery and floor pattern.

Upon the basis of these standard types many new combinations can be made, but a good designer will always respect the natural scale of each, and exploit rather than disregard their limitations.

Construction and *Dramatic Presentation* are two linked but divisible elements of puppetry, and not all puppet enthusiasts are equally skilled or interested in both. The stronger tradition in this country has always been in skilful and ingenious construction, probably last seen at its best in the great Tiller and Barnard Troupes of the late nineteenth century, when contemporary music hall and circus acts were reflected in marionette presentations.

Trick mechanisms can be as fascinating to adults as to children, but increasingly since those days puppetry has tended to become an activity for children only, very well done on television and ably used to further educational and treatment aims, but not an adult art form comparable with that of the Far East.

During the last few years however the picture has become more encouraging. A new vitality in the use of puppetry has been seen in the presentation of puppets alongside live actors, not merely in clever simulation of human movement, but working expressively in a theatre of ideas. Here puppets take a place of major importance, performing once again for adults in new and experimental ways very promising for the future. The construction of such puppets will demand skills of the highest order in modelling and carving from the artists who make them; but in whatever way puppets develop, methods of construction and principles of leverage in movement will still remain based on the traditional skills which I have attempted to describe in this book.

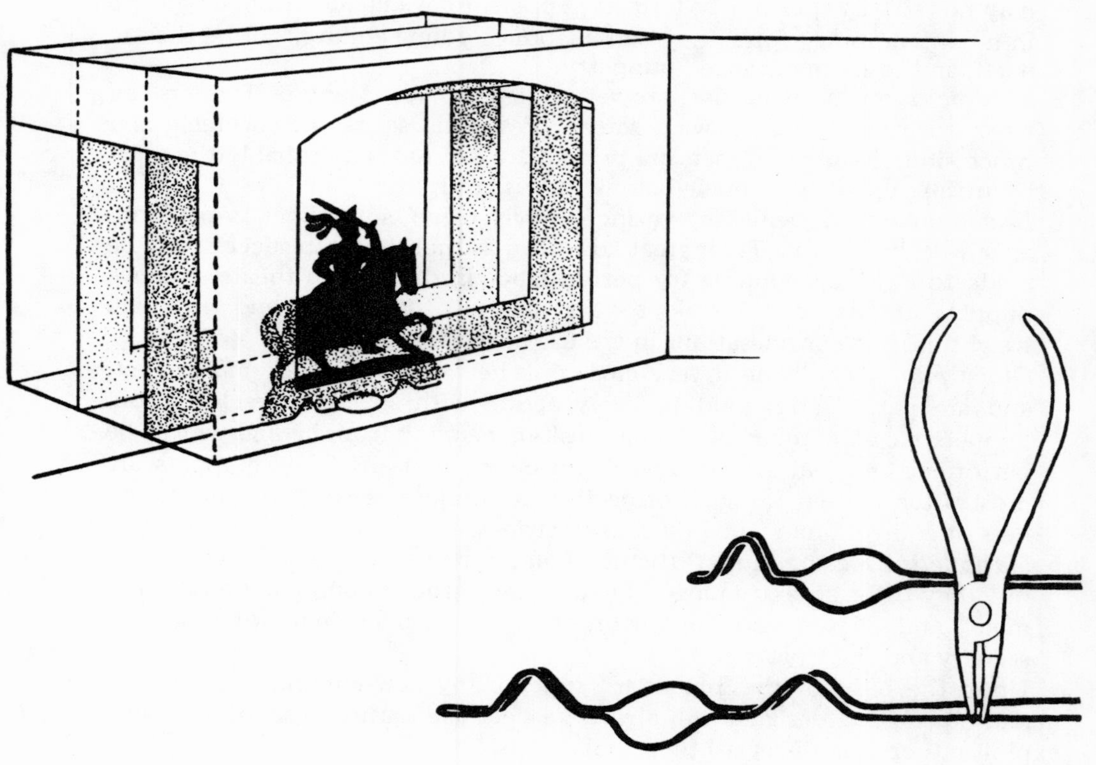

Figure 2 Cardboard theatre and wire bracket holders

The Children's Theatre

The traditional children's theatre belongs to Victorian days. In the nineteenth century prints of characters and scenery from the popular dramas of the time were sold 'penny plain and twopence coloured'. These prints were cut out, mounted on card, each actor being moved on and off the stage by means of a wire from the side of the toy theatre. The Victorian children's theatre has now become the property of the antique dealer, although reprints have occasionally been available. However, modern adaptation of the early children's theatre can give a great deal of amusement as a children's game and is also a good introduction to puppetry and the excitement and make-believe of the theatre as a whole.

The contemporary theatre no longer supplies prints of its scenery and actors, but nowadays there are countless coloured magazines available from which pictures of people, animals, cars, ships, aeroplanes and scenery can be cut and pasted on to card. A child's imagination can soon fit these into a story. For more advanced work characters and scenery can be traced and coloured from illustrated story books.

The theatre in its simplest form is made from a series of rectangular cardboard pierced screens, the front screen being the stage opening. The cut out screens behind form side wings leading to the back screen which is not pierced. A stage floor may be laid across the lower border of the rectangular openings in the screens, or alternatively, the characters may be moved in from the side within the channels between the screens so that no mechanics of operation are visible. If you are using this second method the cut out figures must be mounted on card which raises the actor to the height of the stage opening, otherwise they will be seen only from the knees upwards. The easiest way to assemble the theatre is to cut out each part separately and then paste them together using long strips of thin paper to hinge the joints. Scenery for different performances can be hung from the top of each screen and held in place with paper clips. The general outline of each screen opening is followed, to allow a clear view of the backcloth against the rear screen.

Each actor, when cut and pasted on to card, may have a hinge of the same card turned back underneath, on which to stand. I prefer the wire brackets which give support from both sides of the flat card. These brackets are made of thin wire bent into shape by round-nosed pliers. The actors are easily fitted into these brackets when needed, and removed and packed flat between performances.

Figure 3 Shadow puppets

Shadow Puppets

Shadow puppets belong to the Far East rather than to Europe but they have been seen intermittently in this country. In the late eighteenth century shadow shows known as *ombres chinoises* were very popular in London and Paris, and more recently there have been the shadow puppet films of Lotte Reineger who brings the art to a very high standard indeed.

Shadow puppets are shown in a darkened room, held from below, against a flat semi-transparent screen, with a light behind. The jointed flat figures are cut in outline to make a black moving silhouette. This silhouette can be pierced to add to pattern or detail, and colour can be added by covering pierced work with cellophane or celluloid tinted with thin oil paint. In scenery which is either pinned to a permanent screen, or painted or pasted on changeable screens, degrees of darkness from black to grey can be made by using various thicknesses of paper.

There are two main types of shadow puppet.

1 The Chinese style of shadow figure has a main control rod attached to the base of the neck at the front, and the weight of the body partly hangs from this point. The feet rest on a ledge at the foot of the screen and the screen itself is tilted forward at the top so that the puppets may rest in position without being held. Two further rods are attached to the hands, and a second ledge below the screen supports the rods when not in use.

The amount of jointing in the Chinese shadow puppet can be considerable as the figure will hang straight from the collar attachment. The movement is simple and limited by the use of the three control rods. Although hand movements are decisive, the general body movements are sinuous and flowing.

2 A second type of shadow puppet is supported on a stick held from below and pinned or glued to the lower part of the puppet's body. Limbs are moved by a system of leverage. Thin wire runs from the inner edge of each movable joint down beside the stick, and is then twisted round the stick to make a sliding sleeve. Looking at the picture of the trumpeter you can see that by sliding down the lower sleeve the arm is raised, and by sliding down the upper sleeve the leg moves outwards. The movements of this type of puppet are vigorous and decisive rather than subtle. They are shown against an upright screen without a ledge and depend entirely on the support of the manipulator's hand to stay in position. However, a ledge can be placed below the screen and drilled with holes to house the rods of puppets which are to remain still for any length of time.

A combination of these two types of shadow puppet can be made where the figure is supported on a stick with some movements worked by leverage, and others by extra rods.

Design

In designing shadow puppets it is best to think from the beginning in terms of black and white, as this is how they will eventually appear to the audience. I never draw out designs in pencil, but start straight away with brush and indian ink and aim for a broad carrying effect before getting down to detail.

Shadow figures are most successfully designed from side view, though it is worth trying a front view figure now and again. Greek vase paintings and Egyptian wall paintings deal very well with problems of silhouette design and arrive at a side view of legs and head and arms, and a three-quarter view of the body. The Javanese shadow figures in the Victoria and Albert Museum are well worth looking at too. Costume can be used to fill out silhouettes in interesting and varied ways. The amount of movement in any figure depends on the demands of the character, but the fewer the joints the greater the stability. The height of shadow figures is entirely a matter of choice. Some of the eighteenth-century *ombres chinoises* were only 150 mm (6 in.) high, but Javanese shadow puppets are at least three times this size. Because of the limitation of movement in shadow puppets it may be necessary to design two or three varied positions of one character for different scenes in a play.

Construction

The parts of the figure are traced from your original black and white design on to stiff card which should be black if possible, or painted black. The card may vary in thickness with the height of the puppet, but should remain erect when the puppet is held upright from below.

A Cut out the broad outline of the figure first with a pair of scissors. Details and pierced work are best cut out later with a craft knife or razor blade, the card lying flat on a wooden board.

B Joints are designed on the principle of overlapping circles with a centre shaft. The simplest method of attaching joints is to thread them with fishing twine close knotted at either side. Knots should be painted with thin glue for safety.

C For Chinese shadow figures, I find that fencing wire makes a suitable rod. The end to be attached to the figure is bent into a loop with round-nosed pliers.

D A second loop of fine fuse wire can be passed through the loop on the rod and fixed to the puppet, by being glued under a small cardboard section.

E The free end of each rod should broaden to a handle grip. Adhesive tape bound round the ends soon builds up the substance needed, and can be covered with a whipping of fine cord. There is no rule for the length of the rods, but they usually project below the screen by the length of the figure itself.

With the second type of puppet I use fuse wire which is quite strong enough for the weight of leverage in cardboard limbs, and can hardly be seen where it stands free of the outline of the figure.

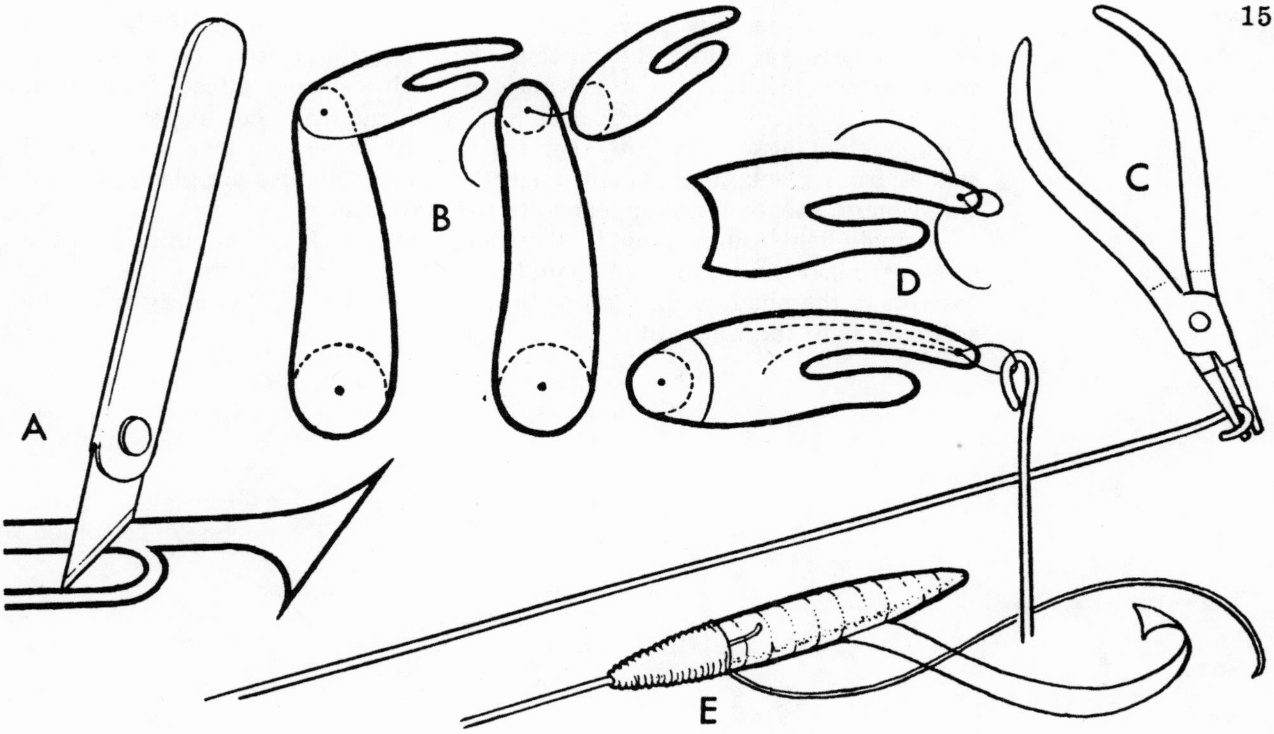

Figure 4 Cutting and jointing shadow puppets

A screen for shadow puppets

The screen for shadow puppets is made from a simple wooden frame on which thin translucent material is tightly stretched. This frame may be fitted into the proscenium opening of any theatre designed for puppets worked from below and for shadow productions the width is more important than the height.

With the Chinese style of shadow puppet, the shadow screen is tilted slightly forward at the top and has a ledge covered with some non-slip material for the puppets to rest on near the base of the performer's side of the screen. The puppet is thus supported in position against the screen and the operator need only move the limbs. A further ledge below the screen can support rods which are not being used. For shadow puppets supported on rods from below the shadow screen need not be tilted.

Scenery for shadow plays may be pinned to the cloth of the screen between acts, or, while the curtain is closed, the whole screen may be removed and another put in its place with the scenery already pinned or painted on. Scenery is quite successfully made from cut paper or card. Various thicknesses of white semi-transparent paper can give a variety of shades from black to grey. Although the shadow figures are placed behind the scenery, they will not appear so to the audience.

A single light source should be sufficient in a darkened room to light the screen from behind. The light should be high enough above the screen not to cast on it the shadow of the operator, and just far enough away from the screen to light the whole of it.

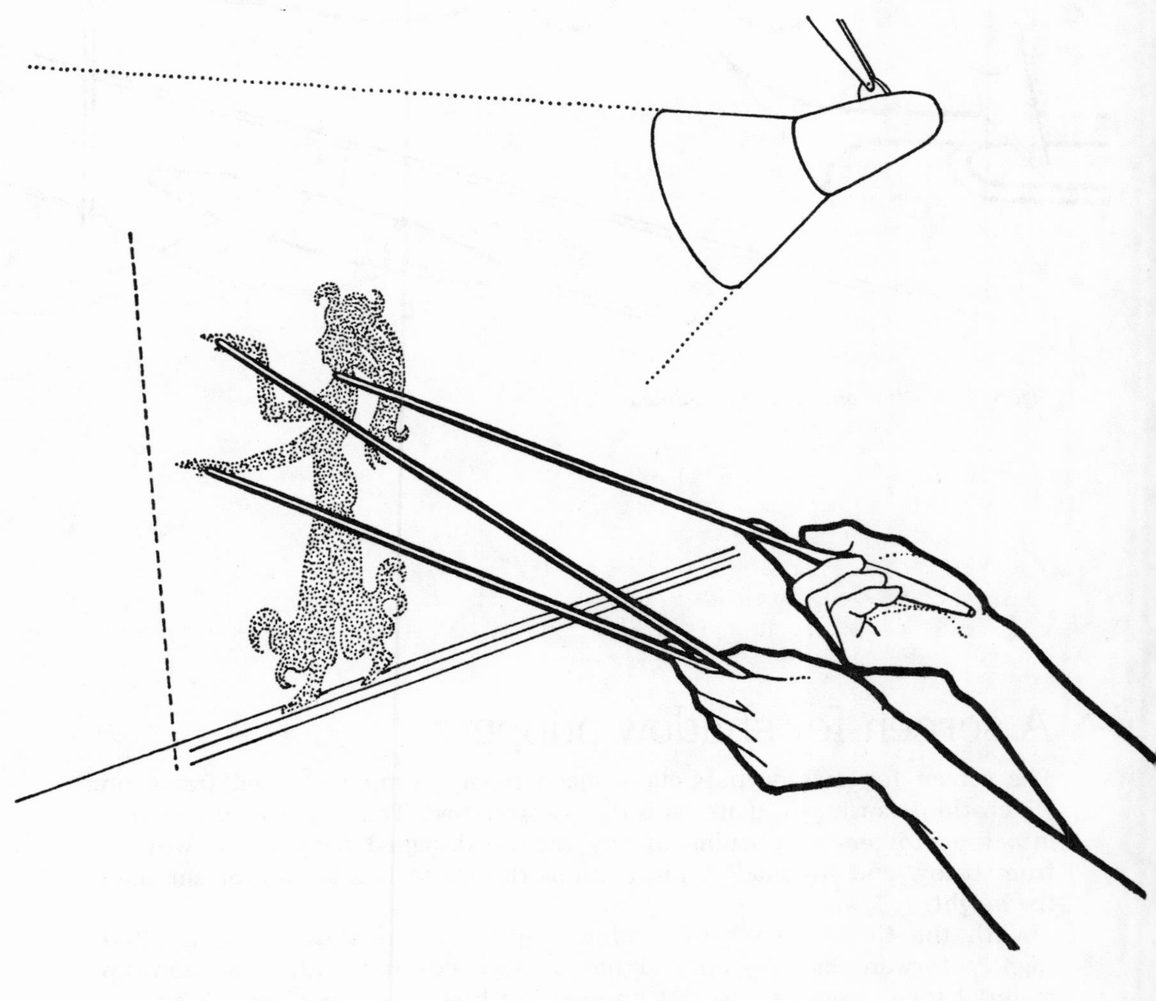

Figure 5

Rod Puppets

Rod puppets, like glove and shadow puppets, are usually worked from below. The manipulator holds the main supporting rod to the body in one hand, and with the other moves the rod attachments to the arms. The puppets themselves may be flat painted figures constructed very much in the same way as European shadow puppets, or made in solid form ranging from a simple development of the glove puppet to fully jointed figures with legs as well as arms.

Rod puppets have only a small part in the European tradition of puppetry, and until recently the best were to be seen in the Far East. However during the last fifty years these puppets have been increasingly used in America in a free and experimental approach vitally related to the contemporary theatre, and many of these productions have visited Europe.

There are certain advantages to be seen in the use of rod puppets today. They can be made to a much larger size than glove puppets whose scale must relate to the human hand, and the weight of large rod puppets is much more easily supported from below than that of marionettes on strings from above. Large rod puppets are viable economically as they can be seen from any part of a normal theatre, and may even be shown in performance with live actors.

For those who ask for movement directly related to speech, rod puppets are well suited for the additional mechanism of moving lips and eyes. Most of such movements relate to a trigger mechanism which fits very easily onto the main supporting rod and is worked by the index finger of the supporting hand. But the most impressive rod puppets I have seen possessed no other mechanism than empty sleeves and gloves into which the operator's free hand could fit while he spoke its part from behind. Well carved and modelled faces posses a life of their own whose expression is changed or intensified by changing light.

The illustrations in this section show a variety of types of rod puppet which may be made of cloth, *papier mâché* or wood. I give no details of these types of construction here as they are fully dealt with in the sections on glove puppets and marionettes. However, because of the ease with which rod puppets can be clothed, and because of the good control of arm movements by rods, I recommend a cloth body and limbs with *papier mâché* head, hands and feet.

When rod puppets are shown in a traditional puppet theatre the manipulator's arm may tire before the action is over. A projecting ledge fixed below the proscenium opening can be drilled to house the supporting rods of the puppets, which can be rotated from side to side in their housings, still continuing to make individual limb and head movements.

Construction

1 (See *figure 6.*) This is a combination of the rod and glove puppet. The head and hands may be of *papier mâché* or wood and the rods of strong wire or umbrella ribs. Umbrella ribs have a hole already pierced in one end and are usually black so that apart from trimming to length they are ready for use straight away. A loop of strong twine or thin wire passes from the rod to the attachment on the hand. With a wooden hand the attachment is a screw-eye in the palm. With a *papier mâché* hand a wire loop in the palm must be part of the original framework.

The glove body is best made from blanket material which gives an appearance of substance over the shape of the operator's hand. The arms are made of stuffed stocking material sewn close at each end, and tied tightly at the elbow joint like a division in a string of sausages. Such a body is quite convincing when dressed in loose clothing which can easily be removed for pressing and cleaning.

The movements of this puppet have more range than those of a simple glove puppet, though both of the operator's hands must be used, one in the glove with the index finger in the neck, and the other to control the hand rods. When either hand of the puppet is not in use the rod may be allowed to hang loose.

2 A short wooden dowel rod passes from inside the glove to the head of this puppet. The shoulder piece, to which the arms and glove covering are attached, is a narrow oval of wood or *papier mâché* drilled in the centre to allow for the passage of the rod. The shoulder piece rests on the index finger of the hand in the glove, and the head has the advantage over the previous puppet in being able to turn from side to side. The control of the rods to the hands prevents the whole body from turning when this movement is made.

3 The third puppet has the addition of legs free swinging from the waist. The legs like the arms can be made from stuffed stocking material but sewn across for a hinge movement at thigh, knee and ankle.

The glove for this puppet is made of dark material to be as inconspicuous as possible behind the legs. The upper part is clothed in the normal way, and the legs only in the lower part. Although there is no controlled movement of the legs, they may be swung over the proscenium ledge if the puppet is in sitting position. This movement can be quite convincing in both glove and rod puppets.

These three puppets are limited in size by the extent of the operator's arm and hands. The length of the rods is measured with the length of the manipulator's arm. When the puppet's hands are fully entended above its head, the rods should still reach beyond the operator's elbow, or the ends will show above the proscenium ledge. Clothing with any of these puppets may be drawn in at the waist to give more shape to the body.

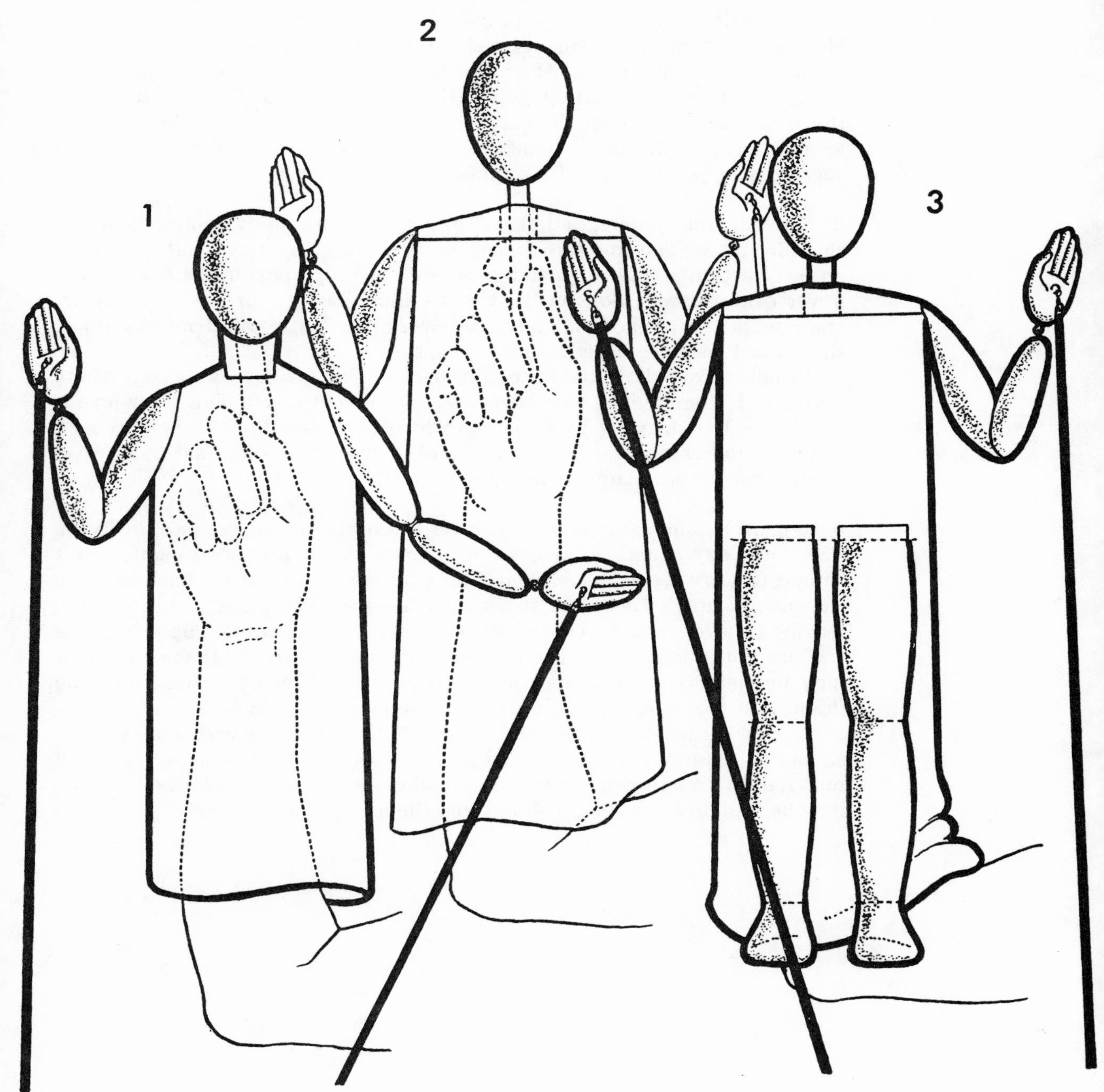

Figure 6 Rod and glove puppets

4 This is a simple design for any long clothed rod puppet of any size and is capable of much adaptation. Since the operator's hand is now held at the bottom of the rod, the shoulder piece must be supported on a disc, either of wood or metal, firmly attached to the base of the neck length. In the diagram shown the only movements performed are arm movements and head rotation. However, any extra movements within the head itself, mouth and eye movements for example, are most easily added to this type of rod puppet. The strings from the mechanisms within the head pass through holes drilled on the neck disc, and down the main control rod to a trigger mechanism convenient to the operator's hand. At the base of the main control rod a suggested supporting ledge for puppets at rest is shown.

5 In this rod puppet a hollow wire framework body hangs from the shoulder piece. The framework may be made in many ways, but here it has an oval section at the waist and another at the hip joint. In the front of the lower oval are two loops in the wire to allow passage for the leg stringing, and also, at this level of the body framework, the centre wooden rod support should be loosely confined within a wire ring.

Stringing from above the knee joint passes up to the projecting edge of the body, and from thence to a screw eye in the centre rod. This screw eye is shared by the stringing to both legs which now pass down the centre rod, though another common screw eye and outwards to each end of a swivel control bar for alternate leg raising movement.

6 Figure 8 is an example of a very large rod puppet, almost two thirds life size. The body is constructed as a wire framework to reduce weight, and is similar to the type just described. The clothing is open at the back to allow the manipulator's free hand to fit into the sleeve or glove of the puppet, leading to a very natural co-ordination of speech and gesture. Puppets of this size are not usually shown in a conventional puppet theatre; the manipulator may be clearly visible as he carries his puppet on an open stage; but the dramatic effect using the right material can be quite compelling.

Puppets of this size may also be made as flat rod puppets with a mechanism similar to shadow puppets worked by leverage. Sheet polystyrene is a useful material for this type of construction. Where weight becomes tiresome, rods may be supported in holders slung from the manipulators' belts.

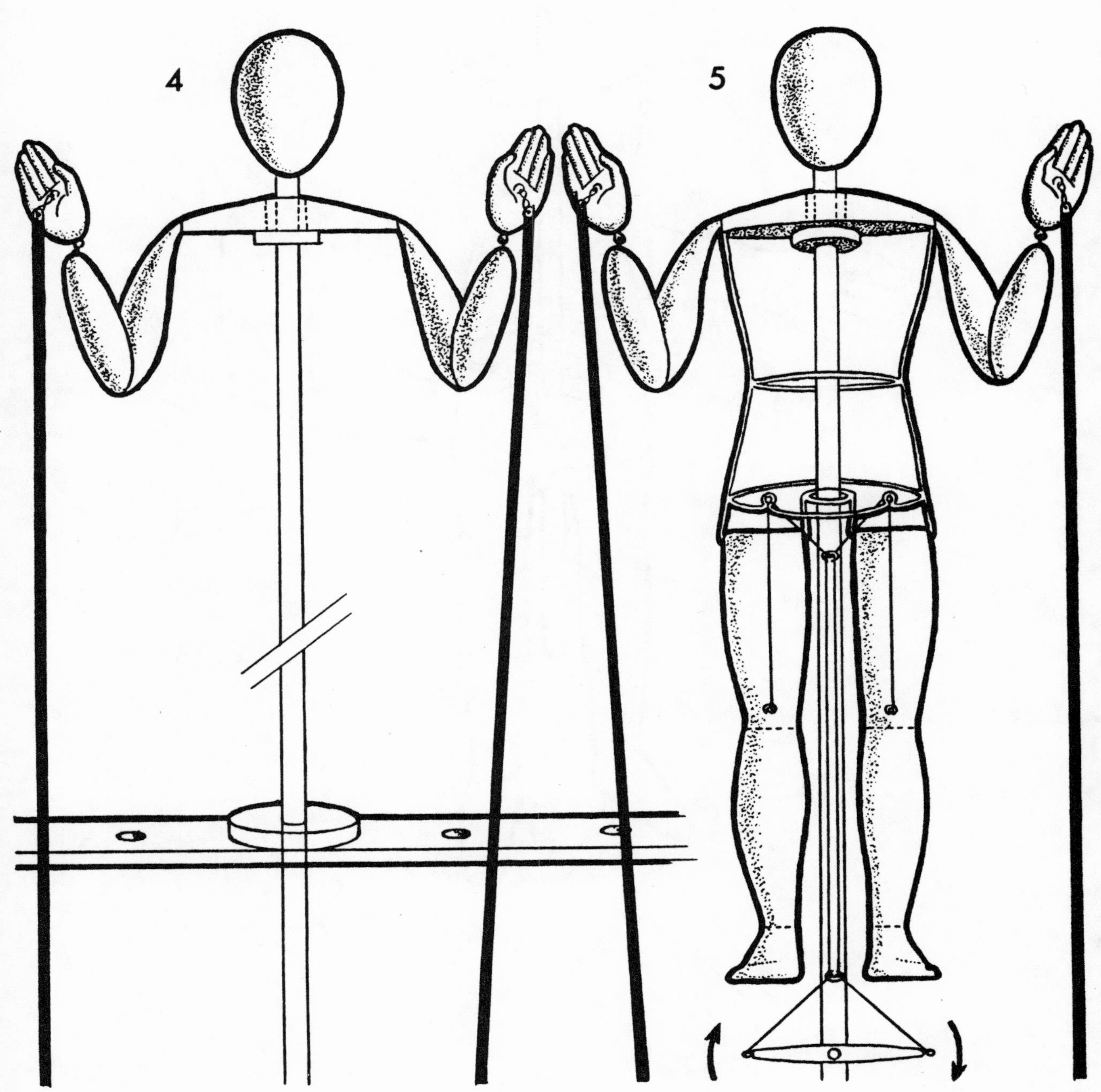

Figure 7 Rod puppets

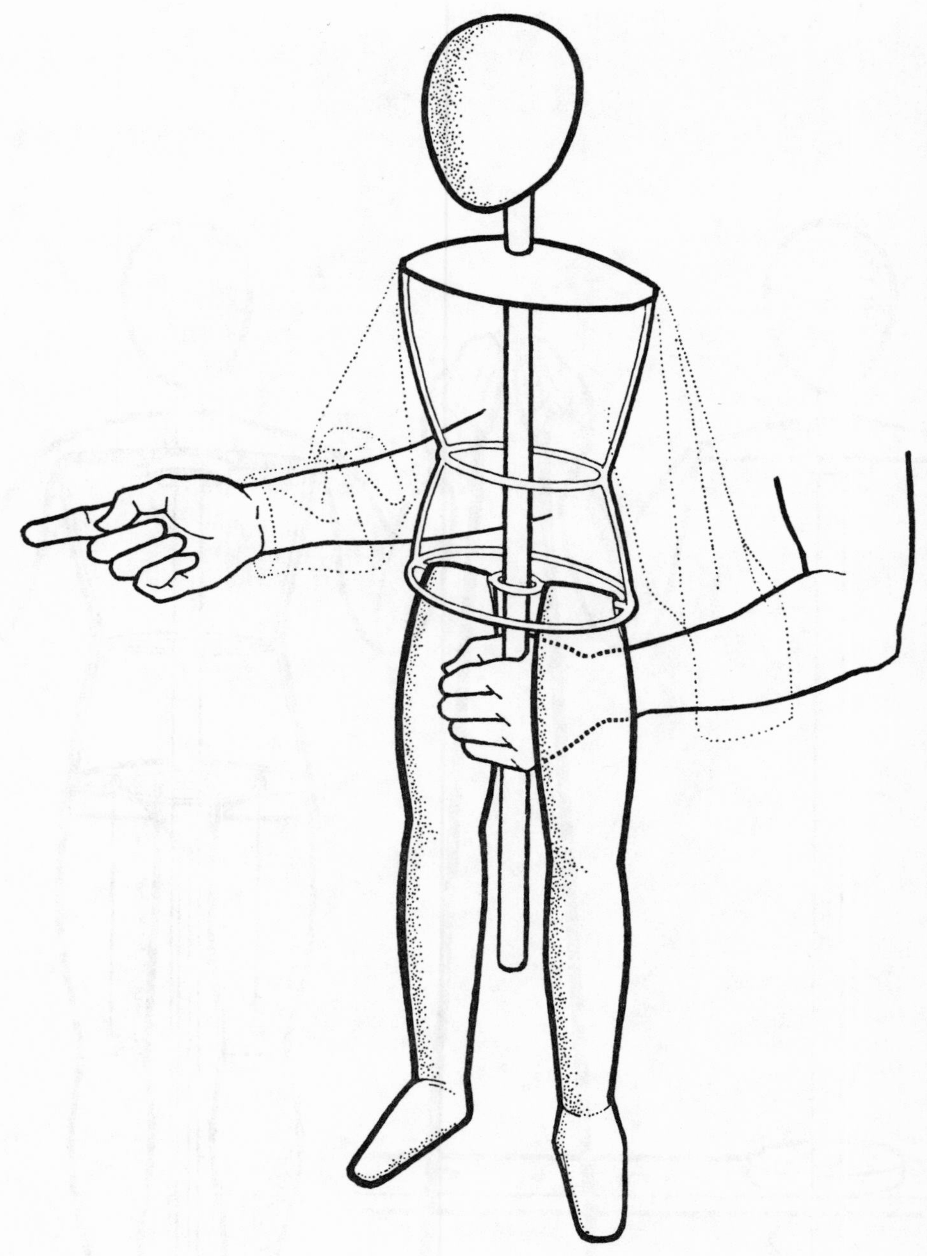

Figure 8 Rod puppet

Special Effects

The ability of the television camera to isolate the details of a puppet for its audience has developed the taste for extra articulation of facial features. The rod puppet is most suitable for this purpose, and for the extra mechanism of a nodding head, moving eyes or lips it is best to work with a strong hollow laminated *papier mâché* head (see *figure 9*).

A The nodding movement of the head is on its own a fairly straightforward mechanism. The space where the supporting rod enters the head is enlarged, and a narrow passage is drilled horizontally through the supporting rod. A wire shaft is passed through the *papier mâché* head from below one ear, through the passage drilled in the supporting rod and out below the opposite ear. The ends of the wire are turned over with round-nosed pliers and concealed under a further layer of *papier mâché*. The head with its wire shaft should now move easily backwards and forwards on its supporting rod.

Two small wire loops are now attached with plastic wood and glued to the front and back edges of the space where the supporting rod enters the head. A small spring or piece of elastic passes from the back loop to a screw-eye fixed in the back of the supporting rod. This holds the head in an upright position. From the front wire loop a length of twine passes through a screw-eye fixed to the front of the supporting rod and down the front of the rod to a trigger attachment at its base. This trigger mechanism is a wire loop passed through a hole drilled in the rod. An extension of the loop can be worked by the thumb alone of the hand holding the rod. Pressure on the trigger lowers the head and on release the pull of the spring above raises the head back to normal position. The joint of head and neck can be concealed by a high collar in the clothing.

B The articulation of facial features involves more detailed work. Again a hollow *papier mâché* head is used, but in this case the modelling is continued downwards to include the hollow shaft of the neck. The supporting rod may be attached to the inside back of the neck, leaving the space inside the head free.

1 The top of the *papier mâché* head is cut off with a sharp knife to allow free entry for work inside. This is easily replaced later and the join concealed by the hair.

2 The circles of each eye-ball and upper lid together are cut out, and also the lower lip with a half circle scoop below it.

3 The cut out eyes with their upper lids are built from behind into spheres with plastic wood, and a wire loop embedded in each at the back. A wire shaft passes through each eye and its ends are placed in small pellets of plastic wood glued to the inside of the head. As the plastic wood dries the

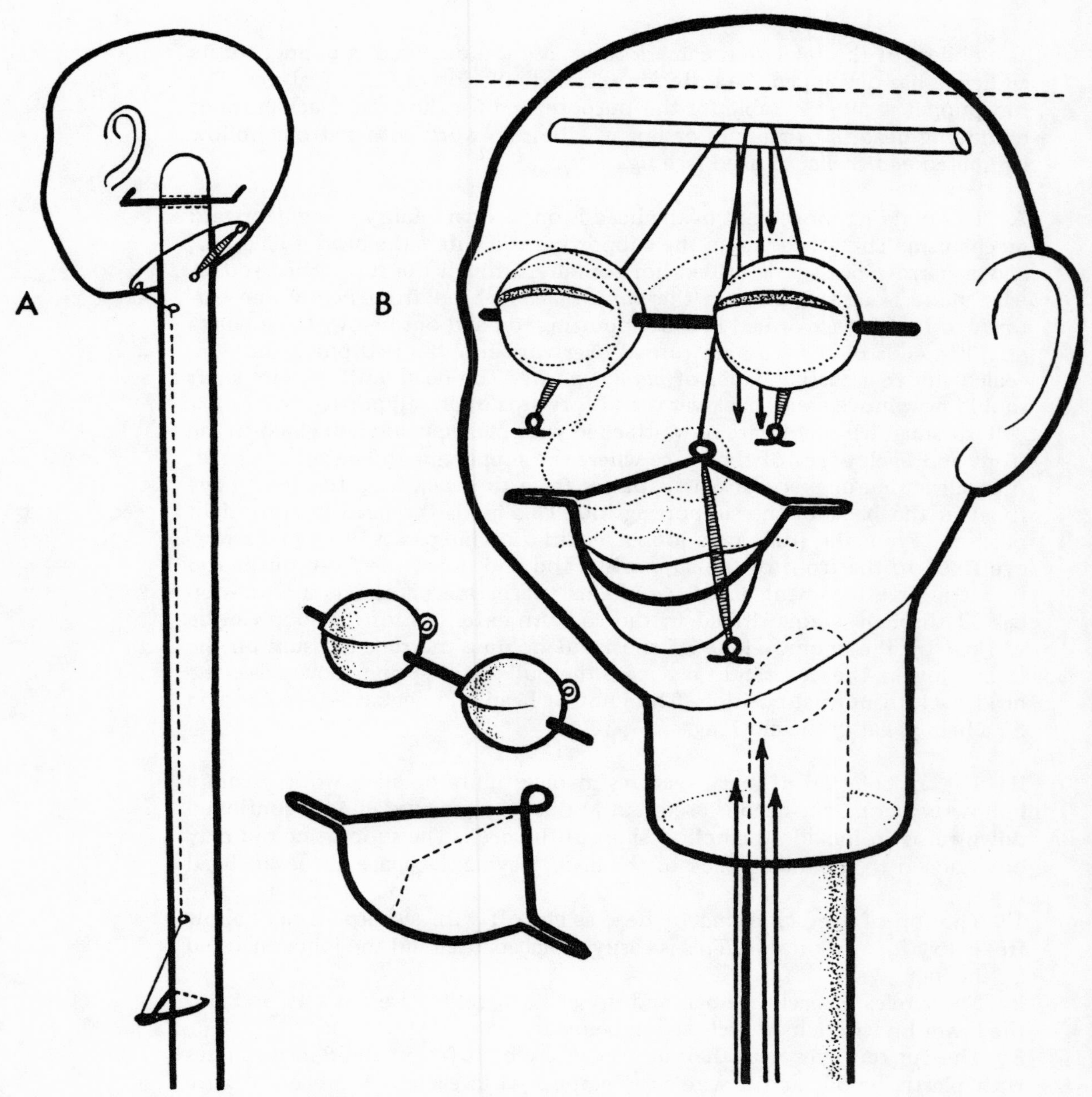

Figure 9 Nodding head. Articulated eyes and mouth

shaft is rotated slightly to form a loose-fitting housing, but the eyes on the shaft must stay fixed.

4 A wire frame, bent into shape with round-nosed pliers as shown in the diagram, is glued to the rim of the lower lip which is strengthened with a coat of plastic wood. The two front pivots of the frame are embedded in plastic wood sockets in the same manner as the shaft for the eyes.

5 A small spring or piece of elastic passes from the loop at the back of the lip frame to the base of the head, keeping the mouth in a closed position. In the same way the loop in the back of each eye is attached to a wire loop behind each cheek and the eyes are held in an open position.

6 Lengths of twine from the wire loops behind the eyes, and from the loop at the back of the lip frame pass over a horizontal length of dowelling fixed in the top of the head, and thence down the front of the supporting rod to trigger mechanisms at its base. Pressure on the triggers closes the eyes and opens the mouth.

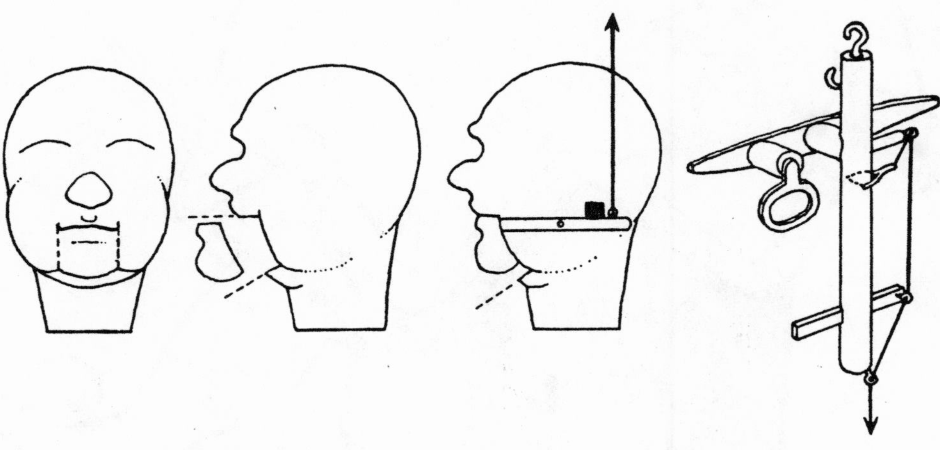

Figure 10 Articulated mouth for a marionette. The mechanism is similar to that described above, but the spring is exchanged for a small weight

Figure 11 Mr Punch

Glove Puppets

The glove puppet may well be called the traditional English puppet, as it has been used continuously in England from Elizabethan times, perhaps from an even earlier date. At periods when marionettes from Italy have gained a more fashionable popularity, the glove puppet has still survived in fairgrounds and in the streets, as it still does today in the Punch and Judy Show.

Glove puppets are worked from below in a booth open at the top in front, and follow the movements of the hand and fingers of the operator. Usually in this country the index finger fits into the head of the puppet, and the thumb and middle fingers fit inside its arms. Some showmen add the fourth to the third finger in the puppet's right arm. This method of operation is not symmetrical in appearance, but the thumb and index finger are most useful in gripping and holding. Apart from striking, throwing, holding and head nodding the individual movements of glove puppets are limited, but they are rapid and decisive being closely linked to the movements of the operator's hand and arm. This directness of control makes the glove puppet particularly suitable for strong characterisation as there is no barrier between operator and puppet. The speech and action of the manipulator are easily carried out together, and the puppet's performance is a direct projection of the performance of the showman himself. These qualities of the glove puppet are part of the reason for the success and durability of the Punch and Judy Show. No other puppet could so successfully carry out the vigorous action and impromptu haranguing of the audience which give it such vitality.

Figure 12

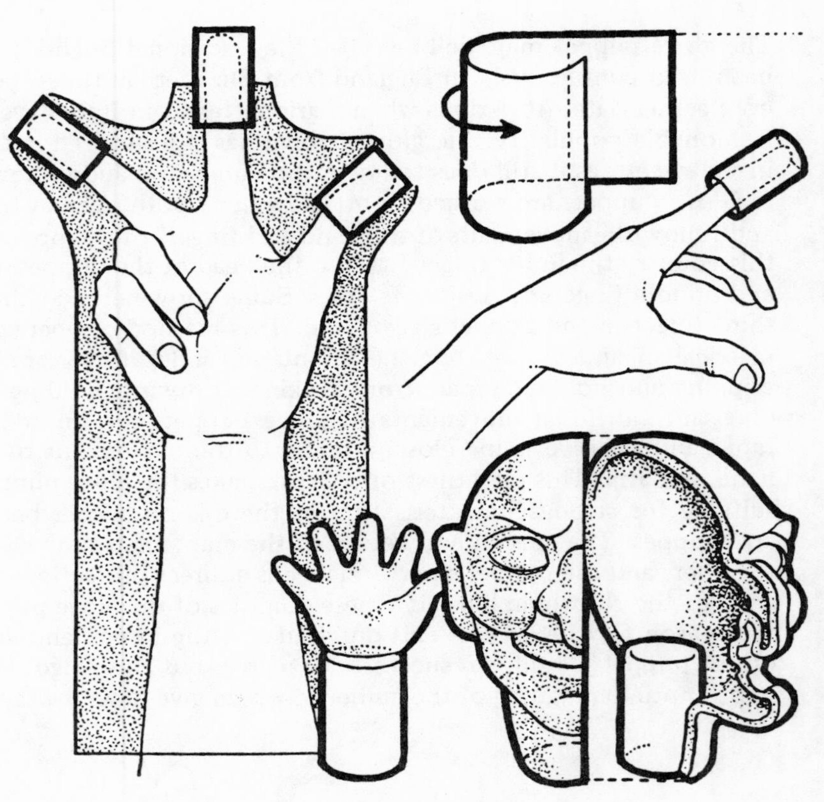

Figure 13 Inside the glove puppet

Inside the glove puppet

The mechanism of the glove puppet is based on three cylinders which fit comfortably on to the thumb, index and middle finger. These cylinders are attached to the head and two hands of the puppet, and are glued into the sleeves and neck of the puppet's body. This principle remains the same in all glove puppets although in wood carving the hollow wrist and hand may be carved in one.

Usually the three cylinders are made of cardboard which is rolled round each finger and thumb for measurement and glued. The card should reach the second joint of each of the fingers, and the first joint of the thumb. The cylinders can be padded inside with thin foam rubber sheet for comfort.

Figure 14

PROPORTIONS

These puppets are limited in height by the length of the performers' fingers, hand and forearm, and have special proportions of their own. In human beings the head as a unit of measurement is not more than one-seventh of the total height. By this rule a glove puppet 460 mm (17 in.) would have a head only 70 mm (2¾ in.) high and features barely visible to the audience! For this reason the heads of glove puppets are made much larger in proportion to their bodies than is found in real life, and are usually a quarter or one-fifth of the total height.

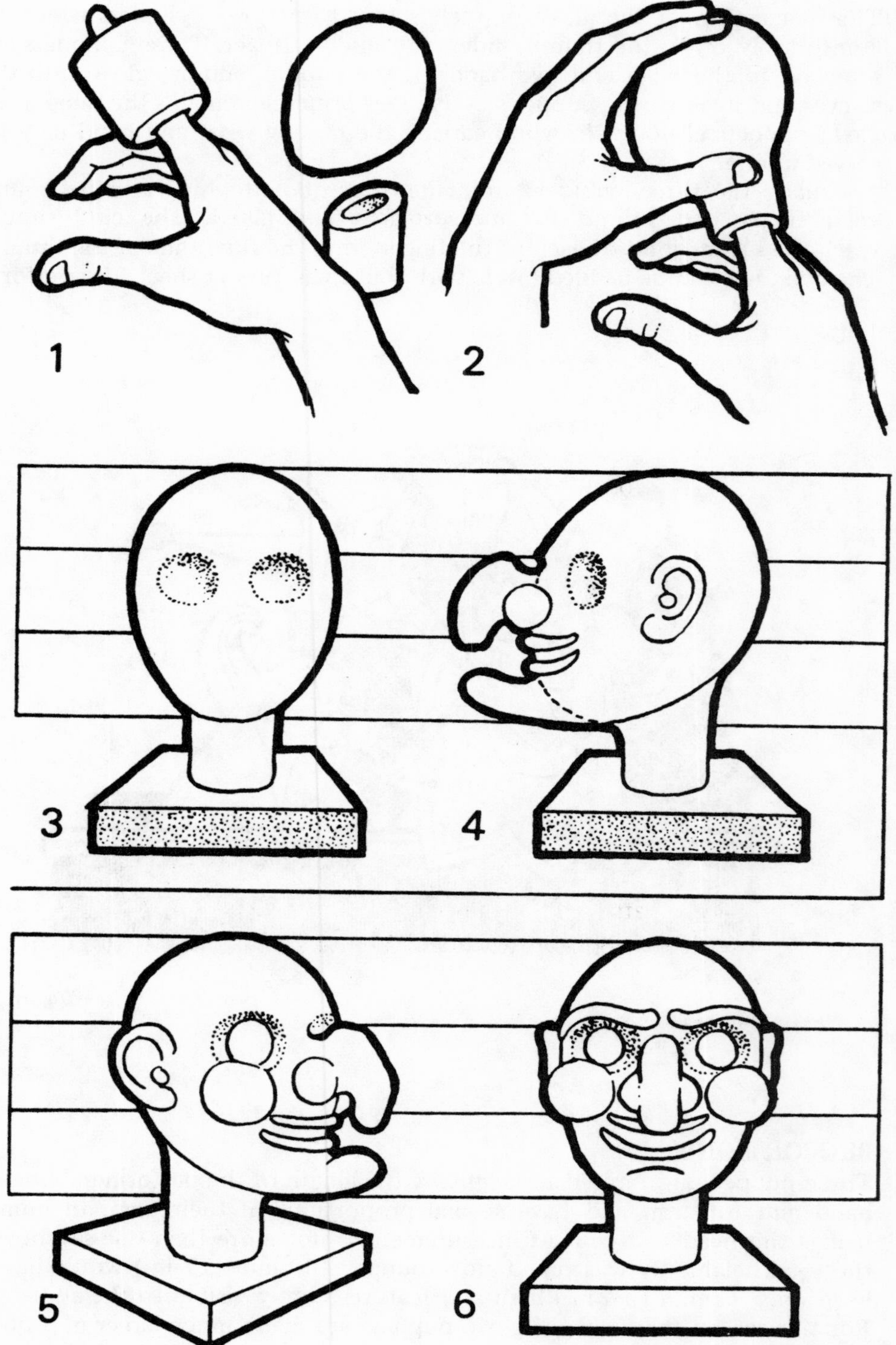

Figure 15 Making a plasticine model

Making the head

There are four commonly used methods of making puppet heads.

1 Direct modelling over a temporary core (plasticine or crumpled paper) which is later removed leaving a hollow head.

2 Lining a plaster of Paris mould taken from a clay or plasticine model.

3 Direct modelling over a permanent core.

4 Carving a head in wood.

The first two methods begin with the modelling of a head in plasticine — also a useful guide for those who carve in wood. At this point it is helpful to have some knowledge of the average proportions of a head. The diagram below (*figure 16*) shows how even the grotesque features of Punch follow a basic plan, with the nose lying in the centre third of three horizontal divisions. Seen from the side the ear also lies in this space.

The facing drawing (*figure 15*) shows how a plasticine head can be built up in simple stages on a 80 mm (3¼ in.) high peg stand. The neck is measured by rolling a ribbon of plasticine round the top half of the index finger; the head is an egg shape 100 mm (4 in.) high. Eye sockets are pressed out with the thumb, and features are built on to this basic shape using fingers and modelling tools.

When a group of people are making heads for a glove puppet play they should decide together on a uniform size of head. A good average height is 100 mm (4 in.).

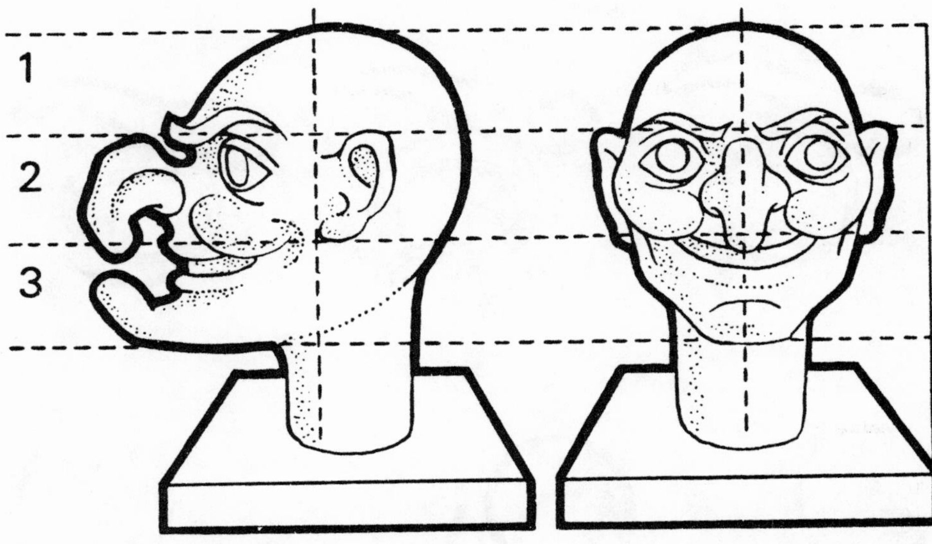

Figure 16 Proportions of the head

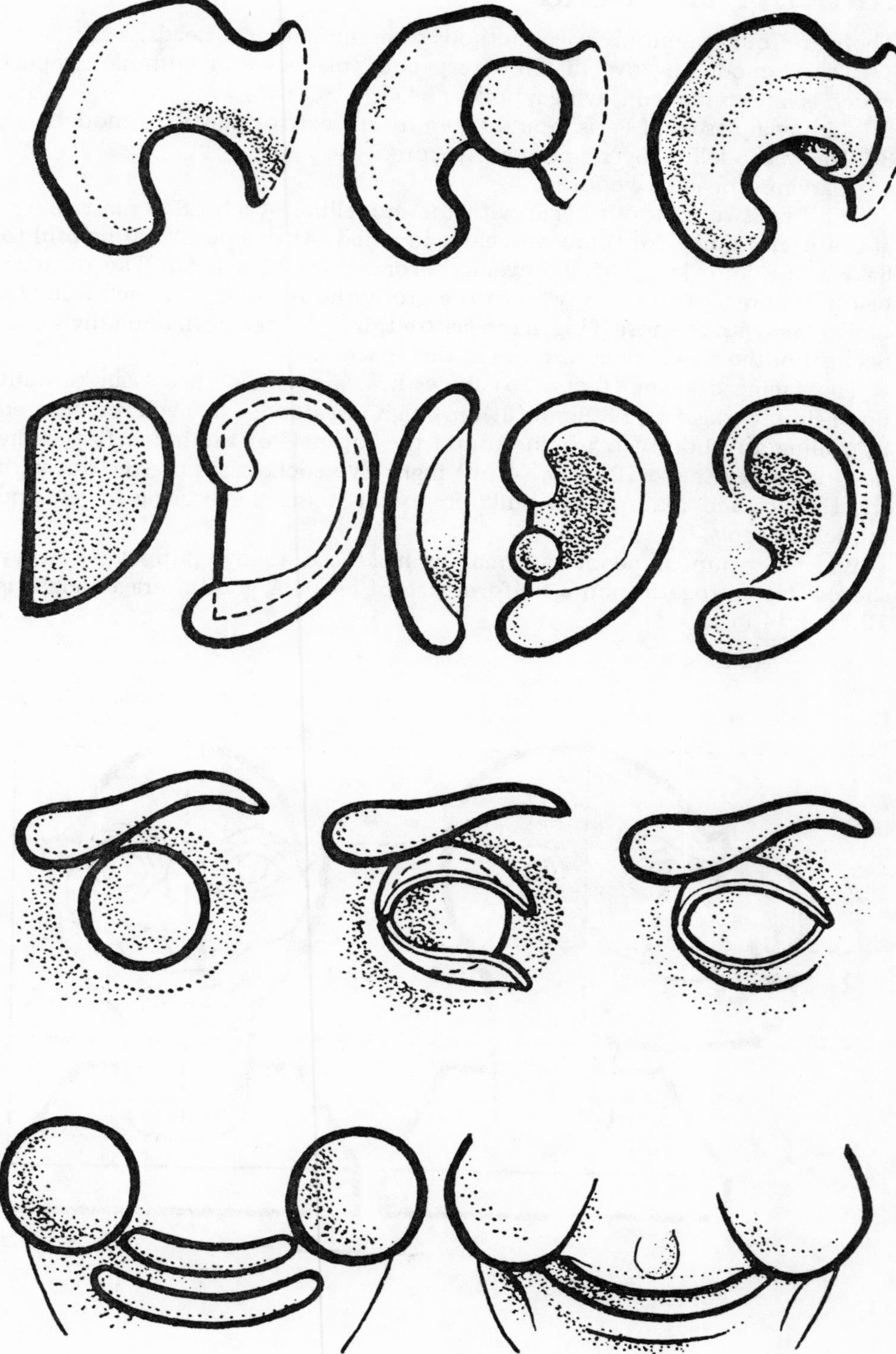

Figure 17 Building up features

MODELLING MATERIALS

The heads of professional glove puppets in the past have usually been carved in wood which can stand up to a lot of hard wear. There are also well established ways of making puppet heads in *papier mâché*, an under-rated medium which is excellent both for direct modelling and for lining moulds. In the last few years many self-hardening water-based modelling substances have appeared on the market, most of which may equally well be used. Many puppet makers still prefer the resilience of wood and the cheapness and light weight of *paper mâché* to the newer products, but this is often because they like what they have been used to. Here is some information on *papier mâché* and other ready prepared modelling susbstances.

Laminated papier mâché is built up in layers. I use torn up paper towelling for the early stages, and torn paper handkerchiefs for later detailed modelling. When covering a plasticine core or lining a greased mould, the first layer is placed without paste. Several further layers are well coated with heavy duty wallpaper paste and smoothed and pressed down with a wetted finger. The finished work is light in weight, but needs strengthening with an inner lining.

Papier mâché pulp is made from newspaper or paper towelling torn into pieces as small as 5 mm (¼ in.) square. The torn paper is soaked in water overnight, thoroughly sifted and rubbed while still in water, then removed and squeezed as dry as possible. Into this bulk of paper fibre quarter parts of modelling clay and ceiling whiting may be kneaded for a smoother pulp, and heavy duty wallpaper paste added until pellets can be rolled between fingers without crumbling.

Papier mâché pulp is stronger than the laminated variety, but is heavier and takes longer to prepare. Both types shrink in drying and show a fissured or pitted surface. This often adds to character, but can be concealed if necessary beneath a generous coat of acrylic paint.

The following are three self hardening water-based clay substitutes which dry on exposure to air.

DAS pronto, which is an Italian product widely sold in most art shops.

CLAYKOS, which is supplied by Dryad Ltd.

COLDCLAY, which is made by Homecraft Supplies.

All may be used for direct modelling over a core, or for lining moulds. Drying of unfinished work may be retarded by covering with a damp cloth.

REEVE'S MOD-ROC is particularly useful for puppet bodies and scenery. Strips of open work cotton cloth impregnated with Plaster of Paris are dipped in water and moulded in layers over wire frame or crumpled paper cores.

REEVE'S SUPERWOOD is a modelling material bought in powder form. Mixed with water it handles like clay and is fairly quick setting. It can be carved and sanded when dry.

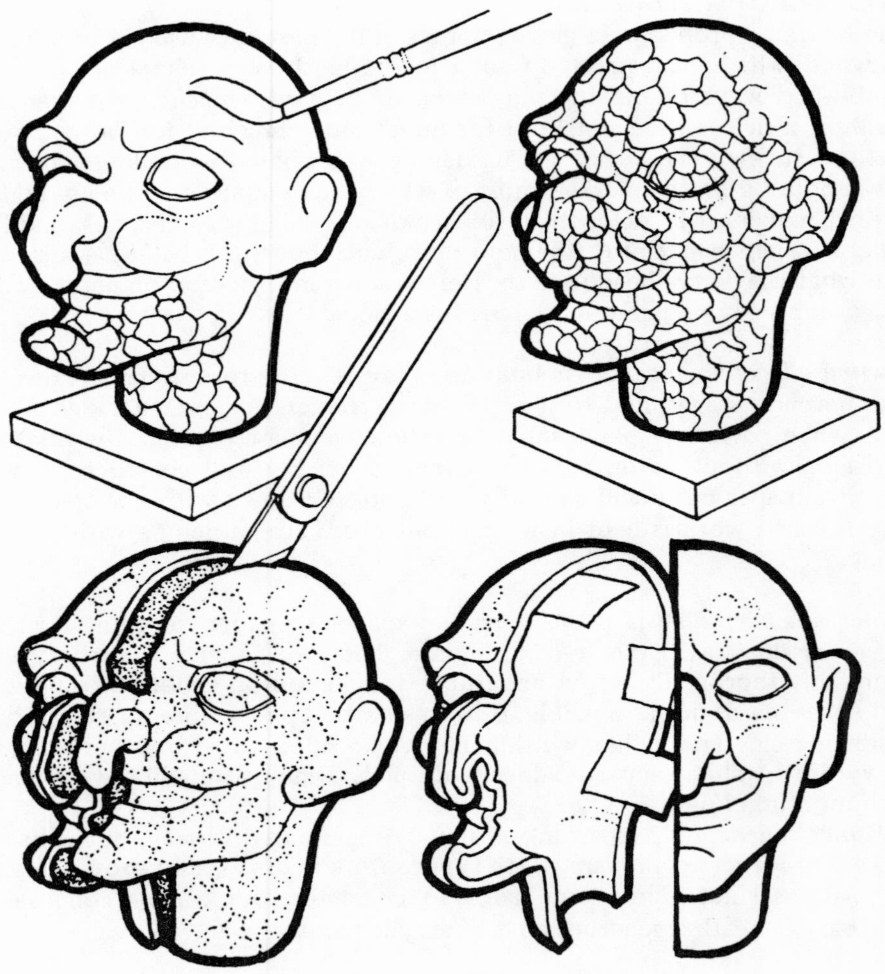

Figure 18

DIRECT MODELLING OVER A PLASTICINE BASE

In this method of puppet-head making, a plasticine base is covered with laminated *papier mâché*. When the covering is nearly dry it is cut in half, removed from the plasticine core, and re-assembled as a light hollow head.

Torn paper handkerchiefs follow a simply contour very well. The model is painted with a thin coat of vaseline which holds the first layer of paper in place. A further four or five layers are pasted over each other, and a wooden modelling tool helps to smooth and define the details.

If the covering is cut from the model before it is quite dry, the two halves can be fitted together while still flexible. Working through the hole in the base of the neck, the halves are attached on the inside with bandage and paste, and the whole inside surface can be strengthened in the same way.

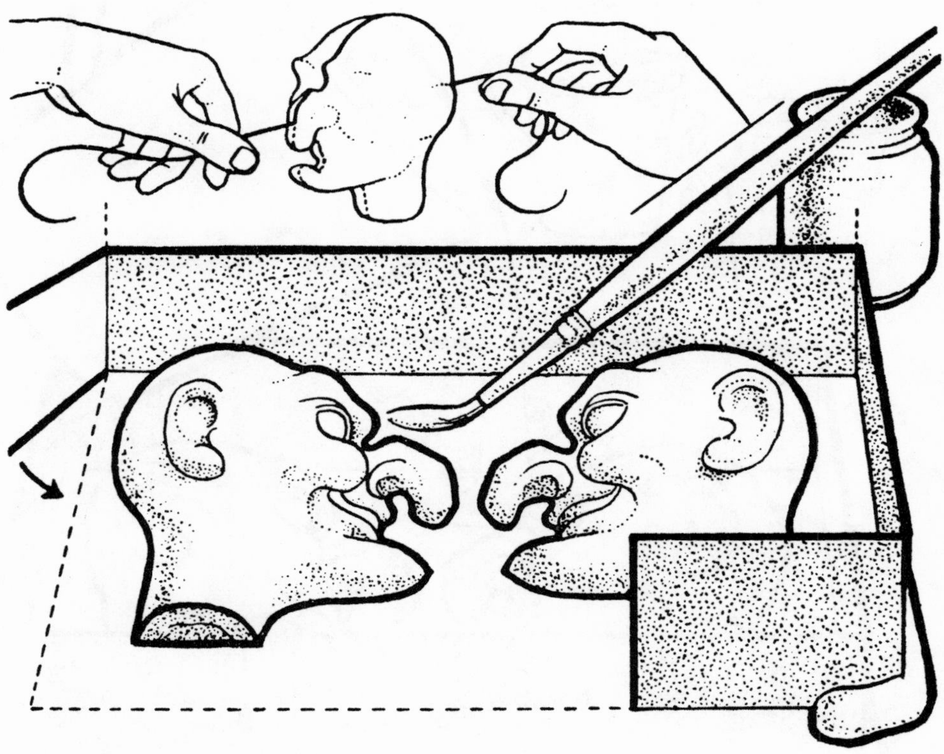

Figure 19a

MAKING A PLASTER MOULD

There are several ways of making plaster of Paris moulds. The following box method is the most easily controlled (see *figure 19*).

1 A plasticine model of the head is cut in two with a length of thin wire. To avoid the undercuts of Punch's nose and chin this cut is made from the front to the back of the head.

2 The two halves are laid flat side down, 13 mm (½ in.) apart on a smooth surface — this may be a sheet of zinc or plastic. A cardboard wall, 13 mm (½ in.) higher than the parts of the head, is placed round the two halves, sealed at the joints with plasticine, and tied round with tape.

3 The surface within the box frame surrounding the two halves is painted with vaseline to allow easy removal of the finished mould.

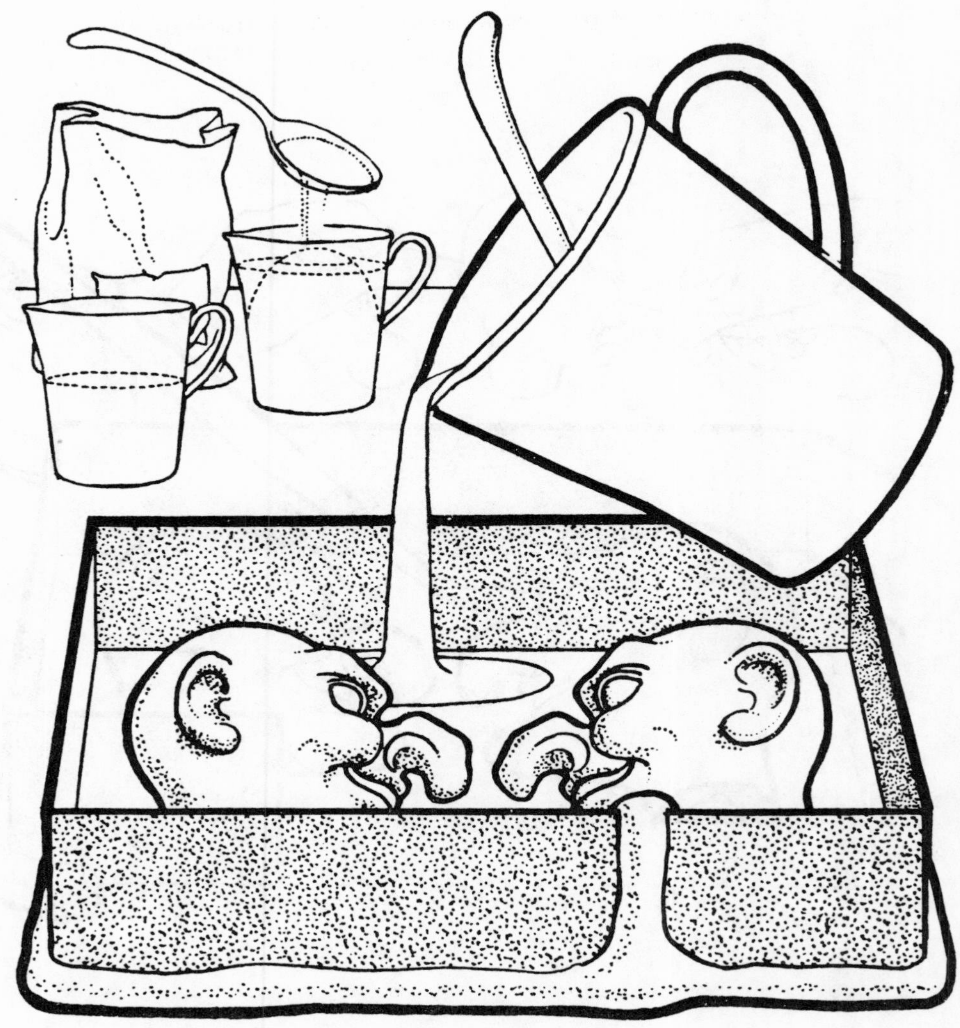

Figure 19b

4 Pour enough water into a large jug to fill the space inside the cardboard surround, and to cover the halves of the head by 13 mm (½ in.).
5 Plaster of Paris powder is shaken rapidly into the water until the sediment shows above the surface. The powder and water are sifted and stirred until smooth and creamy, and in a few minutes the mixture begins to thicken.
6 The liquid plaster is now poured in one continuous flow into the box space and the board or sheet underneath is shaken to release air bubbles. The plaster soon begins to harden and becomes quite warm in the process.

Figure 19c

7 After fifteen minutes the cardboard surround may be peeled away and the hardened mould prized off its greased base. The two halves of the plasticine head are picked out and the inside surface sponged clean with soap and water. The mould can be lined with *papier mâché*, plastic wood, or any hardsetting modelling substance. Before *papier mâché* is used the mould is greased with vaseline; for plastic wood it must be soaked first in water.

Laminated *papier mâché* can be built in several layers of different coloured paper. This makes certain that each layer is completed before the next begins. *Papier mâché* pulp is laid in pellets which are pressed together into a skin fitting close against the shape of the mould. This pressure is repeated during drying to prevent distortion through shrinkage. Other plastic linings are usually laid into the mould in one piece like pastry into a dish and pressed into shape.

The linings are prized out when nearly dry and glued together with paper or cloth hinges inside.

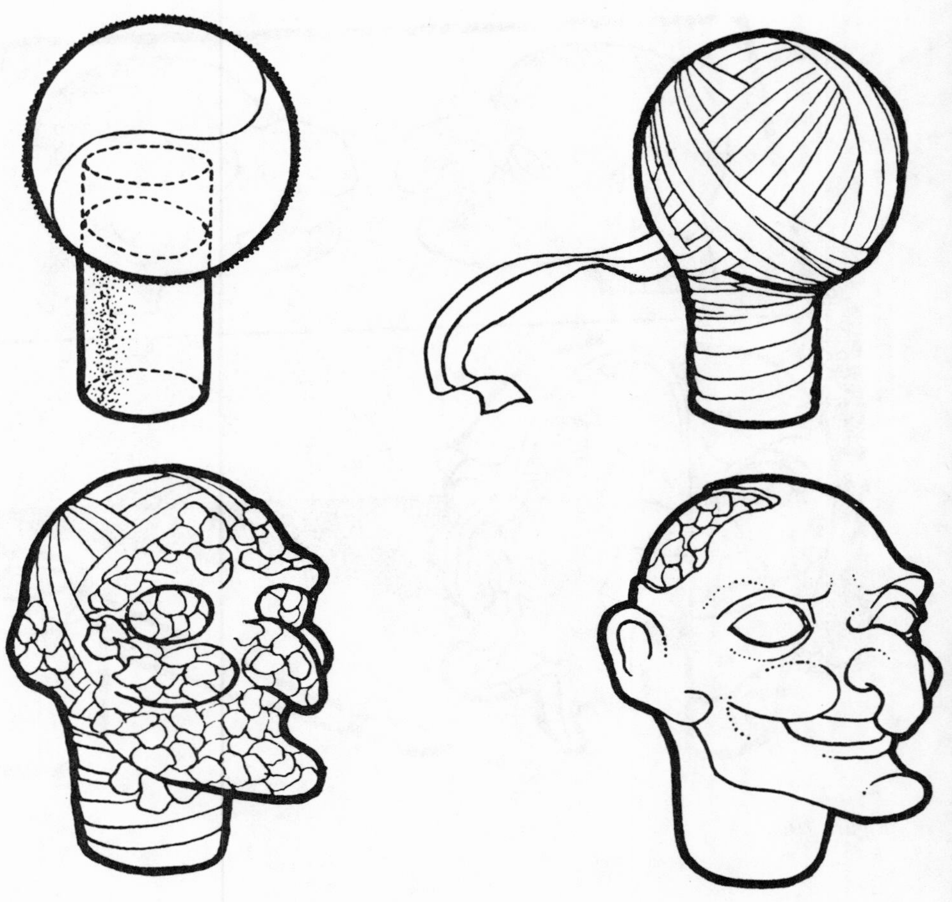

Figure 20

DIRECT MODELLING OVER A PERMANENT CORE

This is the most immediately expressive way of making puppet heads, and is very suitable for work with children.

A tennis ball pierced by a cardboard tube makes a good permanent base for the head and neck (see *figure 20*). The cardboard tube is rolled round the index finger for measurement, and is glued into a hole cut in the ball. Both ball and tube are then bound with torn rag or with bandage, which provides an absorbent base for the *papier mâché*.

Plenty of paste should be used between the bandaging and the first of the layers of laminated *papier mâché* which form the basic shape of the features. When this coat is partly dry, finer modelling in *papier mâché* pulp completes the head. *Papier mâché* pulp is shaped by pinching and pressing rather than by a building up method. When the pulp layer is half dry, a further pressure over the whole surface prevents shrinkage and cracking.

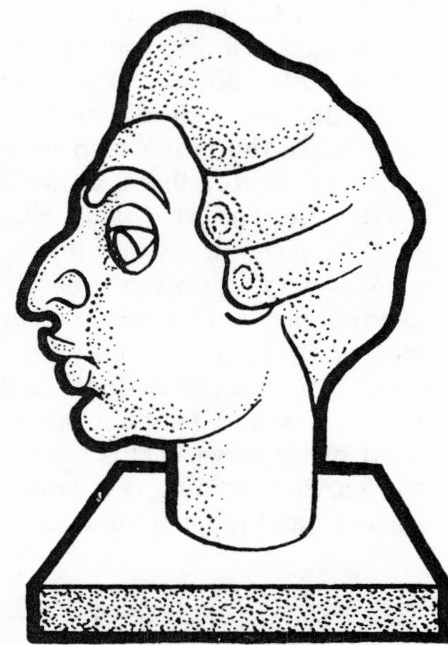

Figure 21

CARVING A HEAD IN WOOD

Unless you are an experienced woodcarver, it is always safest to begin by making a plasticine model of the head to be carved. Then, when you start to carve, you will know exactly the shapes you are aiming for. Carving in wood takes skill and intelligence. A carver must be able to see basic forms under detail, and resist the temptation to start finer cutting before the simpler stages are completed. For those who have not the aptitude for handling wood-carving tools, it is wiser to stick to *papier mâché* construction which is more directly expressive. Balsa wood, which might be considered easy to work, is disappointing as any instrument but a razor blade tends to crush rather than to cut it.

For the sake of clearness I have used the head of the Doctor not Punch, for these drawings. Punch's nose creates problems which are dealt with later. The stages of cutting also are more defined in diagram than in practice where the process is continuous and overlapping.

Choice of wood The detailed carving of a puppet's head and hands demands a wood that is hard and close grained. All fruit woods have this quality, but limewood is by far the most easily cut and has a waxy texture which does not easily splinter. Many Punch and Judy puppets in the past have been carved from ash. Wood bought from a timber yard should be well seasoned and ready to work.

Tools A full set of wood carver's tools is seldom found nowadays and without skilled training cannot be used effectively. For most purposes of carving I find that a 25 mm (1 in.) firmer chisel and a 10 mm (3/8 in.) chisel for finer work do very well if kept properly sharpened. Those who carve frequently will add in time their own set of narrower chisels and gouges where they find a special use for them. Other tools that you will need are a mallet, file, small needle file, and sandpaper where a smooth surface is asked for; also a saw or plane to shape the wood into a rectangle before carving.

It is very important that work should be kept firmly in position during carving, and held without damage to cutting already done. In early stages a vice or G-clamp may be used. If the carving of the ears is left until last, the head can be held in place with pressure at those points. In later stages a block of wood may be screwed as a temporary fixture to the base of the head being carved. This block itself can be held in a vice. I usually complete the carving holding the wood in a cloth in one hand, while the other hand files or hand pares with a small chisel.

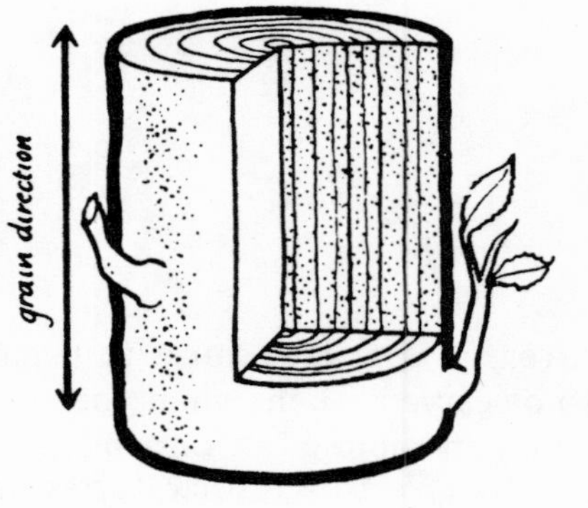

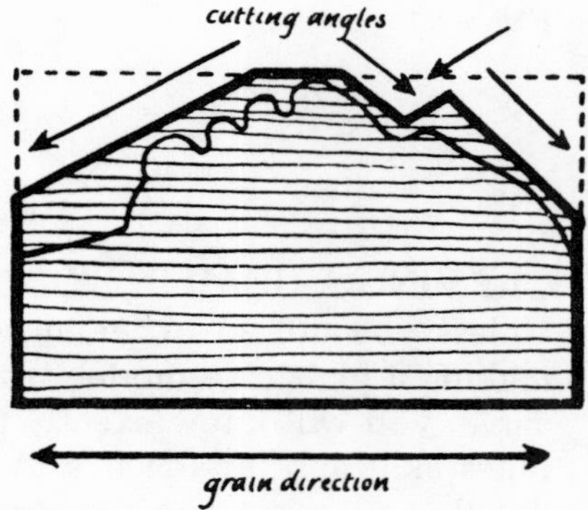

Figure 22

Wood grain An understanding of the grain direction of wood is essential if you are going to carve successfully (see *figure 22*). A cross section of naturally growing wood shows yearly divisions of growth expanding in rings from the centre. A vertical section shows the lines of grain direction caused by these rings. Chisel cuts must always be made at an angle moving in the same direction as the grain. If this principle is forgotten essential parts of the carving will split along the grain lines. In a glove puppet the grain direction is most easily followed when it runs from the crown to the chin in the head, and from the wrists to the finger-tips of the hands.

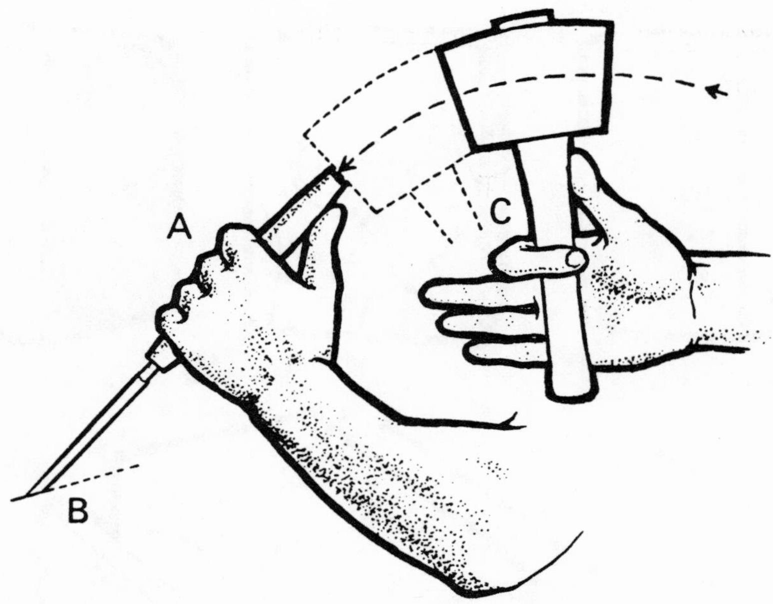

Figure 23 Using a mallet and chisel

Using a mallet and chisel The mallet strikes the handle of the chisel in a series of sharp taps, rather than with great blows which would dislodge the wood from the vice (see *figure 23*). In this way there is more control over the chisel's direction which may be adjusted between each stroke.

A The chisel is held lightly between the fingers and thumb of the left hand and is not gripped hard in the fist.

B For most purposes of carving, the cutting angle of the chisel lies against the wood. Where the flat surface of the chisel is in contact, the cutting direction tends to curve into the work.

C The mallet, like the chisel, is lightly held. The main support comes from the index finger and thumb which also act as a pivot, the three lower fingers working as a trigger. This arc of movement is usually sufficient for fine carving. Movement from the shoulder or elbow is seldom necessary.

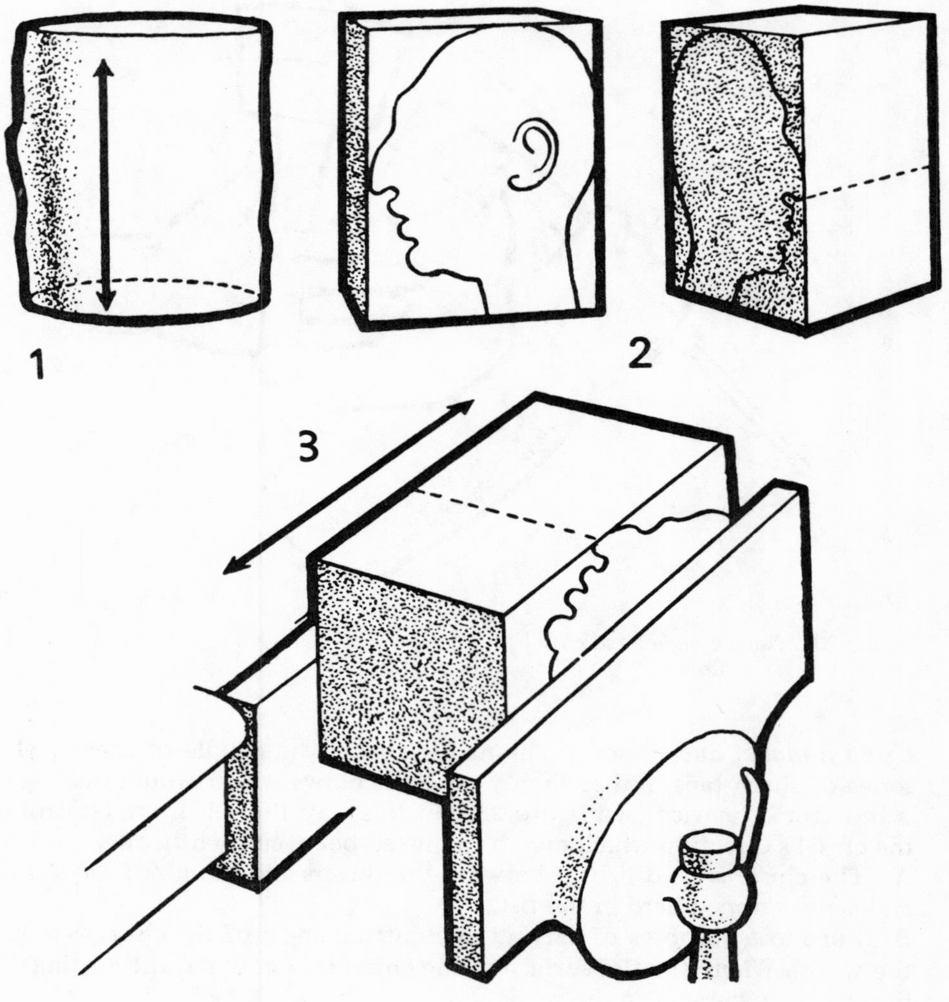

Figure 24a

Carving (*figure 24*)

1 The wood you are going to cut may be circular or rectangular in section. In either case it must be reduced by planing to a rectangular block just over the height and width of your plasticine model. The grain direction runs from the top of the head to the neck.

2 The side profile of the head is drawn on each side of the block and the point of the nose, the most prominent part of the face, is marked in a line across the front.

3 The block is now placed face upwards in the vice ready for cutting to begin.

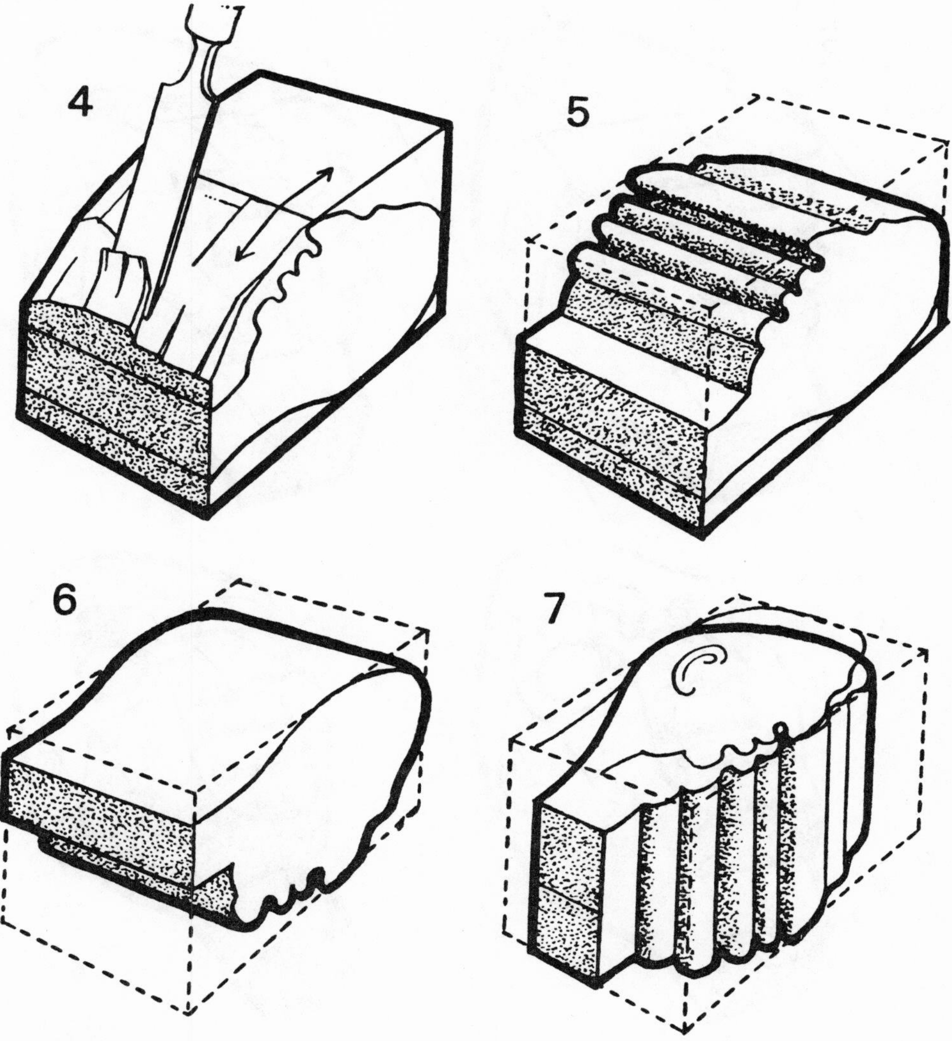

Figure 24b

4 Using a mallet and chisel, two broad planes are now cut; the surface areas from the nose to the neck, and from the nose to the top of the head.

5 All the angles of the features in profile are chiselled out, the direction of cutting altering where necessary to follow the grain.

6 The head is now reversed in the vice, and the profile of the back of the head is cut.

7 The head is turned sideways in the vice and padded with folded rag to protect the nose. The sides of the head are cleared in each direction from the ears.

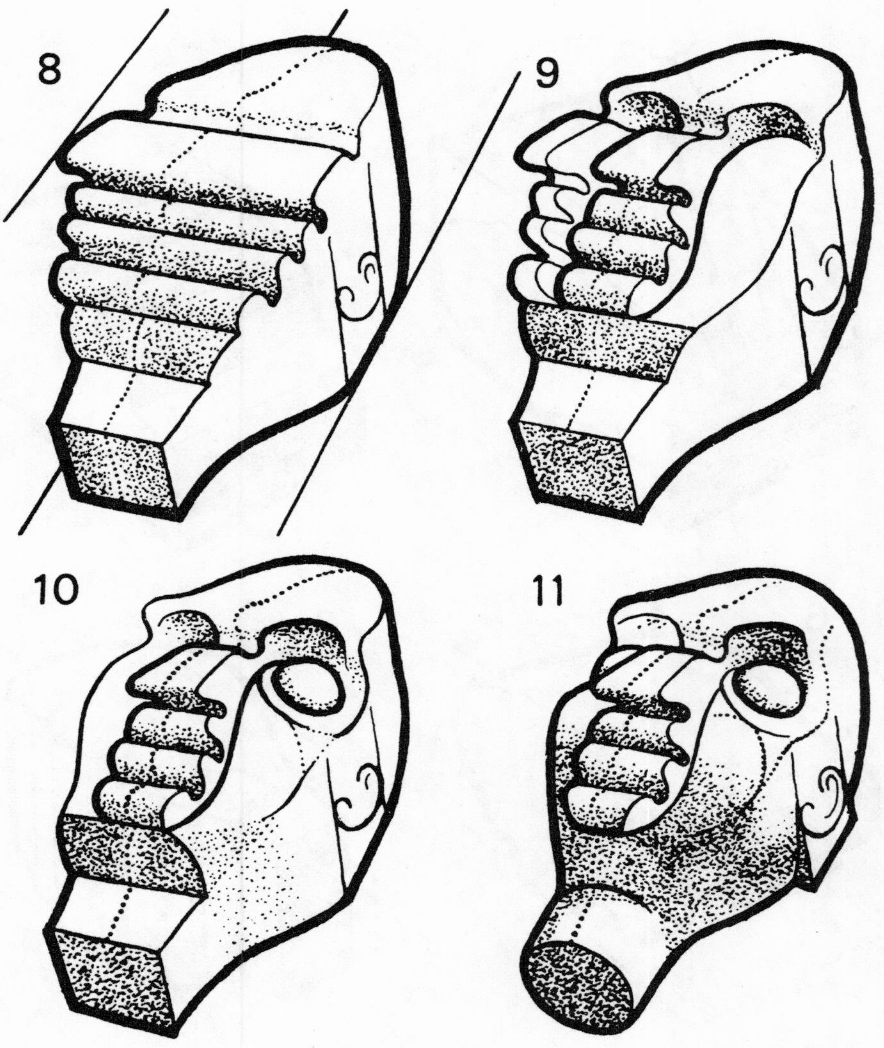

Figure 24c

8 The head is turned face upwards and held in the vice by the ears. The eyebrows and the centre line of the face are marked in pencil.

9 Two deep cuts, starting from the brows, define the width of the nose, mouth and chin. The whole face is lowered on either side of these features.

10 Carefully watching grain direction, a groove is cut round each eye socket, and the rounding of the cheeks is begun.

11 The whole head is rounded back and front. This may be done in the vice with a chisel, or the head can be removed and filed.

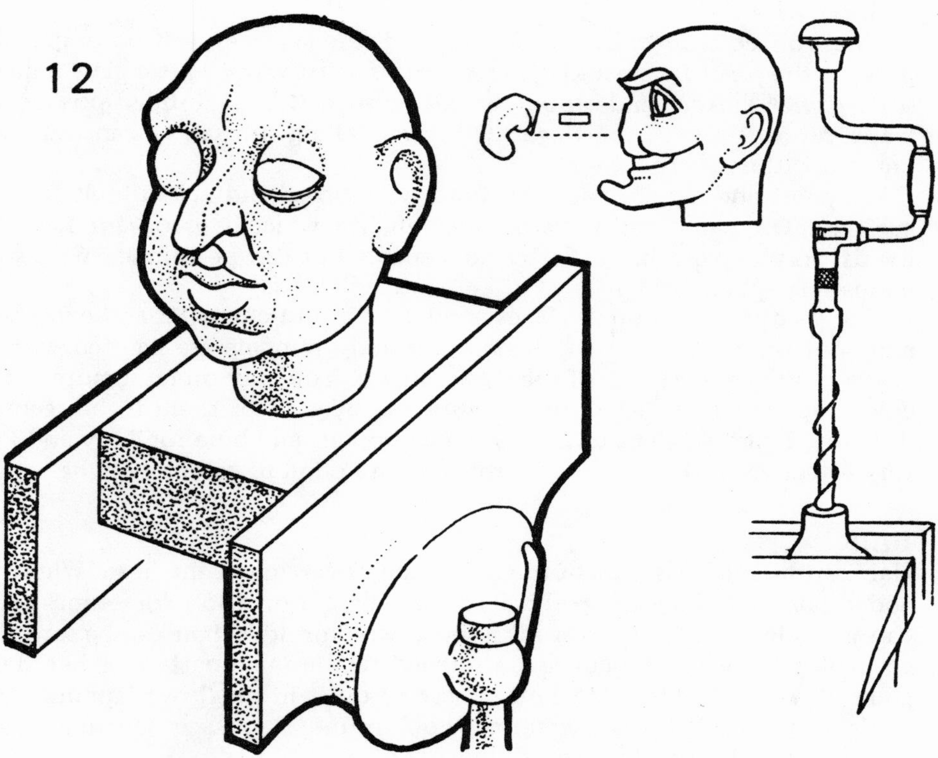

Figure 24d

12 From this stage onwards the head can be held in the hand, or screwed from beneath to a block held in the vice. Details of features are now completed, and you may aim at a smooth finish or leave the natural texture of the chisel marks. Much of the character will depend on added paint and hair.

Experienced wood carvers sometimes prefer to cut the hair in wood as part of the whole head. When making Punch himself it may be necessary to carve the nose separately, as the wood available does not always allow room for nose and head in one.

When carving is completed, the neck shaft is bored with a brace and size 20 mm (¾ in.) bit. To prevent damage to features the head must be wrapped in a cloth in the vice while this is done. Some wooden heads are very heavy, but if the crown of the head is sawn off, much of the inside may be cleared out with a gouge. When the top is replaced the join is concealed by hair.

PAINTING

Before you colour *papier mâché* or wood, the surface must be prepared to prevent the paint from sinking in. A coat of spirit varnish after glass-papering seals *papier mâché*, and wood can be finished with grainfilled powder and water rubbed in with the finger. Other modelling substances can usually be painted without perparation.

Oil paint and acrylic paint are both waterproof and are suitable for most surfaces. Oil paint has a translucent quality which is good for faces and hands; acrylic paint has a flatter appearance but can be thinned with water and is very quick drying.

The painting of puppets' faces should bring out character and expression, and sometimes the faces of Punch and Judy puppets are painted with the crude but lively make-up of the circus clown. You may prefer a more natural colouring, but a strong outline round the eyes helps them to be seen at a distance. I find scarlet outline for male puppets, and blue for Judy and Polly very effective, with a touch of varnish on the pupil to catch the light.

HAIR

Hair can be made as part of the modelling or carving of the head. Where it is added later you may use real hair, dolls' hair, fur or wool. Sometimes a skull cap is made of stiff material into which wool or dolls' hair can be sewn. Fur or lamb's wool can be cut and stretched to the same pattern. When hair is glued directly to the head it is wisest to do it in small overlapping hanks. Curls can be made by wrapping wool round a greased knitting needle, painting it with thin gum, and sliding off when dry.

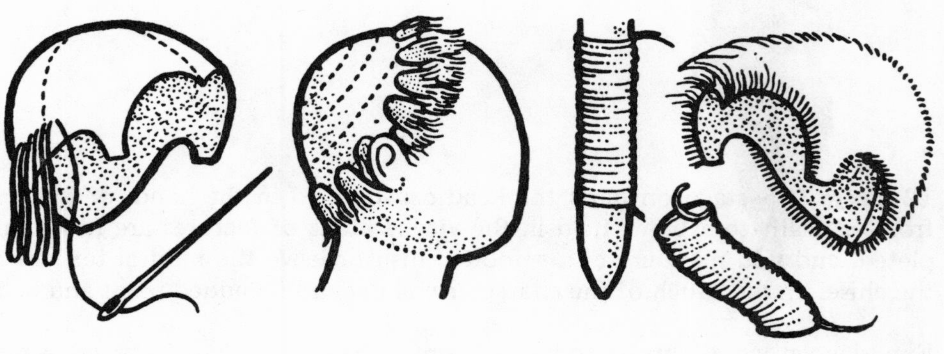

Figure 25

Making hands

The hands of a glove puppet are almost as important as its face in expressing character. Different puppets will have different types of hands; long and narrow, short and square, open or close-fingered. There are several ways of making hands, and each method is suitable for a particular type. The size of hands is a matter of choice. I prefer to make them one-seventh of the total height of the puppet, in proportion to the body rather than to the head.

FELT HANDS

The pattern below (*figure 26*) shows an average shape for a felt hand. The extra length beyond the wrist slides over the cardboard cylinder which fits on to the operator's thumb or third finger. Two pieces (A) are cut for each hand, and stitched together round the edge by oversewing. The whole hand is then turned inside out and stuffed with flock or cotton wool, a knitting needle being useful in turning and shaping the thumb. Finger divisions are stitched in last through the stuffing and the cardboard cylinder is closed at the wrist end (B) before the felt hand is glued into place. Felt hands are easy to make but can only be designed with closed fingers.

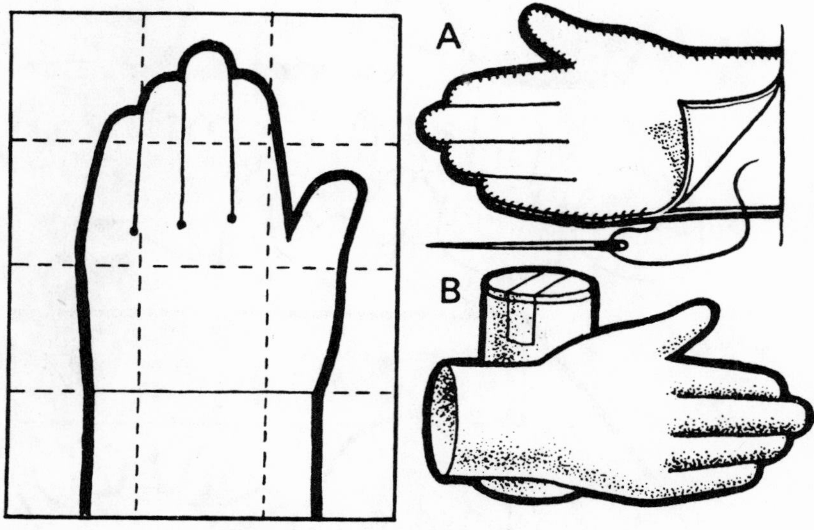

Figure 26

PAPIER MÂCHÉ HANDS

This method of *papier mâché* construction is very suitable for open-fingered irregular positions of the hand.

1 Two curved pieces of wire roughly 102 mm (4 in.) long, are bound together by a third which forms both the middle finger and an attachment to the cardboard cylinder.
2 Strips of rag or roller bandage build up the bulk of the hand and wrist.
3 Fingers may now be bent into any shape or position suited to the character or action of your puppet.
4 The fabric surface is soaked with paste, and covered by a layer of *papier mâché* pulp pressed into shape.

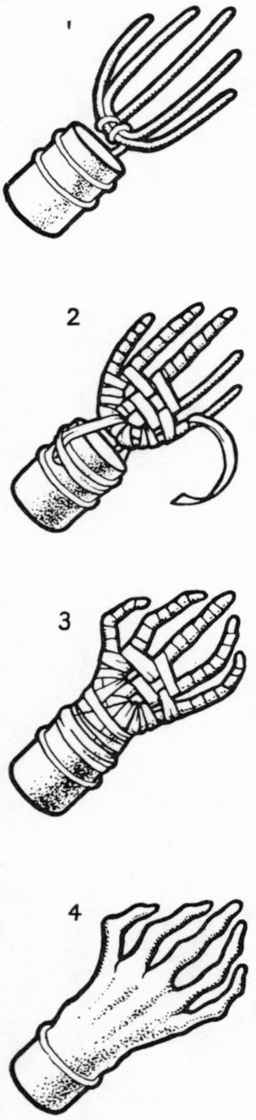

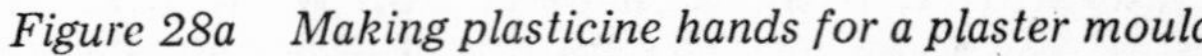

Figure 28a Making plasticine hands for a plaster mould

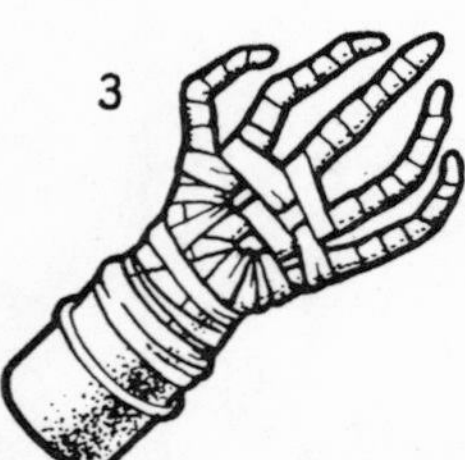

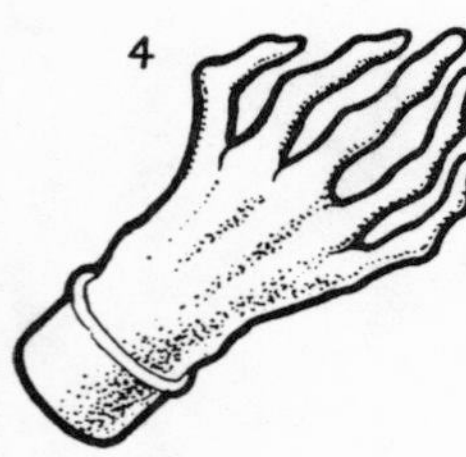

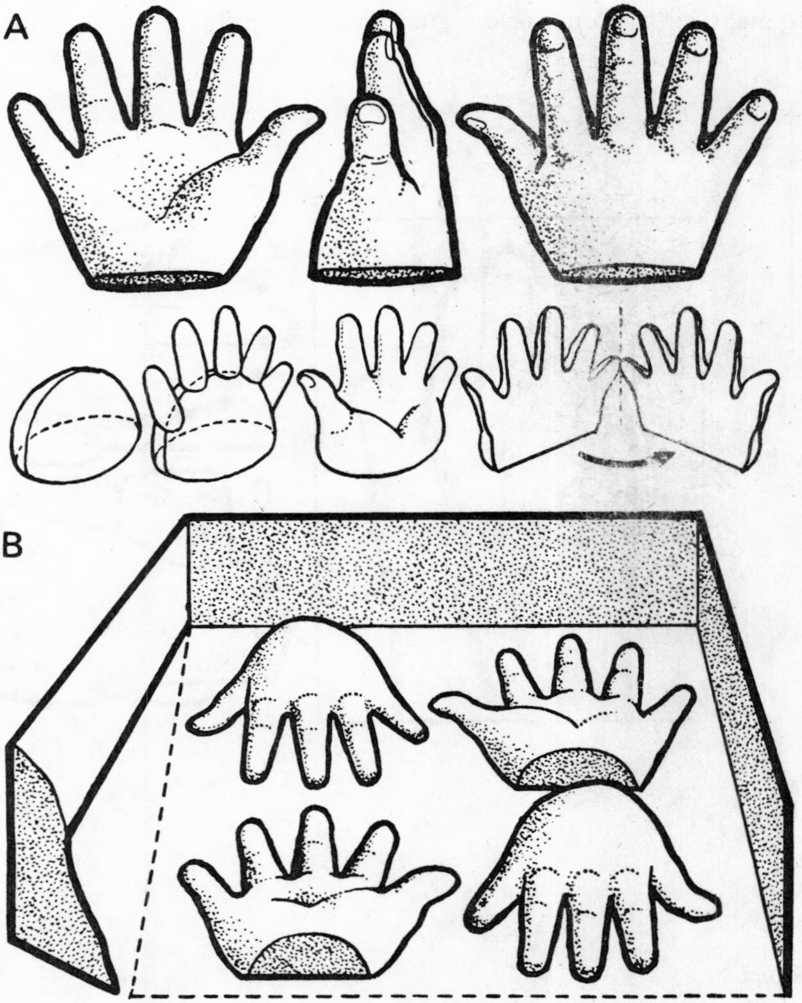

Figure 27

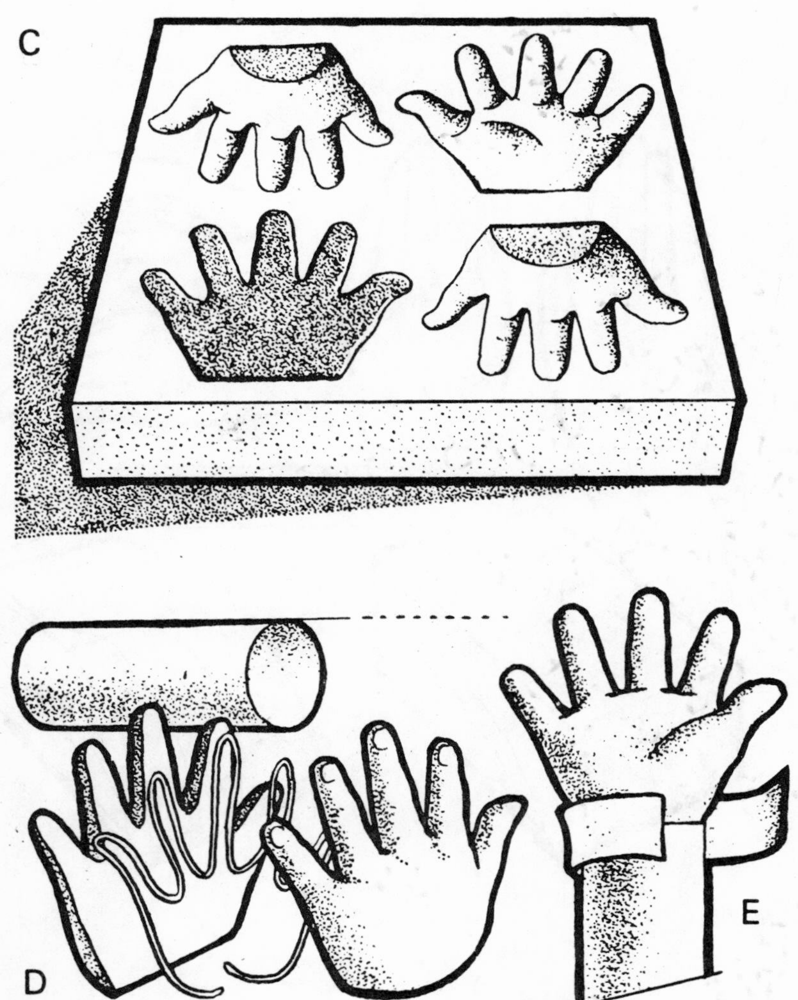

Figure 28b

HANDS MADE FROM A PLASTER MOULD

Hands can be cast from a plaster of Paris mould using the same method described in the making of puppet heads (see *figure 28*). When several puppets are made together this saves time. Two hands are first modelled in plasticine (A). They must be of a shape (short and thick) that can be easily divided. The four halves are laid 102 mm (4 in.) apart in a cardboard surround to make a one piece mould (B).

The completed mould may be lined with *papier mâché* pulp, plastic wood or any hard setting modelling substance (C). Hands, being small, are usually made solid. If *papier mâché* is used, it is safer to add a core of thin wire (D), when the two halves are sealed together. When each hand is glued in position on the end of its cardboard tube, the joint is strengthened with a strip of tape round the wrist (E).

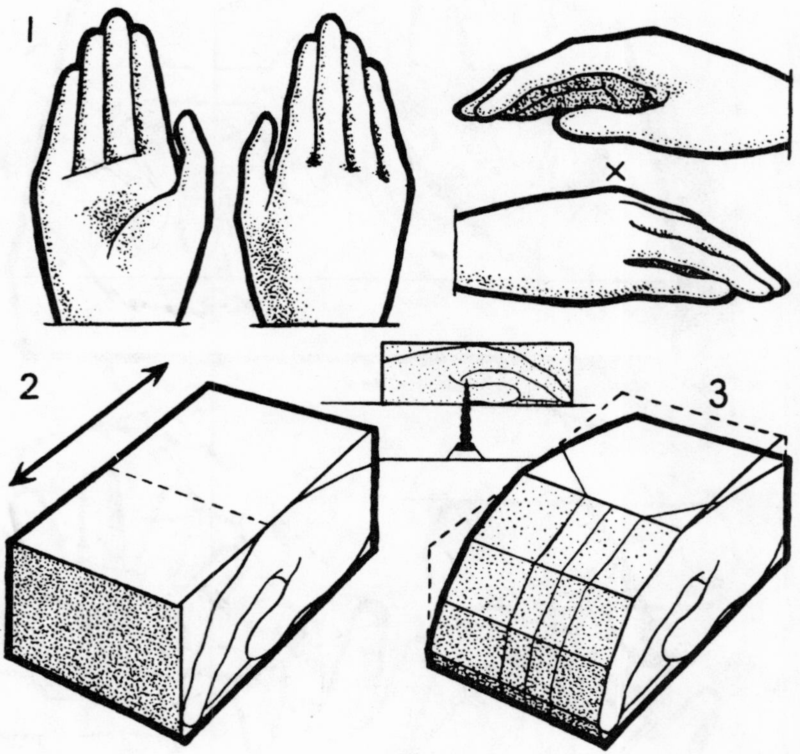

Figure 29a

WOODEN HANDS

If you have successfully carved a puppet's head in wood you will find the planning and cutting of hands very similar (see *figure 29*).

1 A plasticine model shows the basic form of the hand. This is the best position for a beginner to attempt, with the palm hollowed and the knuckle of the index finger at the highest point.
2 A block of close-grained wood is marked with the side profile of the hand, and a line across the top marks the knuckles. The grain direction runs from wrist to finger-tip.
3 The hand is held in position on a block of wood in the vice by means of a screw through the palm. The top of the hand is cleared in either direction from the centre, and the positions of index and middle finger marked in.

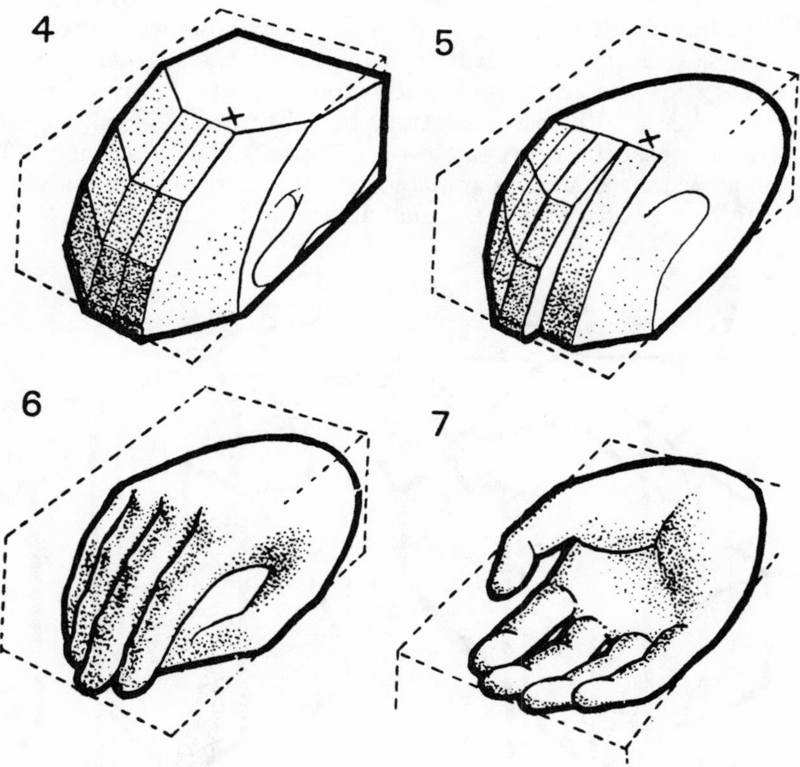

Figure 29b

4 The wood on either side of the index and middle finger is cut back to the thumb and fourth finger.
5 The index finger is now cut back leaving the middle finger forward. Working in the opposite direction the back of the hand is rounded with a chisel or file and the fourth and fifth fingers and thumb marked.
6 A fine chisel cuts the surface divisions betwen the fingers, and between the index finger and thumb.
7 The hand is unscrewed from its block, turned over and from now on held in the hand. Paring from the finger-tips and wrist towards the centre, the palm and thumb are cleared. The finished hand is glued to its cardboard cylinder and the joint strengthened with tape.

Making the body

Here are two kinds of glove puppet body. Type A, often used in work with children, has an identical back and front with side-projecting arms. Type B has sleeves set in facing forwards. When in use the simpler pattern tends to gather between the arms, while the second pattern follows the shape of the operator's hand with less distortion. In either case wide sleeves tapering to the wrist conceal the different levels of thumb and third finger. The use of thick material gives an appearance of substance to a glove body, which with the addition of collar and cuffs, may also serve for clothing.

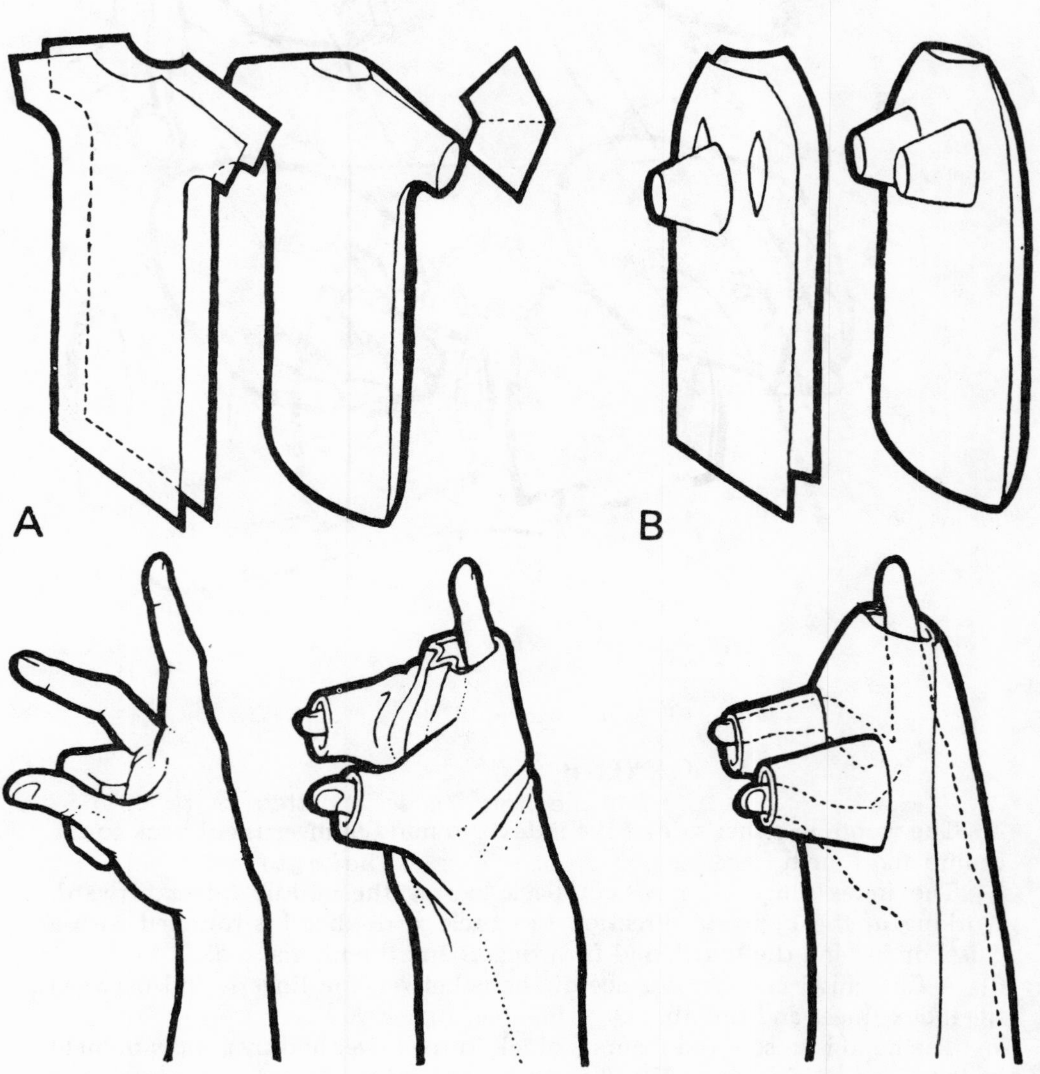

Figure 30

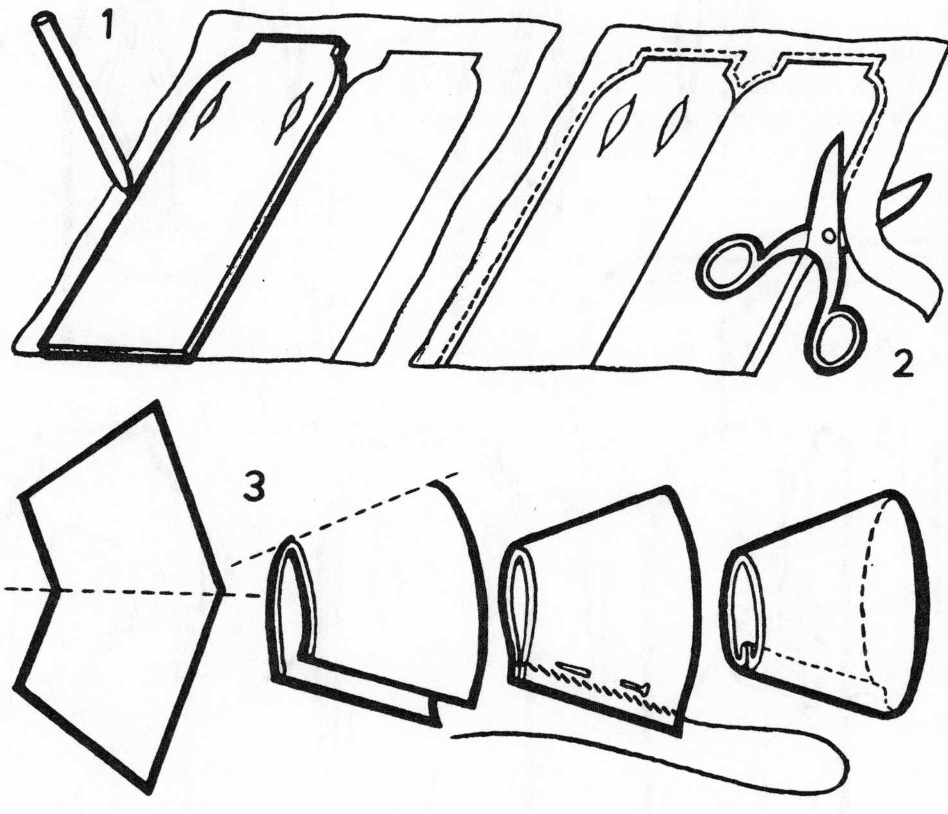

Figure 31a

CUTTING AND SEWING TYPE B

1 A cardboard template is made from the scale pattern of type B body (*figure 32*). This template is stencilled on to a piece of material wide enough to hold the front and back pieces side by side. The length of the glove body should extend to three quarters of the length of the operator's arm.

2 Allowing an extra width of 6 mm (3/8 in.) for sewing, cut round the outside of the pattern, leaving the joining of the two halves to be folded later. The spaces for the two sleeves are also cut out at this stage.

3 The sleeves are now cut from a stencilled line, folded, and sewn along the border.

4 Working from the inner side of the material of the body, the sleeves are pinned into place and sewn.

5 With the sleeves facing inwards, the body is folded across so that the front and back are in position.

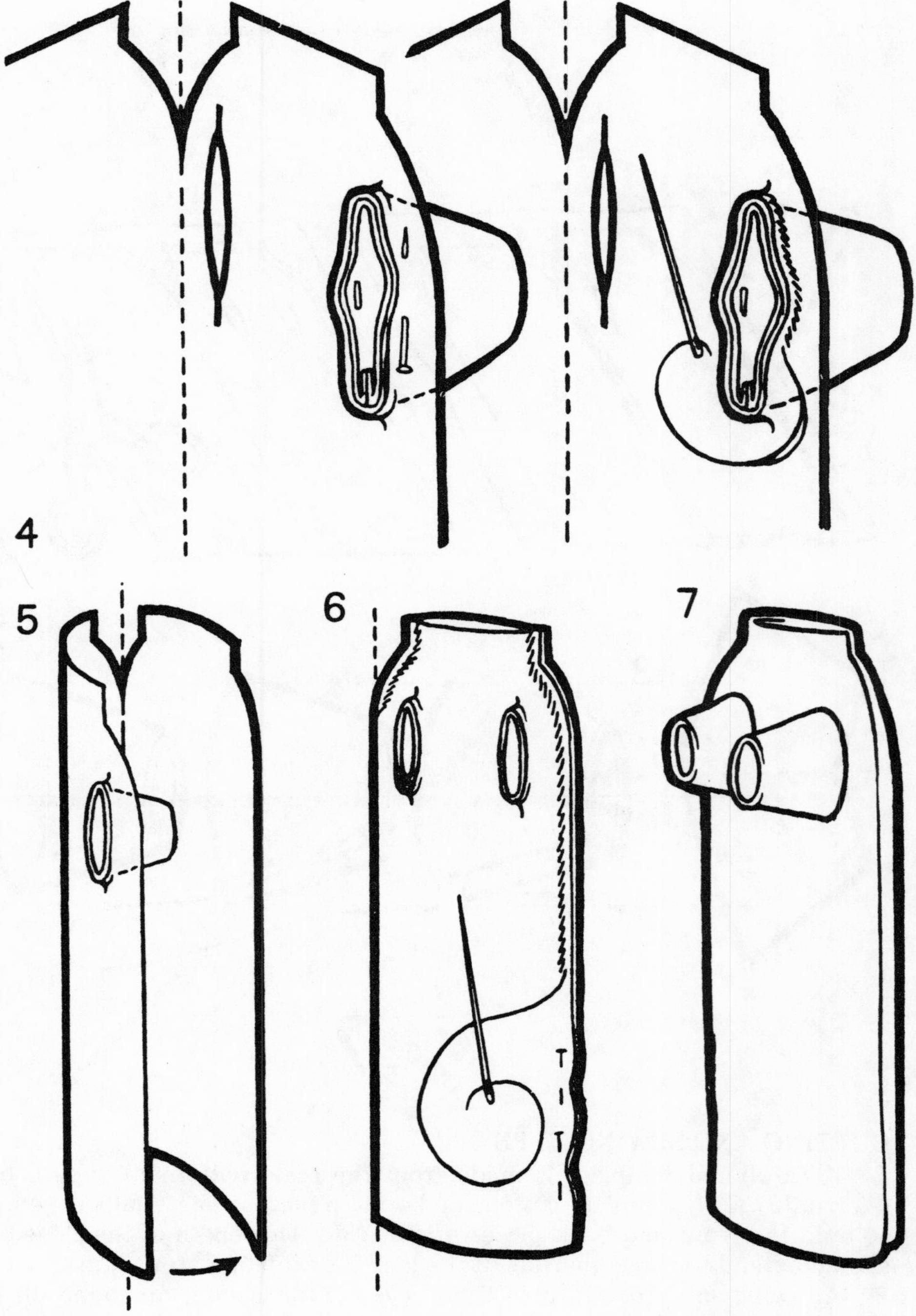

Figure 31b

6 The open side of the body and both sides at neck and shoulder are pinned into position and sewn.
7 The glove body is finally turned right side outwards, ready for the attachment of head, hands, and a hook to hang by.

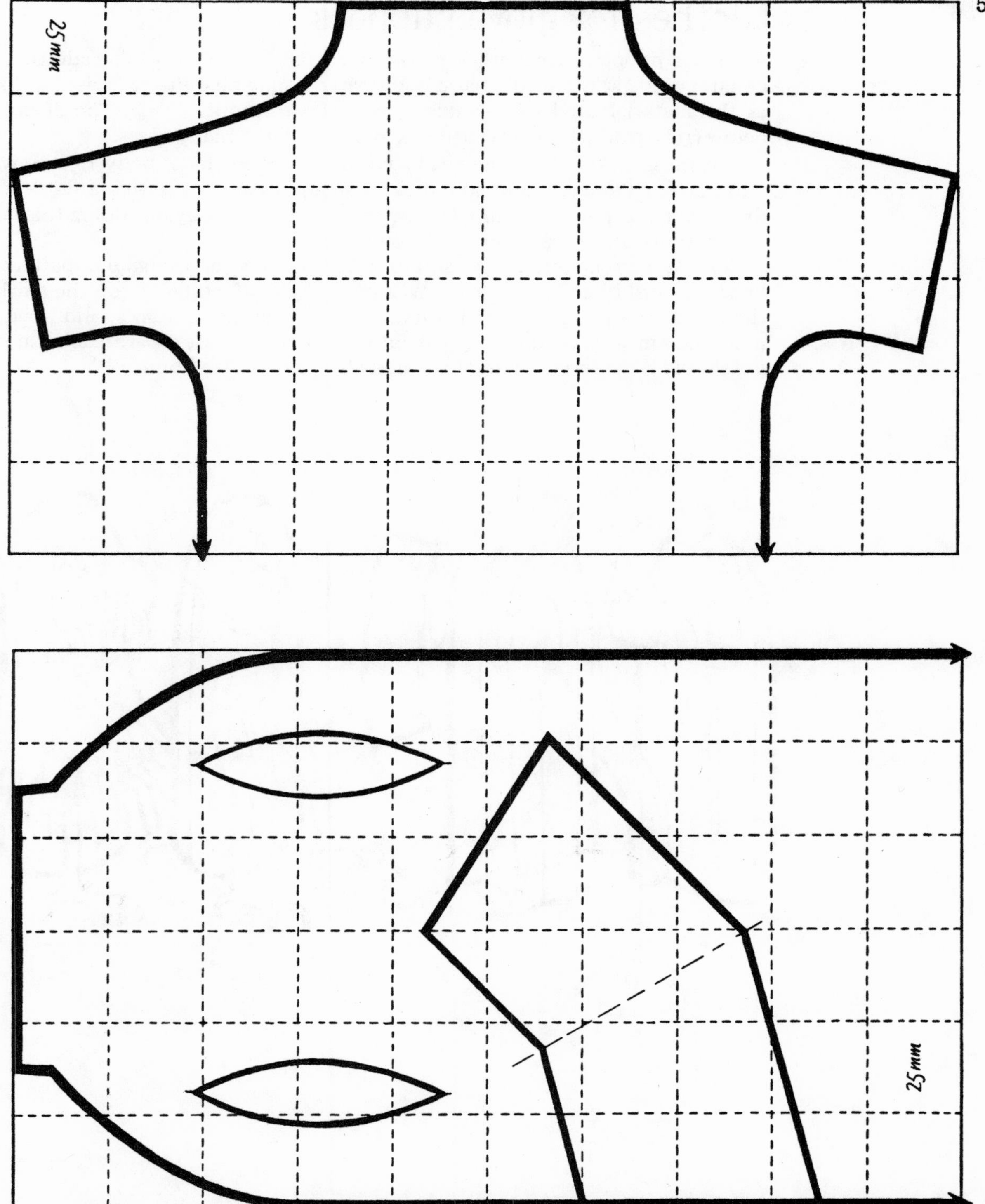

Figure 32 Pattern for body type A and B

Clothes for glove puppets

For glove puppets, the clothes and body can be of one piece. The addition of collar, cuffs and hat to the basic body pattern may be quite sufficient as long as the material used has enough substance to keep its shape. The diagrams below (*figure 33*) show how little extra is needed in many cases.

For those who prefer removeable clothing over the basic body I have given patterns for Punch's coat and hat to fit an adult hand. I use this wide-sleeved dress over most of my puppets; but there are many ways of doing this, and the costume of each puppet has its own problems.

Almost any materials are suitable for puppets' clothing, but patterned material must be correct in scale. With so many cloth adhesives on the market there is no need for elaborate stitching except at stress points, and braid or nylon lace may be used to conceal cut edges in some cases. Cardboard stiffening should be used in making hats, and also for Punch's hump.

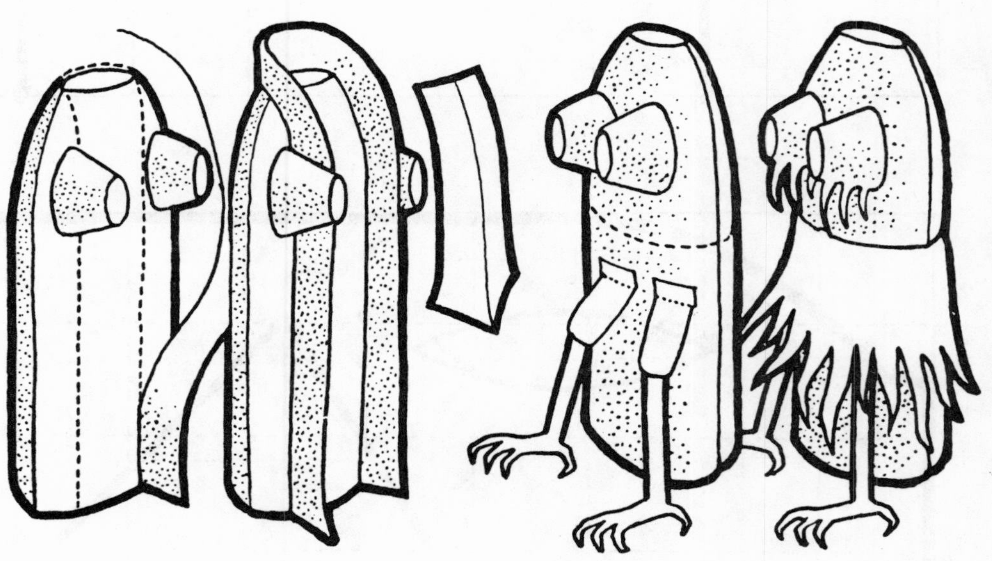

Figure 33

Figure 34 Pattern for Punch's coat (back) (front)

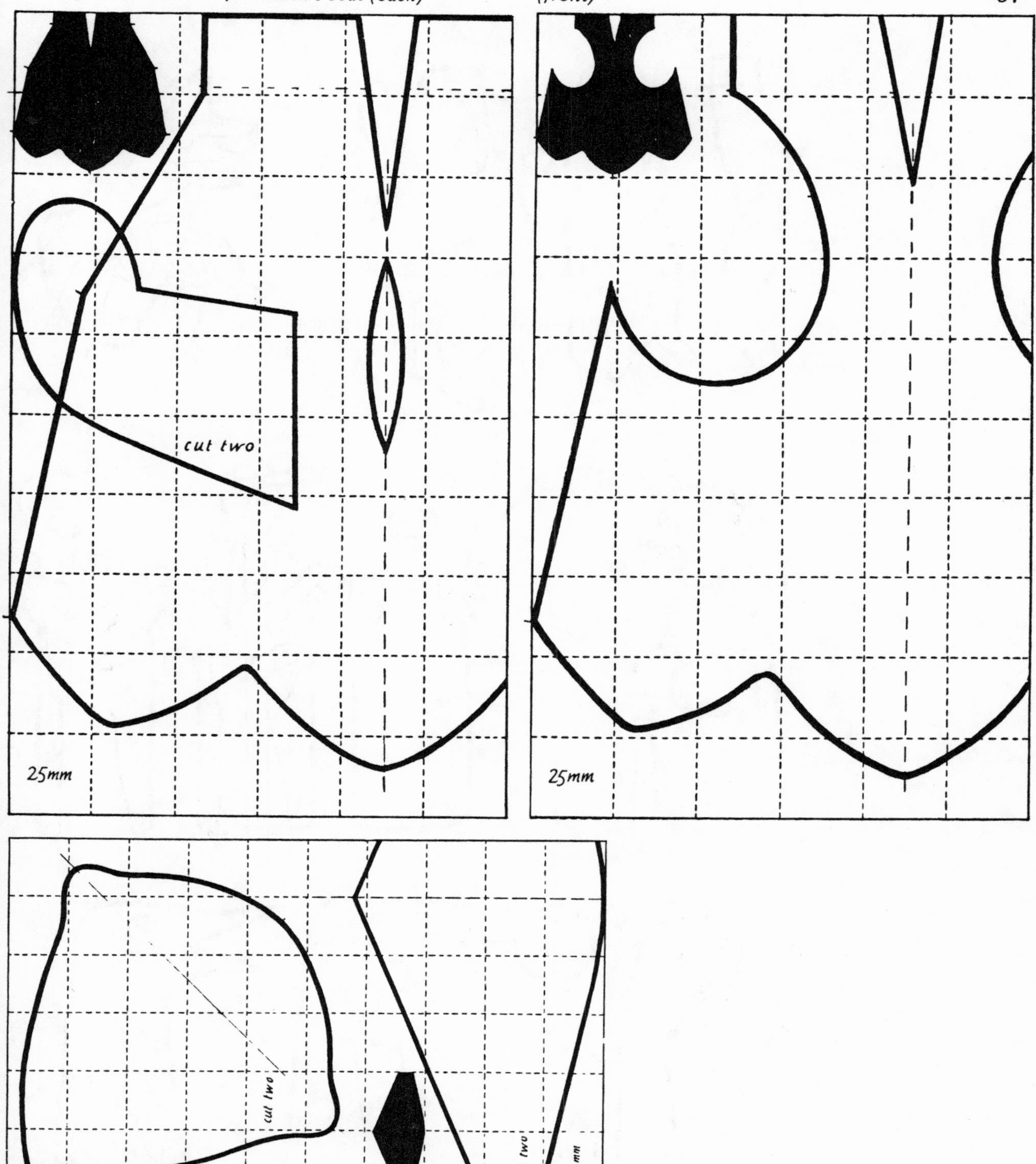

Figure 35 Pattern for Punch's hat and sleeves

Figure 36

Trick glove puppets

Several irregular glove puppets appear in Punch and Judy shows, and in any glove puppet presentation some variation gives interest (see *figure 36*):

A Shows how legs may be added to the basic glove. They can be made of felt, wood, *papier mâché* or any other modelling material, the upper half being of the same material as the body. Legs of this type hang over the edge of the play board.

B Shows legs that are made in the same way as the arms, and are manipulated by the operator's spare hand. They may swing loose at other times like type A.

C Most animal glove puppets look best when modelled with a wide neck fitting over the body and a cylinder fitted inside for the operator's index finger. There are many patterns for animal gloves on the market where a stuffed head is made from the same fabric as the body.

D For puppets with heads that can look from side to side or even be knocked off, a strong cardboard ring is fitted into the collar of the body. A turning head is fixed to a free moving piece of wooden dowelling held by the operator's spare hand. A removeable head is held temporarily in position on the operator's index finger.

E Shows a development of the glove puppet where, instead of fitting into neck and arms, the manipulator's thumb and fingers are used to carry out mouth movements. A strong cardboard disc is folded in half, (the hinge may be strengthened with leather), and glued into the end of a sock or sock-shaped head and body. This type of puppet is most successful in the representation of birds and animals where the basic body is easily disguised with feathers or scales, or cut from the outset in fur fabric. The mouth mechanism is less well suited to human characters, but can be made more natural looking by the addition of a beard.

These puppets may be made in their simplest form by children, but can become quite large and elaborate with the addition of open-backed clothing, allowing the manipulator's free hand to fit into the puppet's sleeves or paws in just the same way we have seen used with some large rod puppets.

Marionettes

Marionettes are puppets worked by strings from above, and are the most ambitious attempt in puppetry of the portrayal of the whole human figure. These puppets were introduced into England from Italy in the second half of the seventeenth century and rapidly became more popular than the traditional glove puppet which survived mostly in the form of Punch and Judy. At the same time the material for puppet plays developed from folk lore sources into much more sophisticated dramatic productions.

Marionettes are probably the most difficult to make and to control of all puppets, as the mechanism is comparatively remote from the figure. There can be various grades of difficulty in making marionettes, but I would never advise a beginner in puppetry to tackle even the easiest until he has had some experience with rod or glove puppet making.

Marionettes may be made of *papier màché*, cloth or wood. Whatever the material careful planning is important, and some understanding of the function and proportions of the human body is essential for good design.

The height of marionettes may vary considerably. Usually they are not less than 460 mm (18 in.) and not more than 915 mm (36 in.). The movements of very small marionettes are not visible at any great distance, and with larger marionettes, the weight becomes unwieldy.

Figure 37 Marionettes for a nativity play

Proportions of the head and body

In designing a puppet, it is helpful to have some idea of the general proportions of the figure. Sometimes distortion or exaggeration adds to character, but this should be consciously done.

Too often the head is mistakenly tackled first by a beginner making a puppet, and the height and proportions thought of later. This may lead to the head and hands being far too large for the rest of the body. Now this may not matter in the case of glove puppets where the overall length is undefined; but the marionette expresses itself with the whole body, not the head alone. When too much emphasis is given to one part, the significance of the movements as a whole are lost. A head is seldom more than one-seventh of the complete body height in an adult, and a scale drawing should be made of the whole puppet before work begins on any one part.

Just as the head, hands and feet, are parts of the complete figure, so the features of the head are related to each other. In looking at the average head, we should remember that a slight deviation of one feature from the normal can be more telling than a set of exaggerated features, each one crowding for attention.

Seen from the front, the head may be divided horizontally into three equal sections:

1 From the top of the skull to the brow line
2 From the brow to the base of the nose
3 From the base of the nose to the chin

The mouth is placed a little above the middle of the lowest section. The ears lie within the limits of the centre section. The distance between the eyes is the width of one eye.

Seen from the side the head may be divided vertically in two. The ear lies behind the centre division. The eye is set well back in its socket from the bridge of the nose. This distance may be as much as the width of the base of the nose.

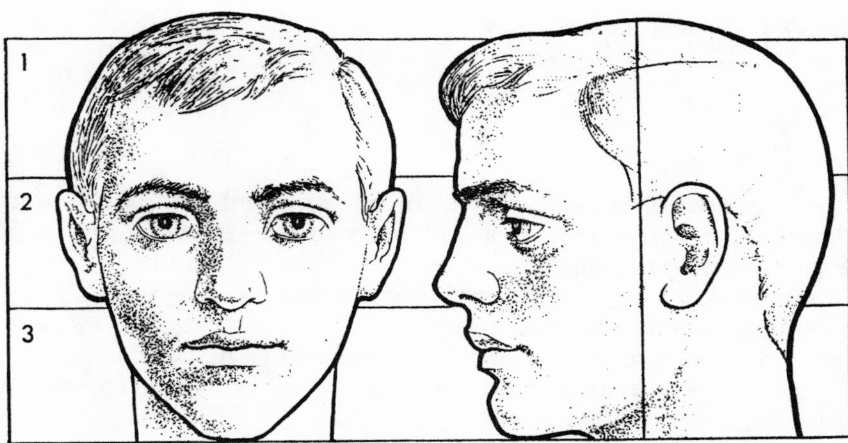

Figure 38 Proportions of the head

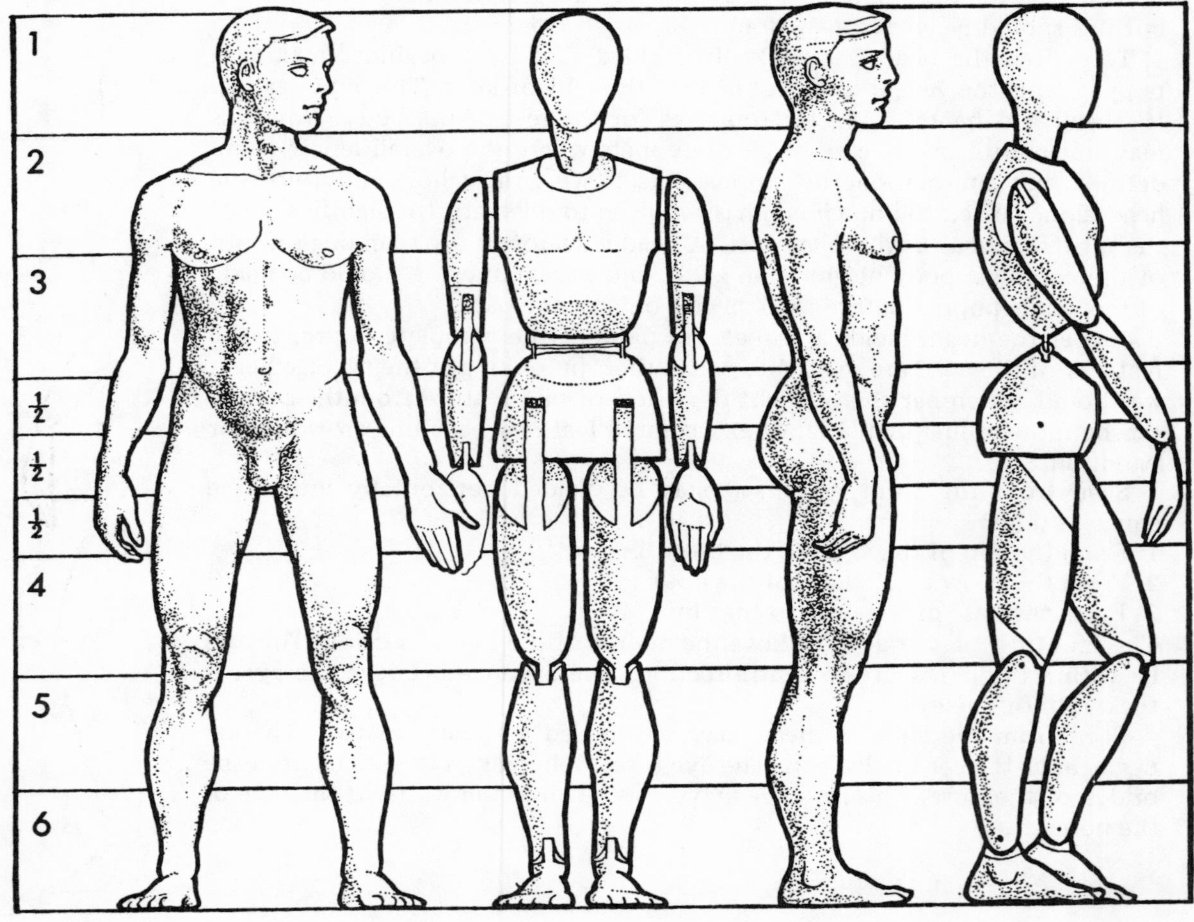

Figure 39 Proportions of the male figure

The head is usually taken as a unit of measurement, and in the average male figure there are seven and a half units in the complete height. The following points may be remembered and noted in the diagrams:

a The division of the legs is at the mid-height level of the body.
b The elbow joint is level with the waist.
c The shoulders are two units wide; the hips one and a half units.
d The arm divides into three units—armpit to elbow, elbow to wrist and wrist to finger tips.
e The hand is the length of the chin to hairline.
f The feet are slightly more than one unit long.

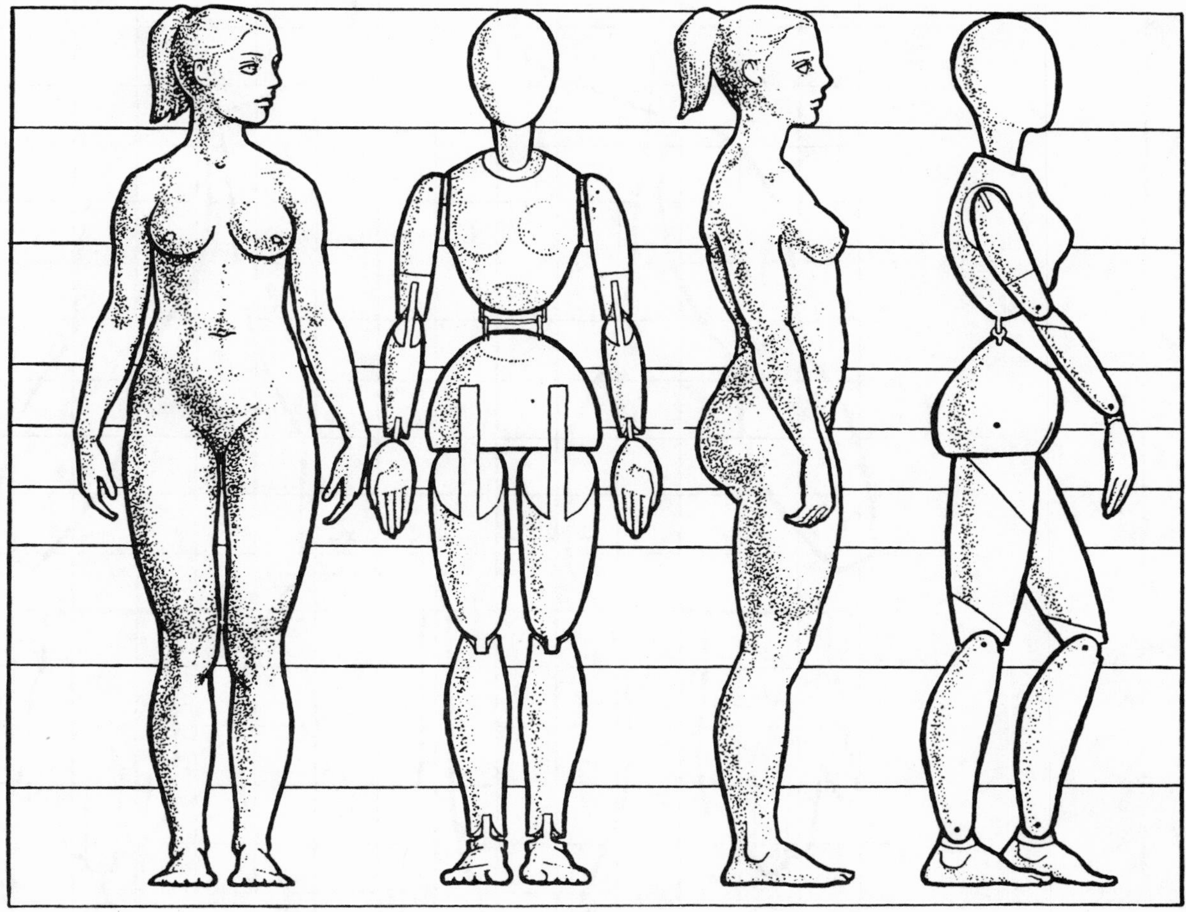

Figure 40 Proportions of the female figure

The female figure is more variable than the male, but the following comparisons are usually true.

a The shoulders are narrower and more sloping.
b The hips are wider.
c The waist is narrower.
d The legs are proportionately shorter, altering the line of mid-height.

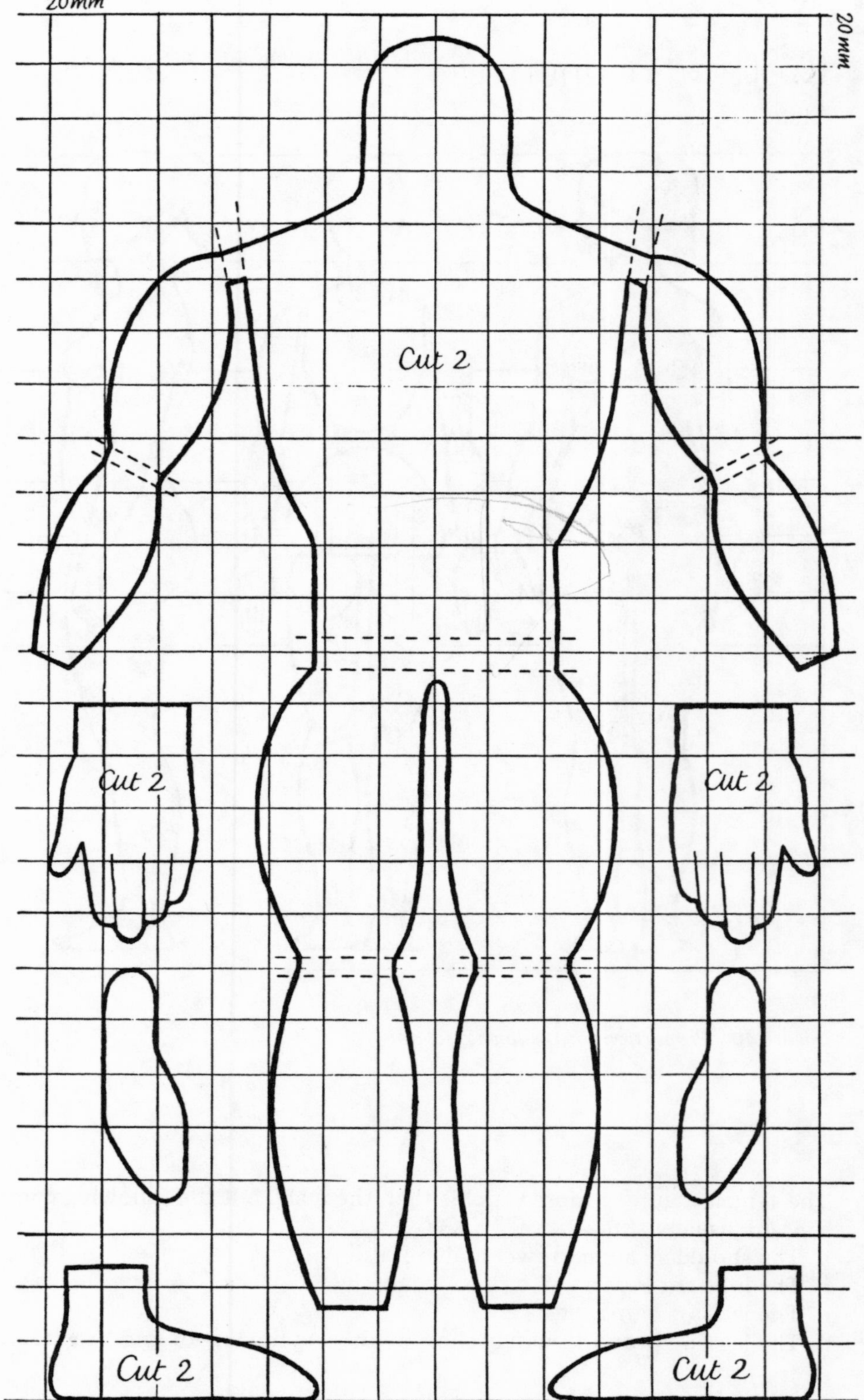

Figure 41 Pattern for a cloth marionette

Cloth marionettes

There are many ways of improvising cloth puppets. For those who prefer to follow a pattern, I have drawn one which can be copied on to 15 mm (½ in.) squared paper for a puppet 460 mm (18 in.) in height, or 20 mm (¾ in.) squared paper for a 600 mm (23 in.) puppet. When the pattern has been traced on to material it should be cut with an extra width of 5 mm (¼ in.) all round so that the stitching can follow the drawn line (see *figures 41* and *42*).

The two parts of the body are sewn together round the edge, leaving openings at the neck, wrist and ankles. The body is then turned right side out and stuffed. Double rows of stitching at knee, elbow and thigh make good hinge joints, while the narrow spaces between the rows of stitching at the shoulders are tightly bound with thread to make freely moving joints. The head, hands and feet are most successfully made in felt, and are turned inside out and stuffed in the same way as the body. They are then fitted over the neck, wrists and ankles and sewn or glued in place.

Ears, eyes and mouth may be completed in felt appliqué or paint; sometimes a *papier mâché* mask is fitted over the felt head. Hair can be stitched directly onto the head, and the divisions between the fingers of each hand are tightly sewn after the hands are stuffed.

Cloth marionettes, usually light in weight, are easier to control if small pieces of sheet lead are placed in the hands, above each knee joint, and at the base of the back for ballast. In spite of careful weighting, cloth puppets are difficult to control. They appear most successful when combined with rigid apparatus, (as the stilt walker and unicyclist), but the simple stringing

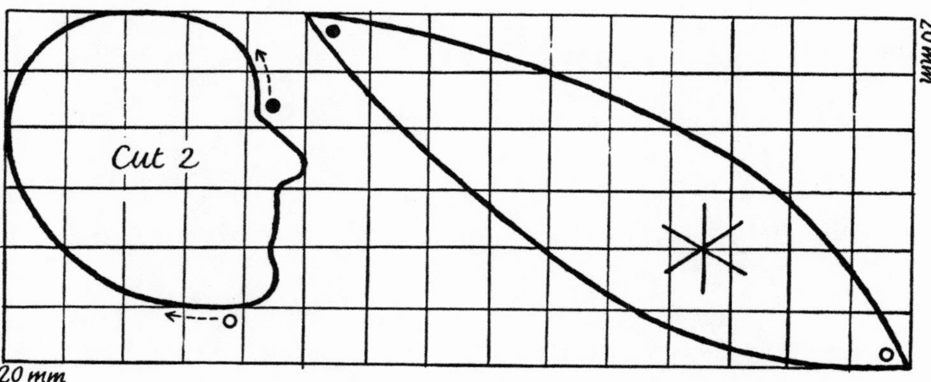

Figure 42

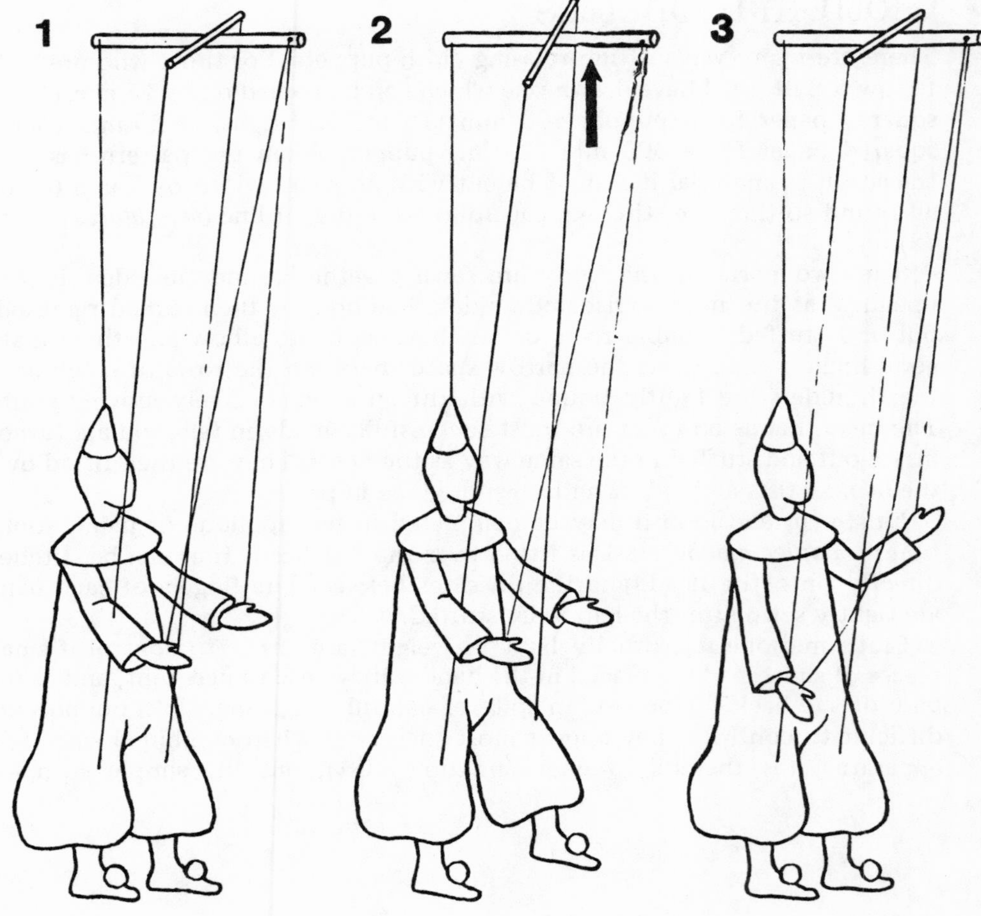

Figure 43

described below is often used in puppetry with children.
In *figure 43:*

1 One string to the head supports the clown's weight; strings from the cross bar are joined to each knee, and the hands are half raised on a running string through a hole in the main bar.
2 The main control bar is rocked from side to side for a walking movement.
3 The hands are raised or lowered by pulling on the running string.

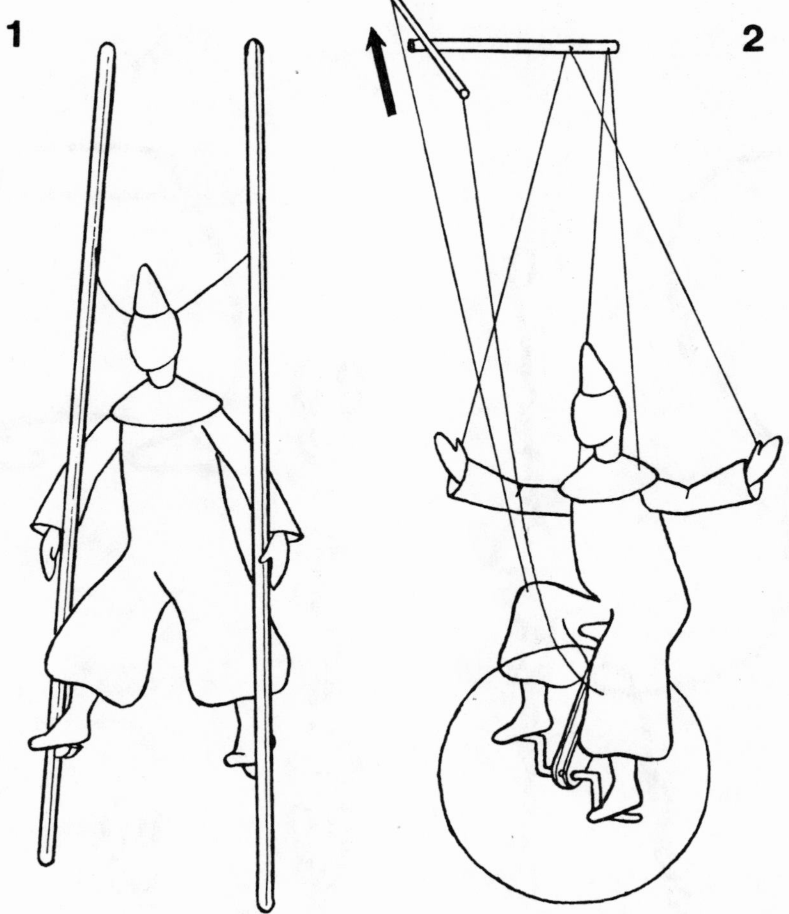

Figure 44

In *figure 44:*

1 The hands and feet of the stilt walker are fixed to the stilts, while his head is supported on strings to each side. The manipulator's hands hold the stilts out of sight of the audience. This is a simple and most effective circus puppet, particularly when performing in a group.

2 The unicyclist is literally glued to his saddle, and his feet are fixed to the pedals of the wheel. The arms are raised on a running string through the main bar which rocks to raise and lower the knees. The shoulder strings support the main weight of this wobbly but convincing performer.

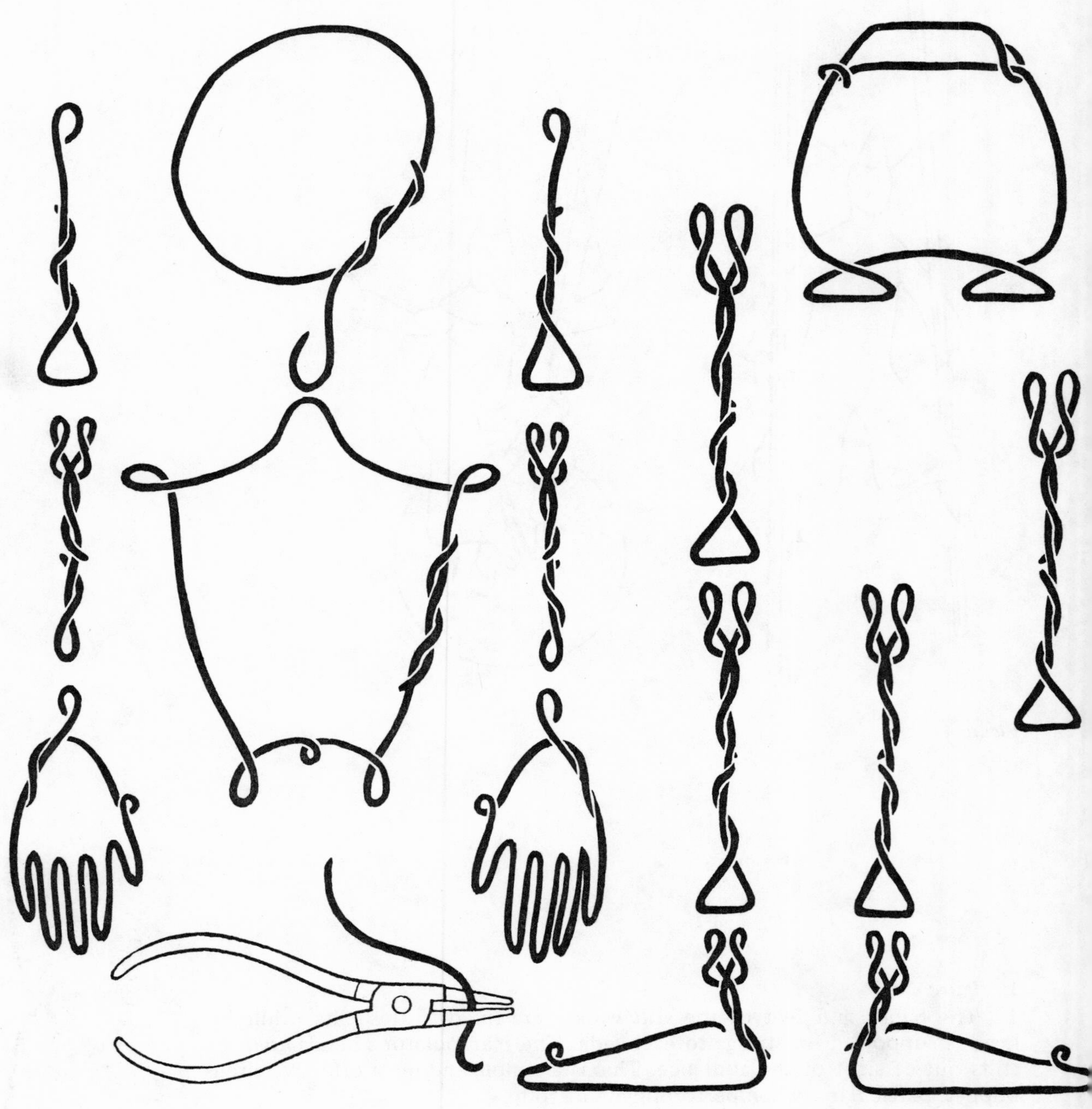

Figure 45 Wire framework for a papier mâché marionette

Directly modelled marionettes

The diagram opposite (*figure 45*) shows a suggested wire framework for a directly modelled marionette. For convenience in copying I have drawn the parts separately, but before modelling begins the parts should all be interlocked, except for the head and hands which can be attached later. The drawings of the building up of the head (see *figure 46*), show the method used for all parts of the body. The wire frame is either filled or surrounded with paper soaked in thin size or watered gum and the whole part bound tightly with bandaging. On this core the features and finished surface are built, using laminated and pulped *papier mâché*, or one of the plastic modelling substances described on page 33. When this layer is dry it can be sandpapered smooth and sealed with spirit varnish ready for painting.

Screw eyes for string attachments can only be used safely with wooden puppets, so hooks for stringing must be included in the wire framework. When this has not been done, wire loops may be bedded with extra glue in the modelling material before it is dry. The hinge joints at knee and elbow are limited in range by the shape of the modelling; the joints at neck, shoulder and wrist are freely moving.

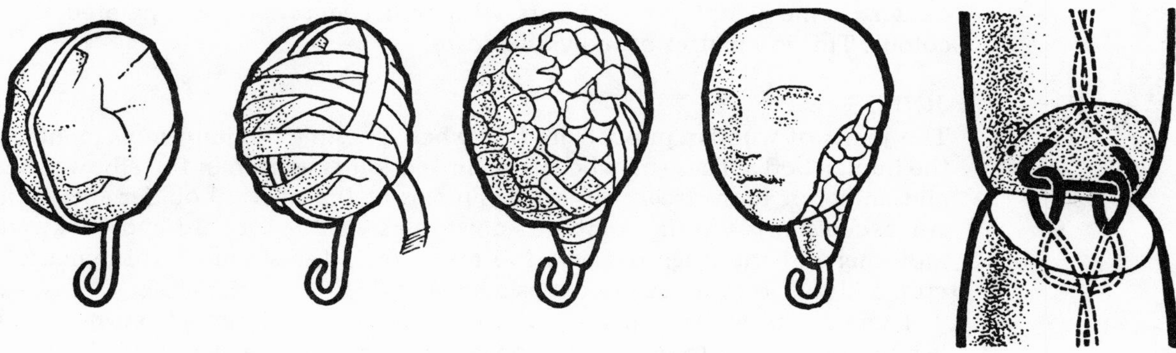

Figure 46

Wooden marionettes

THE PARTS OF THE BODY

The carving of a wooden head and hands has already been described. In principle, the carving of the feet and parts of the body are exactly the same, provided you have a front and side profile clearly marked on your block of wood. I have given diagrams of both a male and female wooden marionette of just over 460 mm (18 in.) high as a guide for drawing these profiles.

Although head, hands and feet are cut in close-grained hard wood because of the detail involved, all the parts of the body may be carved from soft wood which is much easier to work. The grain direction of the whole wooden marionette is vertical from head to ankle, the exception being the feet where the grain direction is horizontal. The carving of the parts of the body may be done with a mallet and chisel, or a spokeshave, but an electric sander works very quickly through soft wood. This cannot strictly be called carving, but it saves a lot of time.

If your marionette is to be clothed entirely except for hands, head and feet, there is no reason at all why you should not use wooden dowelling for the legs and arms. I have found 19 mm (¾ in.) dowelling for legs and 13 mm (½ in.) dowelling for arms quite suitable. If the weight of the completed marionette is too great, holes can be bored through from front to back of thorax and pelvis, or these parts may be sawn in two and hollowed out with a chisel.

The plans given are of two marionettes carved for a nativity play. They are only 460 mm (18 in.) high as the play had a large cast and was presented on a 2 m (6 ft.) wide stage. Real hair was used for the shepherdess, and a piece of goatskin was soaked and moulded to be glued on the head of the shepherd.

It is by no means necessary to use one type of joint throughout the whole marionette. I prefer string jointing for shoulder and elbow and tongue and groove for knee and ankle joints. It is best to be guided by what is most suitable for the particular movements required by individual puppets. In the instructions of the different types of joint, I have given the example which is most typical of its kind, although there are variations within each type of joint. Some types of waist joint belong to none of the varieties above, but are dealt with in their place in the plans of the wooden marionette. If a joint is well made, it should, like the stringing, be an acceptable part of the whole design. Some people cover joints with thin *chamois* leather painted flesh colour. This is a matter of individual taste.

JOINTS

The joints of wooden puppets imitate where possible the joint movements of the human body. These may be either hinged joints as seen in the elbow, knee and ankle, or more freely rotating joints as at the neck, shoulder and wrist. An exception is the hip joint. A sideways as well as forward and backward movement of the thigh detracts too much from the stability of the marionette, and this joint is usually cut as a hinge.

There are three principal ways of jointing a wooden puppet—string joints, leather joints and tongue and groove joints cut in the wood of the limbs themselves. I have arranged them in order of difficulty.

String joints are the most flexible type of jointing, and are best used where movement is to be sideways as well as forward and backwards. A combined string jointing at shoulder and elbow makes for excellent arm movement with the ability to move across the front of the body. This is not easily accomplished by any other type of jointing. Sometimes a free-moving waist joint is made, using strong cord which can be continued upwards to make the neck joint. I am not very happy however about string jointing where there is any weight below the joint, and string jointing is not suitable for the more rigid hinge joint of the knee.

Leather joints make a very good hinge where movement is forward or backwards only. Good examples of this are the knee, elbow and ankle joint. Where a more freely moving joint is wanted, leather is less successful. It can be used for the shoulder joint, though I prefer other types of jointing here, and also for the waist joint if no great sideways movement is wanted. The leather used must be strong and supple. For very small puppets *chamois* leather is sufficient, but for larger puppets men's gloving leather is best, or even book-binders' morocco. Hide and calf are too thick and not flexible enough.

Tongue and groove joints are the most difficult joints to make. A carpenter would more correctly name them flexible saddle joints. These joints give a more natural appearance than other types of jointing, and give the satisfaction of meeting a technical challenge. In the plans of the two wooden marionettes which follow, I have shown tongue and groove joints with their variations throughout as they need to be most carefully planned. I often cut profiles in card of tongue and groove joints, and rotate them around a pin to see what range of movement I may have. The tongue and groove joints in the following instructions are stopped on one side so that movement is in one direction only. This is the most complicated tongue and groove joint to make and it is used at the elbow and knee.

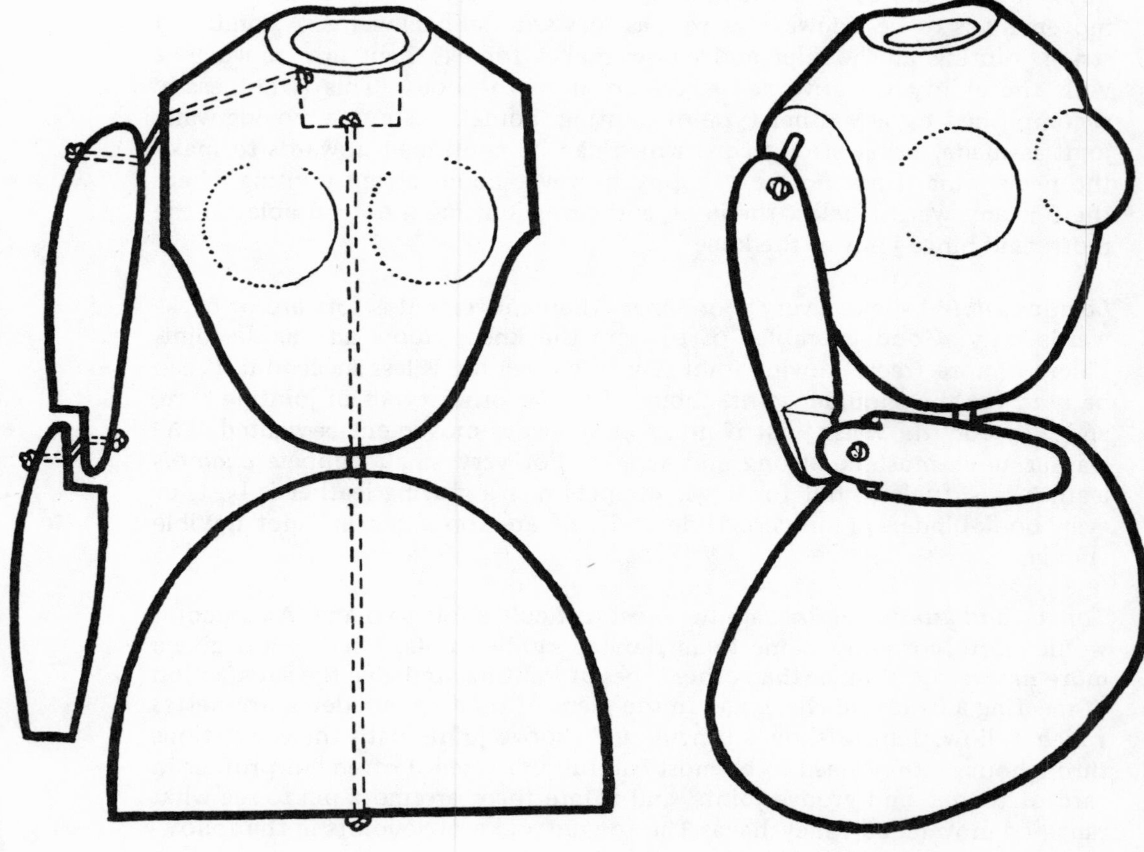

Figure 47 Some useful string joints

MAKING A STRING JOINT (*Figure 48*)

Tools needed: bench saw, hand drill, file.

A Two saw cuts remove a little over half of each end to be jointed. When the two ends are fitted together there is a narrow vertical space between them. The first cut is made with the wood fixed in a vice, the second on a bench hook.

B A hole is drilled through the centre of each projecting tongue at the joint ends. These are best drilled separately, fixed with a G-clamp over a piece of waste wood. An opening for the drill is first made with a sharp pointed tool.

C The projecting tongues at the joint ends are filed or sandpapered round.

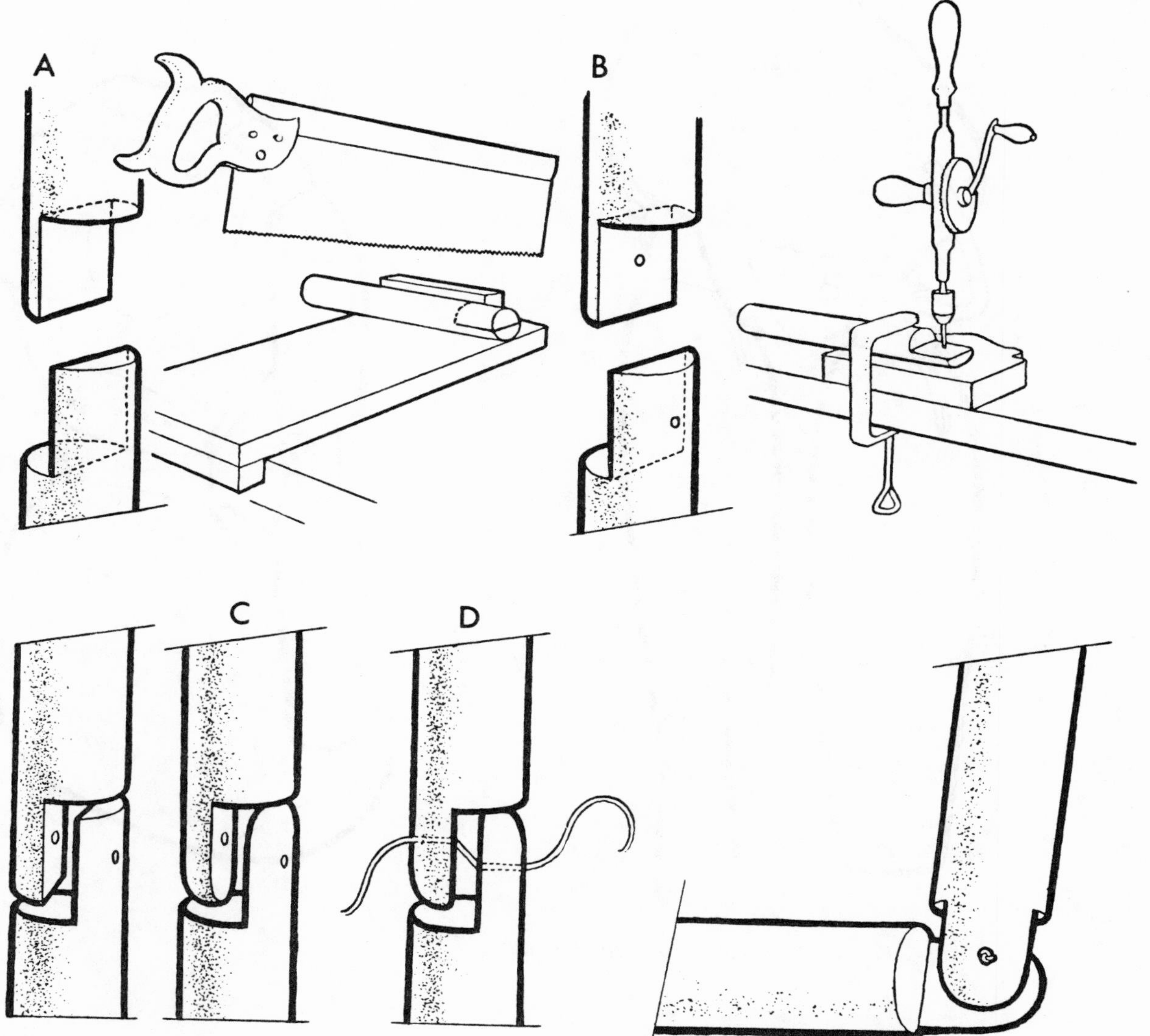

Figure 48   Making a string joint

D String is passed through the drilled holes from one side to the other of the joint. Inside the joint the space between the tongues is loosely strung, and the outside ends of the string are knotted and cut close. It is always safer to paint the finished knots with glue. The string used must vary with the size of your puppet, and must be strong enough to take the weight of the lower limb of the joint. *Macramé* twine makes a rather large knot, but lasts a long time without fraying. The cord in string joints must be renewed from time to time.

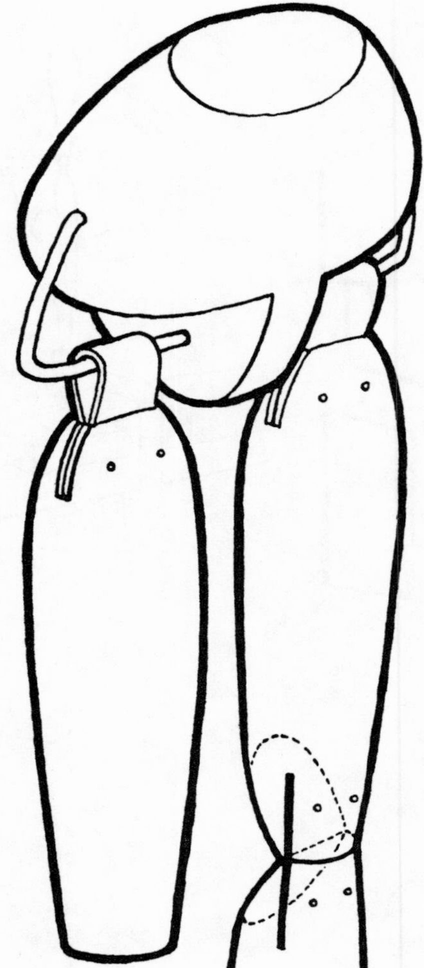

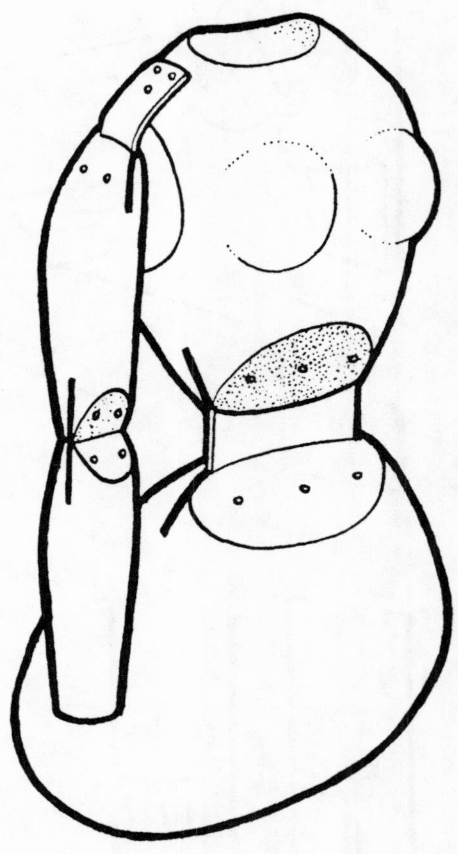

Figure 49 Some useful leather joints

MAKING A LEATHER JOINT (*Figure 50*)

Tools needed: bench saw, file. razor blade. hammer.

A A straight saw cut is made down the centre of each part to be jointed. These saw cuts should be exactly opposite each other. The cut made should be of the same thickness as the leather which is to be used, so for small joints with *chamois* leather a hacksaw is sufficient. For larger joints with thicker leather a tenon saw makes a wider cut.

B One half of each part to be jointed is filed to an angle. This may be done with a chisel if you prefer. The degree of the angle controls the range of movement in the finished joint.

C A square cut piece of leather is eased into each groove in turn, until the two halves of the joint fit closely together. A little glue is run into the bottom of each groove but kept clear of the joint ends.

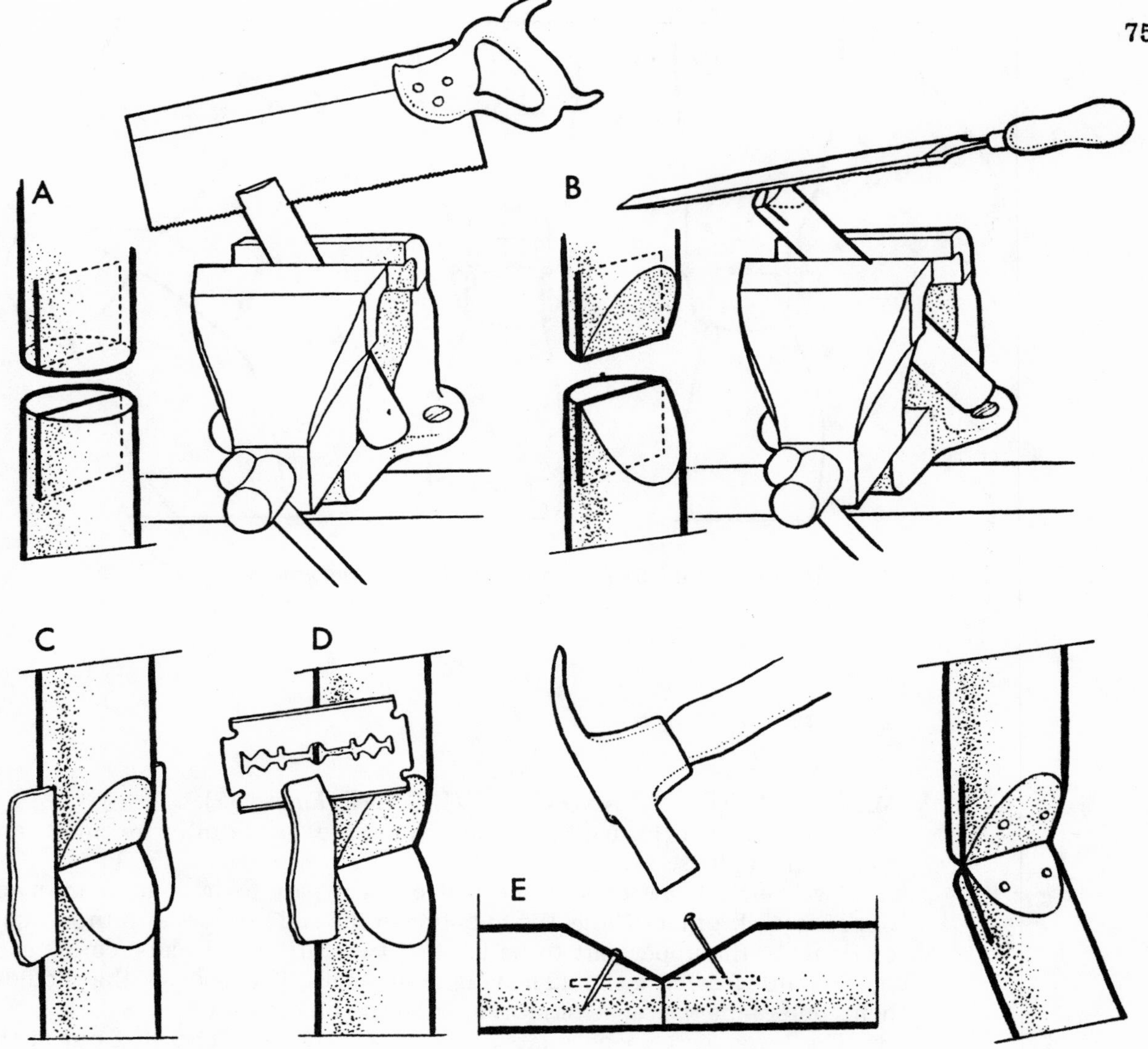

Figure 50 Making a leather joint

D The overlapping leather is trimmed with a razor blade close to the sides of the joint.

E After testing movement to make sure that the joint is not too tight, two small pins are tapped into each filed surface of the joint to pierce and fix the leather. Picture framer's pins are best for this purpose. If they are too long they can be cut with wire cutters, and driven in with the cut end lying across the grain of the wood.

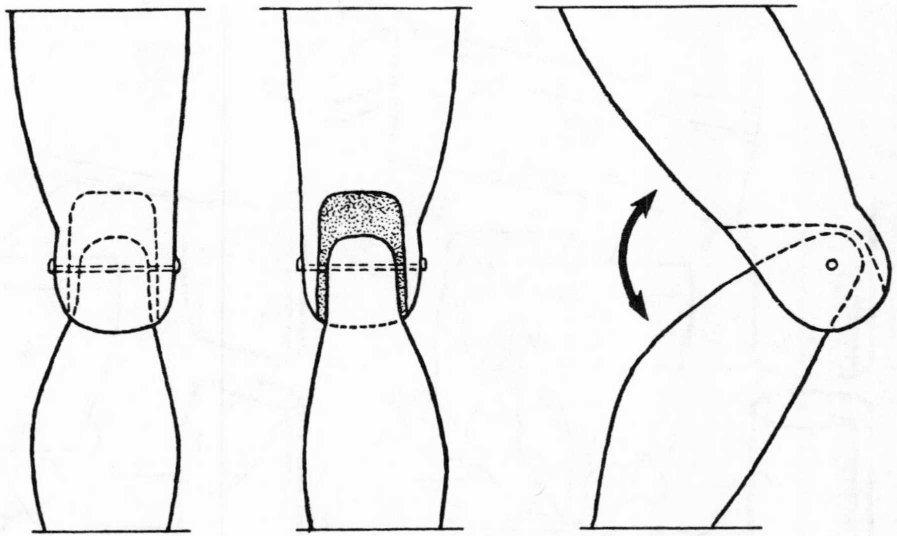

Figure 51 Concealed knee joint; a modified tongue and groove

MAKING A TONGUE AND GROOVE JOINT (*Figure 52*)

Tools needed: bench saw, mallet and chisel, file, hand-drill, wire cutters and round-nosed pliers.

A Two vertical saw cuts in the end of each part to be jointed are made opposite each other. These saw cuts divide the end surfaces into three equal sections. In the upper part to be jointed, two further side cuts remove each outer third leaving a shoulder lying at an angle. The angle of the shoulder helps determine the range of movement in the finished joint.

B The lower part to be jointed has the centre third chiselled out at the angle shown. Use a chisel of the same width as the groove to be cut.

C A small notch is cut from the short side of the tongue, and the groove in the lower part of the joint is deepened to allow the tongue to fit.

D The end of the tongue is filed round, and the surfaces of the lower half of the joint are also rounded.

E The tongue and groove are fitted into each other. If they are tight they are better left so at present; if slack then the joint should be wedged with paper to keep it in position for the hand-drill. While you are using the drill the joint may be held in position by a G-clamp over a piece of waste wood, or you may ask someone to hold it in position for you. The size of the drill bit should be the same as the wire to be used in fixing the joint.

F Make sure that the tongue can move easily in its groove. If the fit is too tight, the sides of the groove must be cleared further with a chisel. A short length of wire is inserted through the joint, cut, and turned over at each end to form a loop too wide to slip back into the shaft.

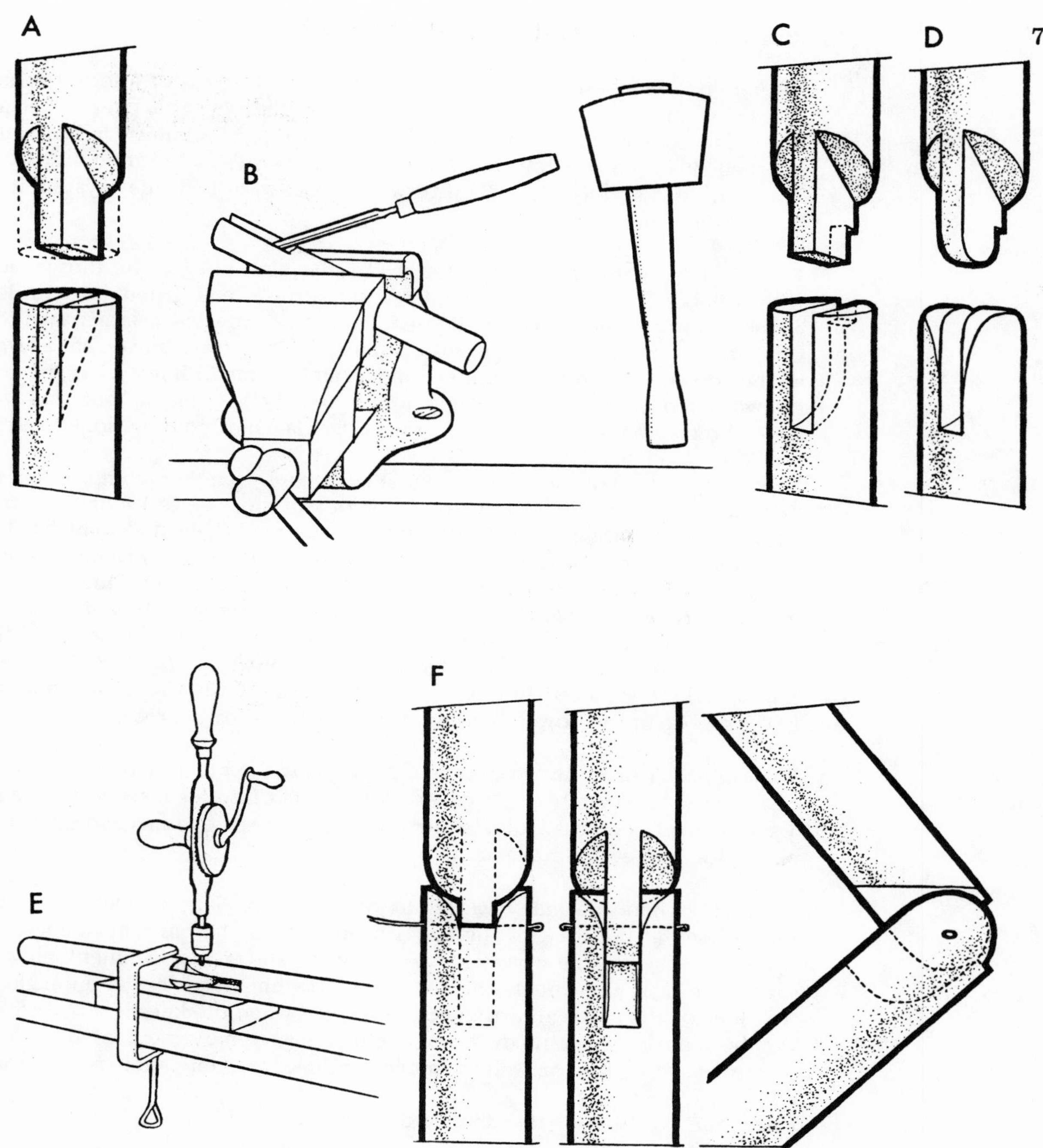

Figure 52 Making a tongue and groove joint

Neck joint The base of the neck is attached to the base of a socket in the thorax by means of two cup hooks which are closed with pliers when in place. The socket is most neatly made by a brace and 19 mm (¾ in.) bit, and widened slightly at the top with a chisel used sideways to the grain direction. The movements at this joint are forwards, backward and sideways, limited by the rim of the socket.

Waist joint There are many variations to this joint, but I prefer those made with thick wire passed through large screw eyes and fitted into drilled channels in the woodwork. If the opening in the screw eye is larger than the thickness of the wire there is a certain amount of sideways movement as well as the forward and backward hinge movement. A metal hinge joint gives no sideways movement, and a string joint possibly too much, but this will depend on the actions necessary to the performance of your marionette.

Shoulder joint The shoulder joint shown here is rather complicated to make and is used with upper arm rotation. In most cases I much prefer a string joint at shoulder and elbow, but this more complicated joint has the advantage that the shape of the shoulder is preserved whatever the movement may be. A housing for a short piece of 13 mm (½ in.) dowelling is drilled into the thorax at shoulder level. One half of the piece of dowelling is cut into a tongue to fit the groove of the upper arm. The other half of the dowelling has a groove filed round it. A small length of thick wire or very fine dowelling is passed through the top of the socket in the thorax, and lies in the groove of the dowel, holding it in place but allowing rotation.

Wrist joint This is an open tongue and groove joint. The tongue is most easily cut as a separate piece of wood and glued into a socket in the hand. Variations of the wrist joint show a wire and screw eye mechanism which allows some sideways movement.

Hip joint There are many variations of this joint. The tongue and groove joint closed at the back of the pelvis probably has the best appearance and control in the walking movement. A screw eye and wire attachment allows a slight sideways movement. and the screw attachment of legs at an angle to the sides of the pelvis allows an outward splay when the knee is raised which can be amusing if wanted. A complete sideways movement at the hip is seldom attempted as the walking movement becomes impossible to control.

Knee joint This is a straightforward closed hinge joint.

Ankle joint The variations in the ankle joint are of appearance rather than function, as all that is needed is a limited hinge joint. The amount of drop allowed to the foot may be controlled by the stringing, or by the shape of the joint itself. In all constructions of the foot and ankle it is necessary to attach the foot at an angle slightly outwards from the shaft of the leg to avoid the risk of the feet getting in each others' way when walking. It is sometimes necessary also to add weight to the front sole of the foot to make it drop when the knee is raised. A small piece of sheet lead is suitable for this.

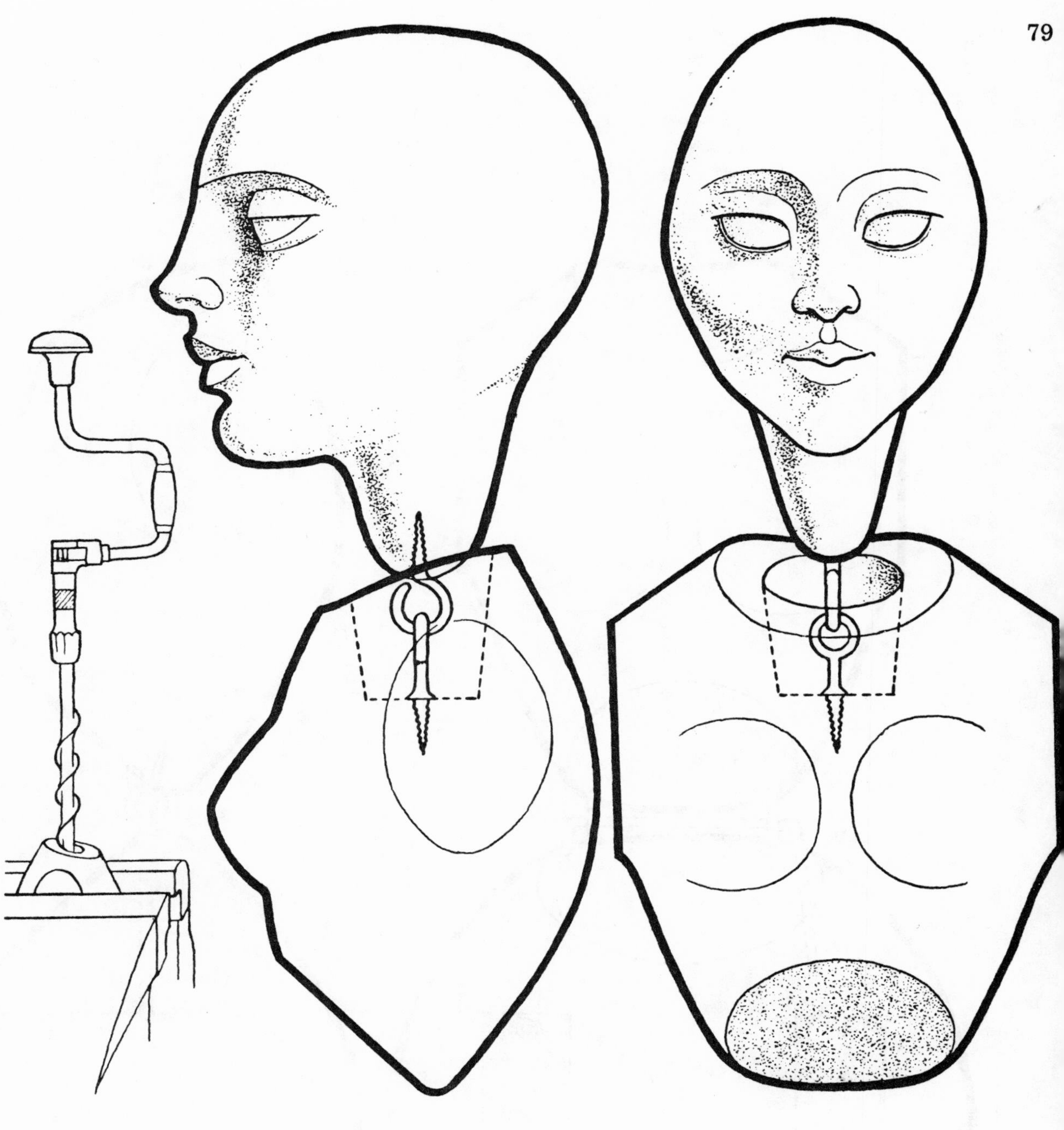

Figure 53 Head, thorax and neck joint

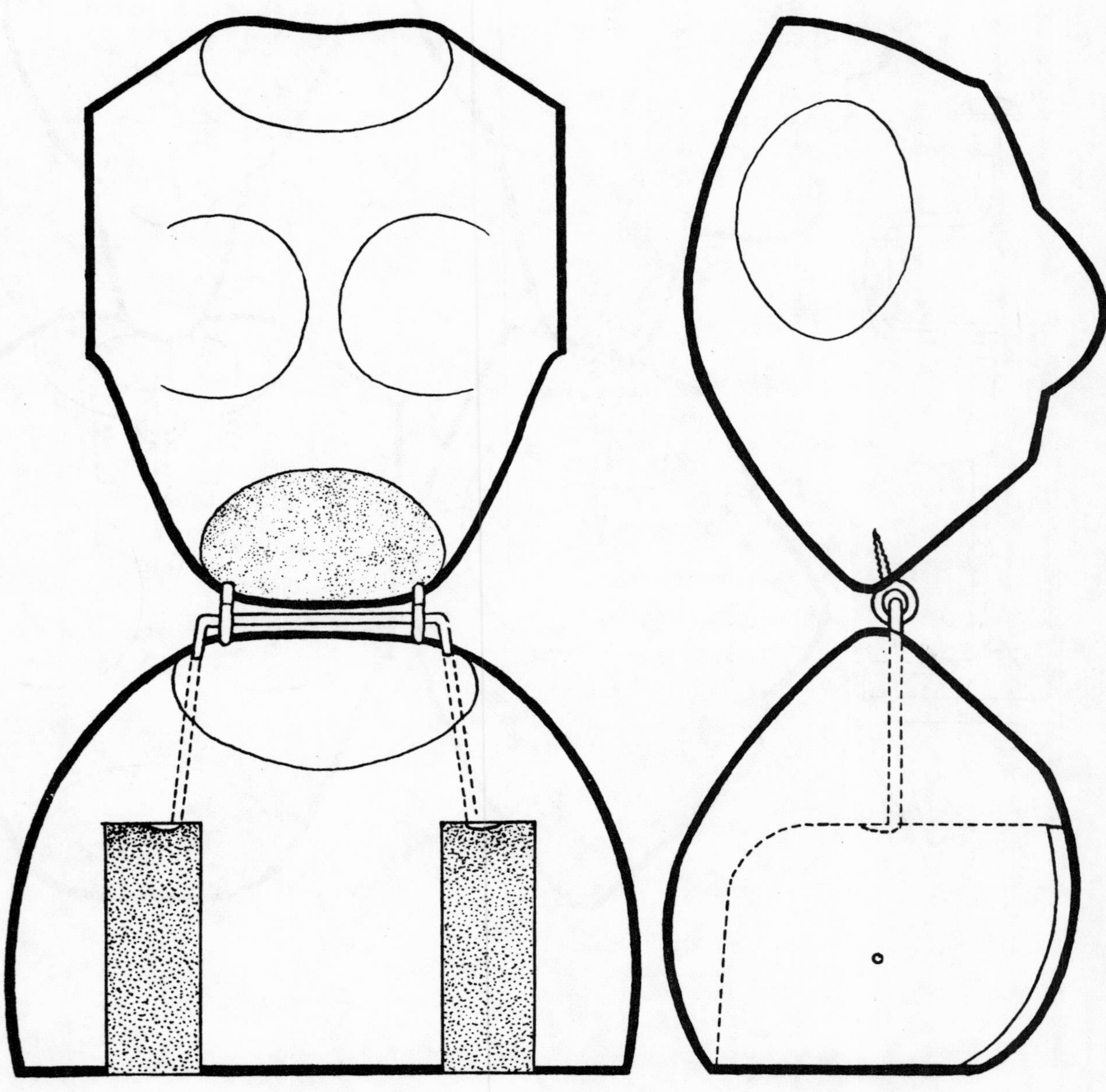

Figure 54   Thorax, pelvis and waist joint

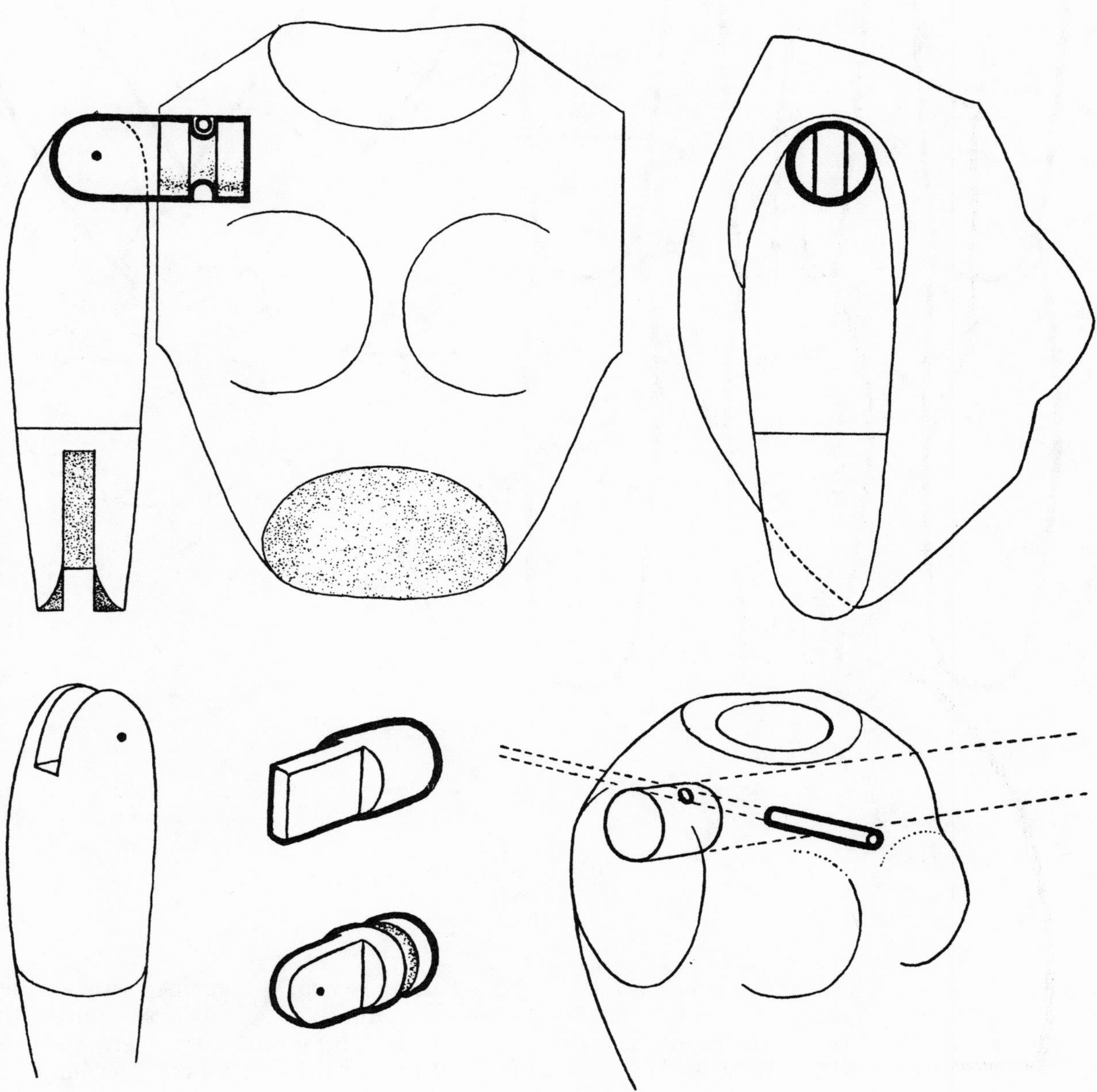

Figure 55 Shoulder joint

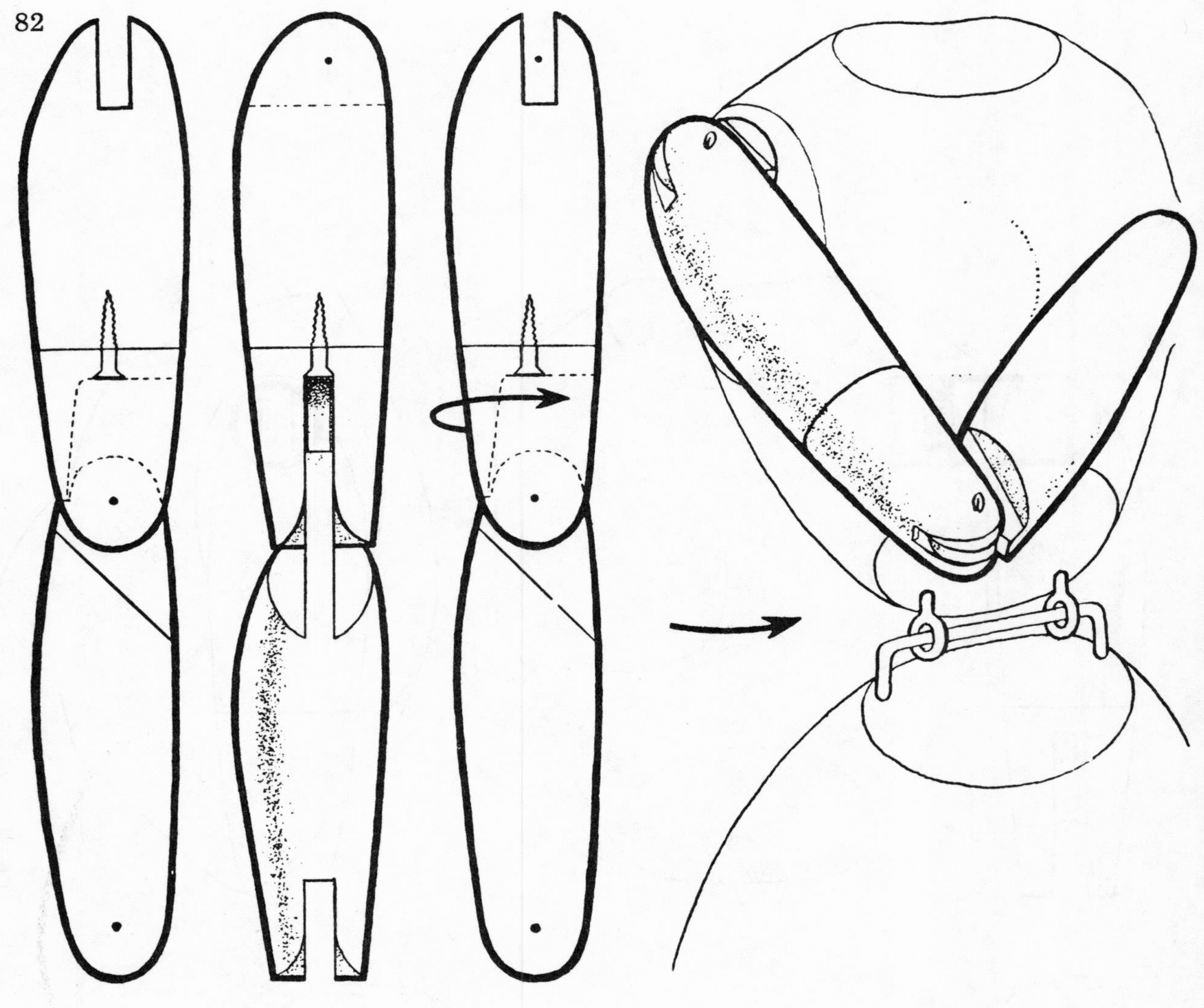

Figure 56

Upper arm rotation (Figure 56) This movement is combined with a closed hinge joint at the elbow and allows the arm to move across the front of the body. The upper arm is cut into two, at a distance above the groove of the elbow joint equal to the unthreaded part of the screw shaft. The thread of the screw is fixed firmly in the upper part of the arm, and the lower part of the screw passes freely through a shaft drilled from the groove of the elbow allowing a circling movement.

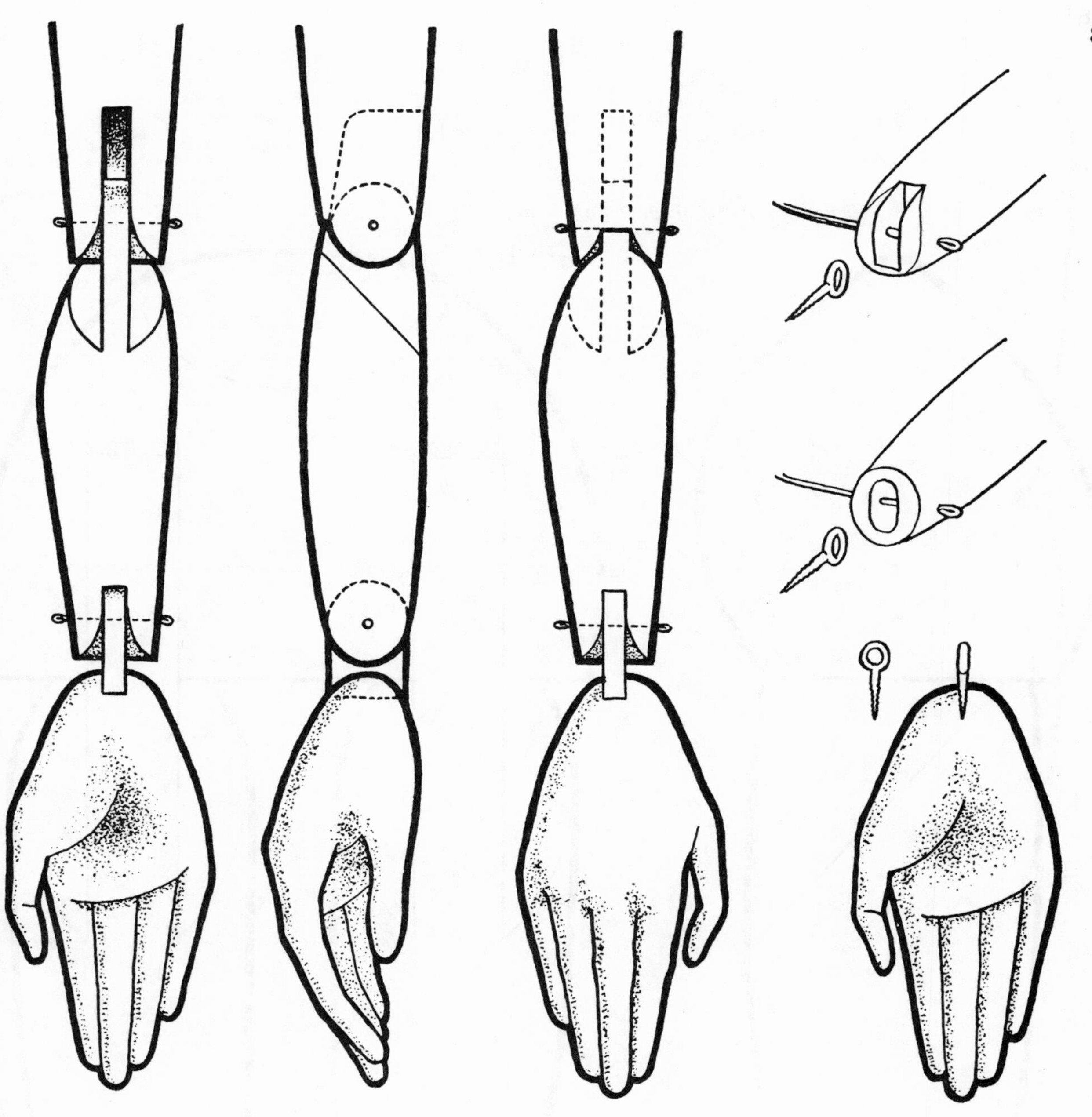

Figure 57 Forearm, hand, elbow and wrist joints

Figure 58 Pelvis, thigh and hip joint

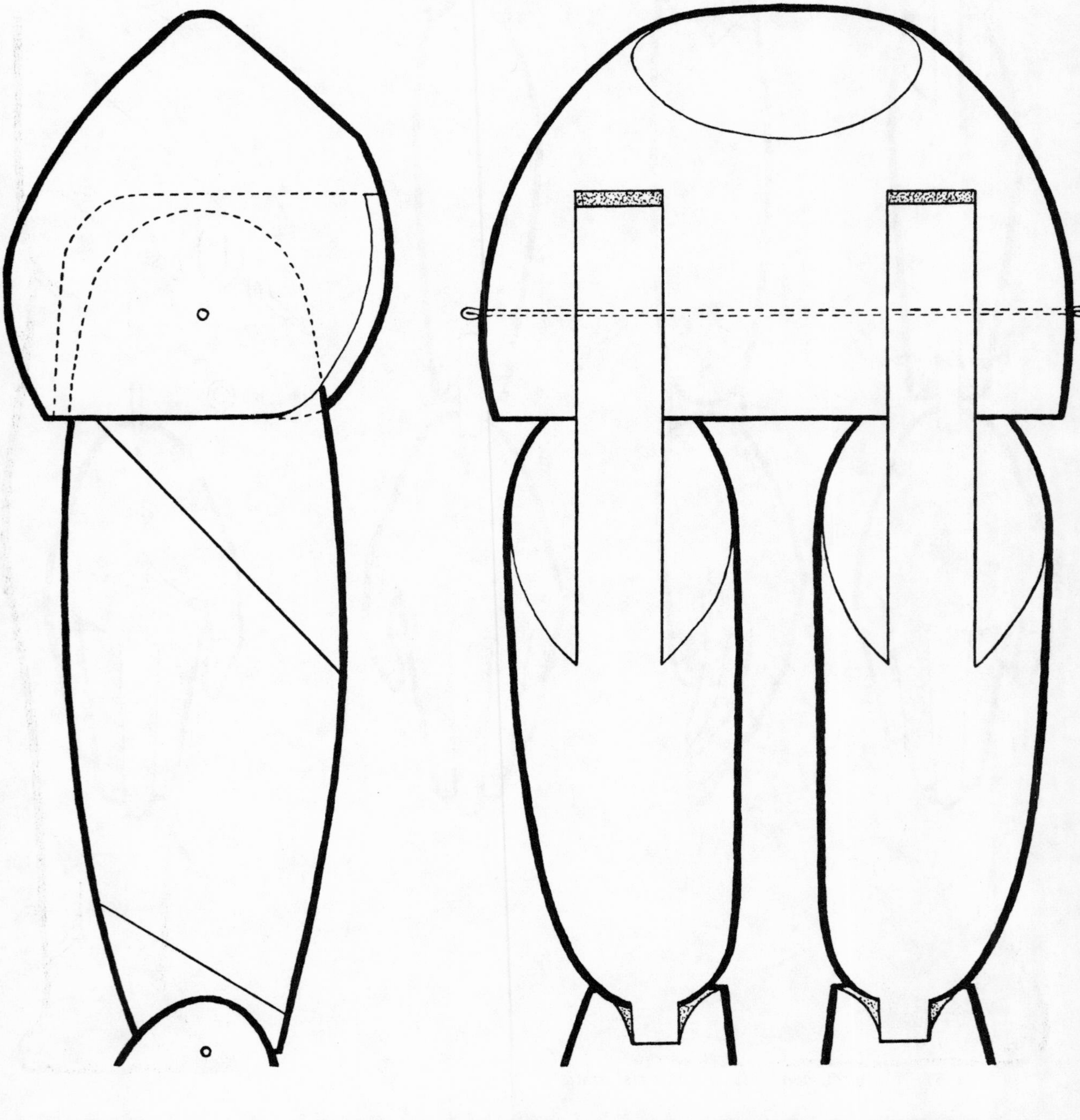

Figure 59 Lower leg, foot, knee and ankle joints

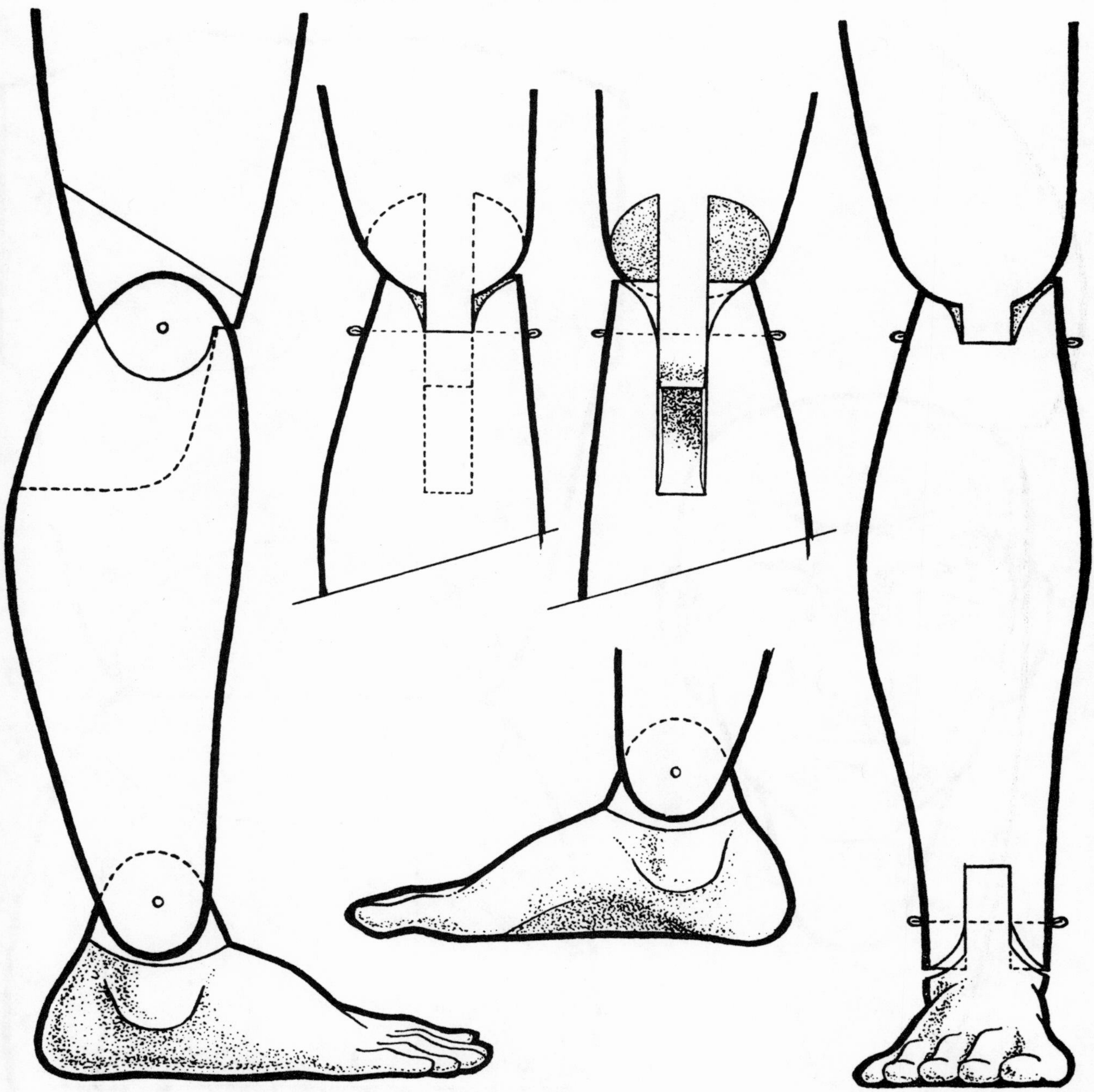

Figure 60   Parts of the shepherd marionette. Actual size. Front view

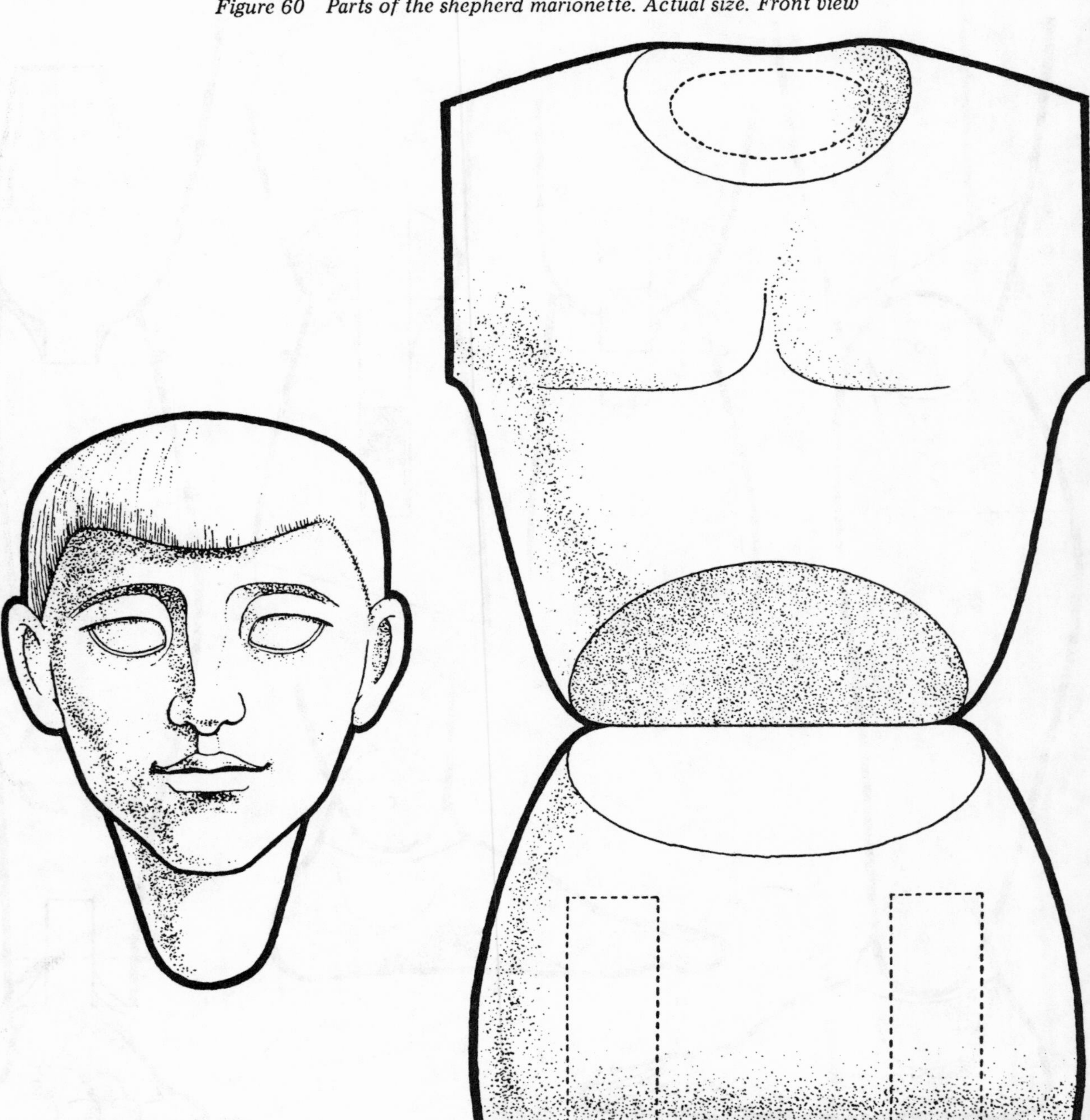

Figure 61 Parts of the shepherd marionette. Actual size. Front view.

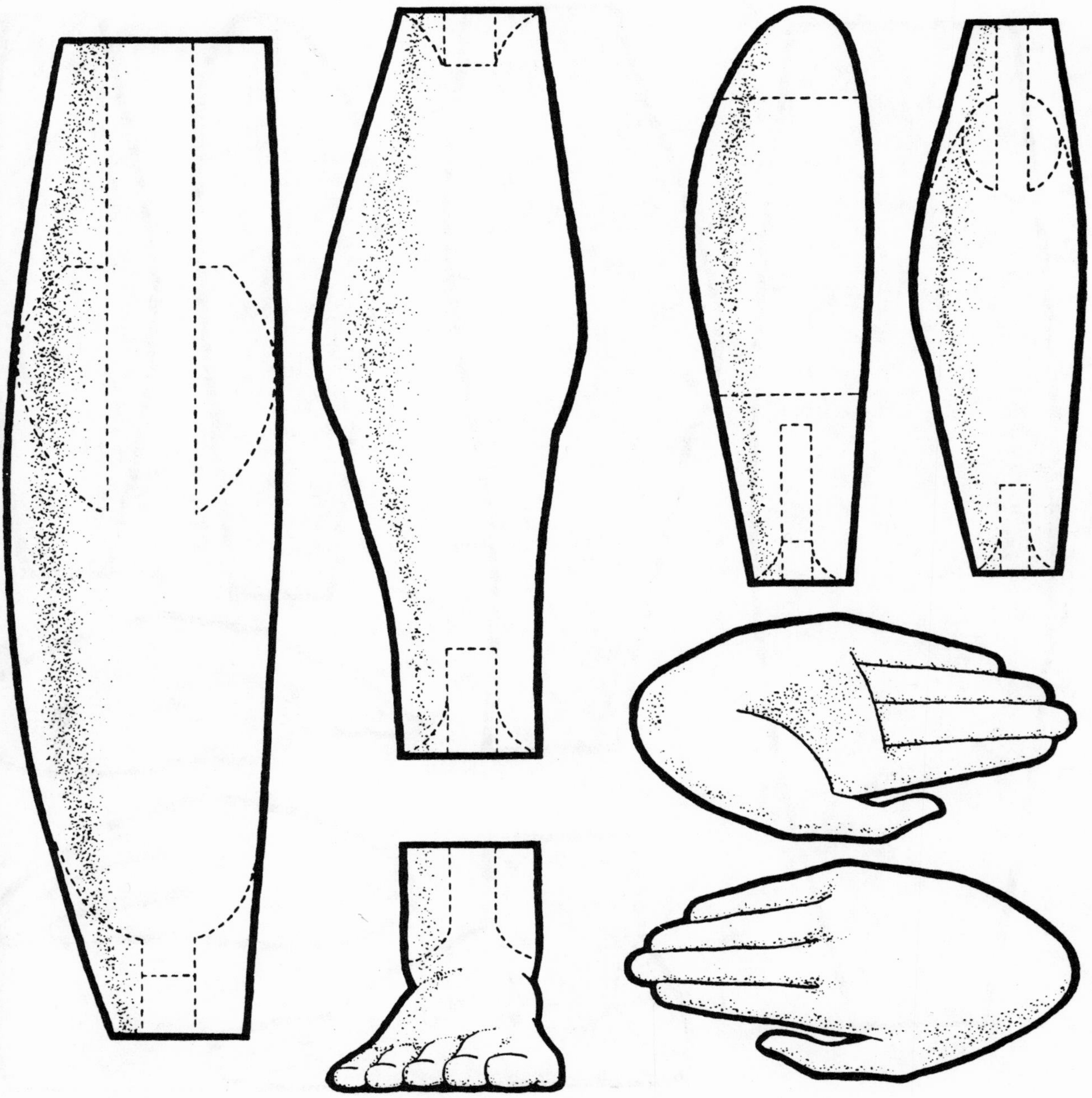

Figure 62   Parts of the shepherd marionette. Actual size. Side view

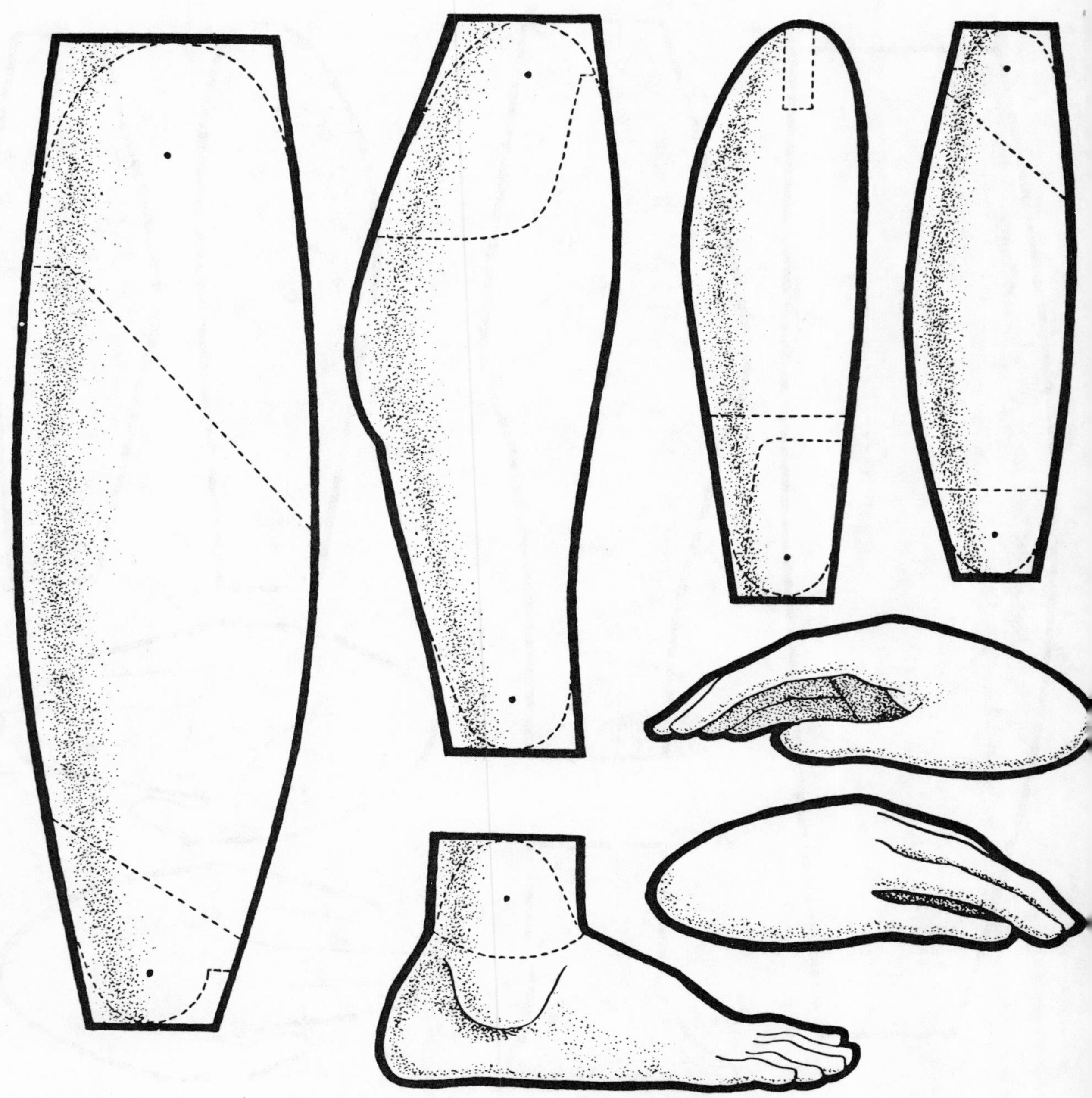

Figure 63 Parts of the shepherd marionette. Actual size. Side view

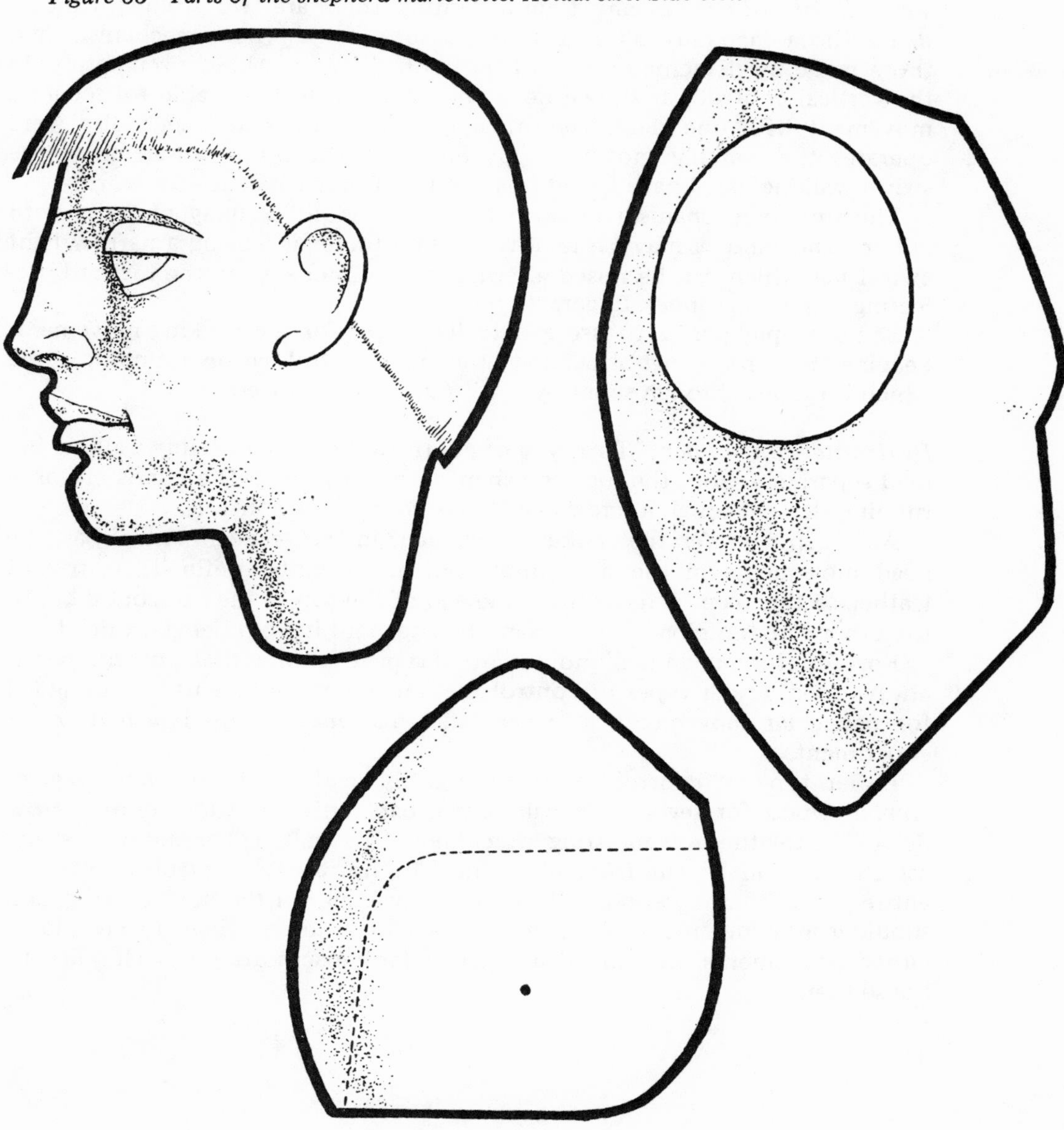

Controls

The mechanism for moving the strings of the marionette is known as the control bar, crutch or perch. There are two main types--vertical control bar and the horizontal control bar. The vertical control is most commonly used in Europe, and the horizontal in America, and there are advantages and disadvantages in both.

Vertical control bar In any type of control there are two groups of movement—those made by altering the position of the whole mechanism and those made by detaching a part of the controls and working it separately. In the vertical control bar shown here, the hand bar is detachable for separate movement with one hand. The other hand holds the main mechanism, and operates the walking movement by means of the thumb insertion in the swivel walking bar. I have found this a fairly effective balance for work.

The thumb mechanism in the walking bar is not equally effective with either hand, and it may be removed if you prefer it leaving a narrow light swivel bar which can be raised alternately on either side by the forward projecting thumb and index finger.

Some people prefer to use a detachable bar for the walking movement, keeping the hand strings attached to the main control bar on a running string which is looped through screw eyes without being knotted.

Horizontal control bar This type of control shows a detachable walking bar held separately from the main mechanism when in use. The hands are on a running string through a screw eye at the front of the controls.

Although I prefer the walking movement in the vertical control bar, the head movements in the horizontal control are better defined. A strip of leather or tape can be fixed from one end of the top of the horizontal bar to the other across the back of the hand to safeguard it from being dropped.

For four-legged animal movement a type of horizontal control bar is always used. Other types of control are not typical and are usually designed for particular movements in a particular marionette. This is a matter for experiment.

Either type of control bar is quite easily made. A broom handle gives enough wood for several vertical control bars, with the addition of narrow dowelling for the bowing string attachment. The walking bar and head string attachment can be cut from plywood. The horizontal control bar may be entirely cut from plywood with narrow dowelling for the bowing string and shoulder attachments. Washers must be used in the screwing of swivel bars. Other attachments are pinned and glued into spaces drilled or chiselled to house them.

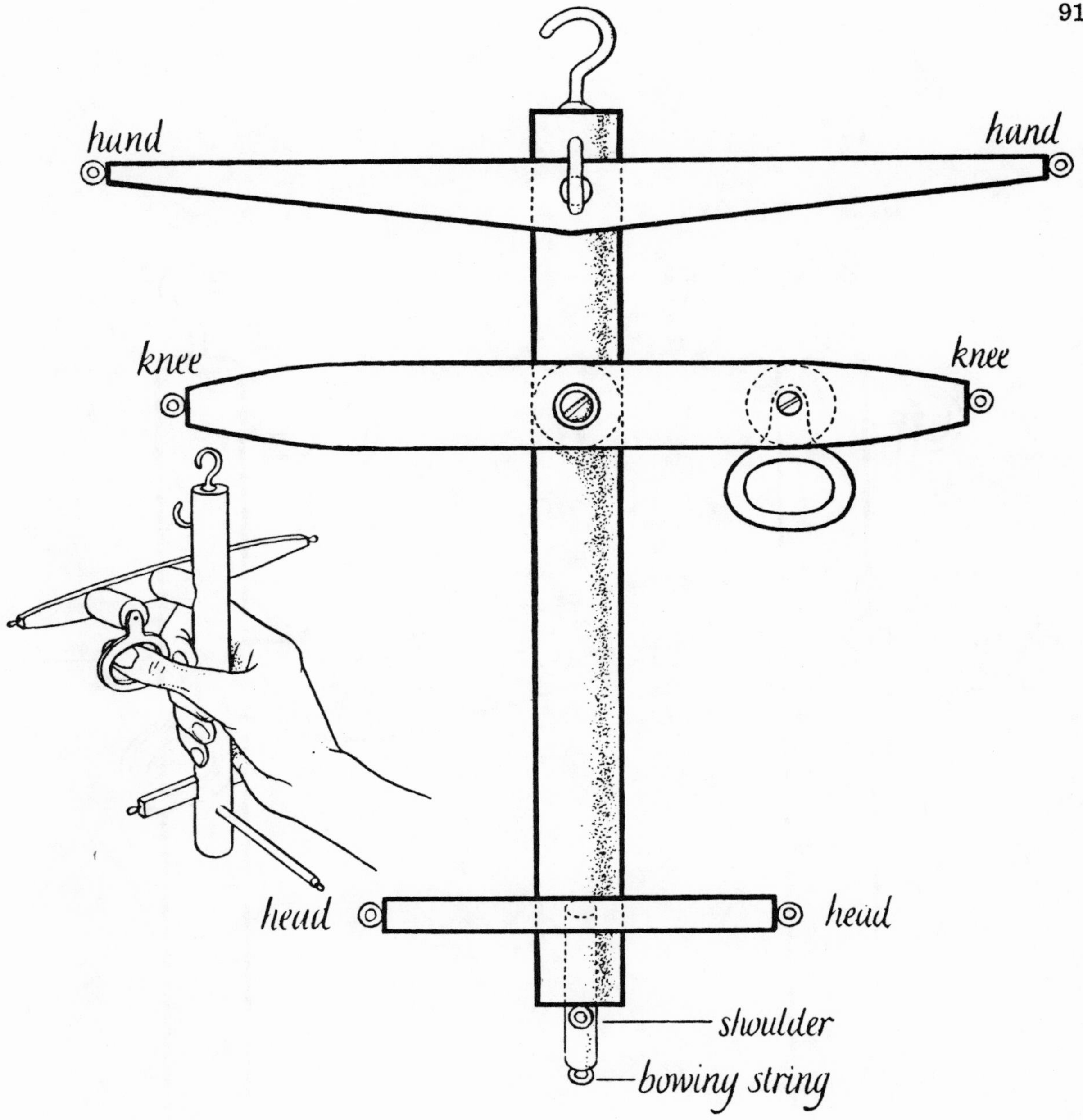

Figure 64 Vertical control bar. Half actual size. Front view

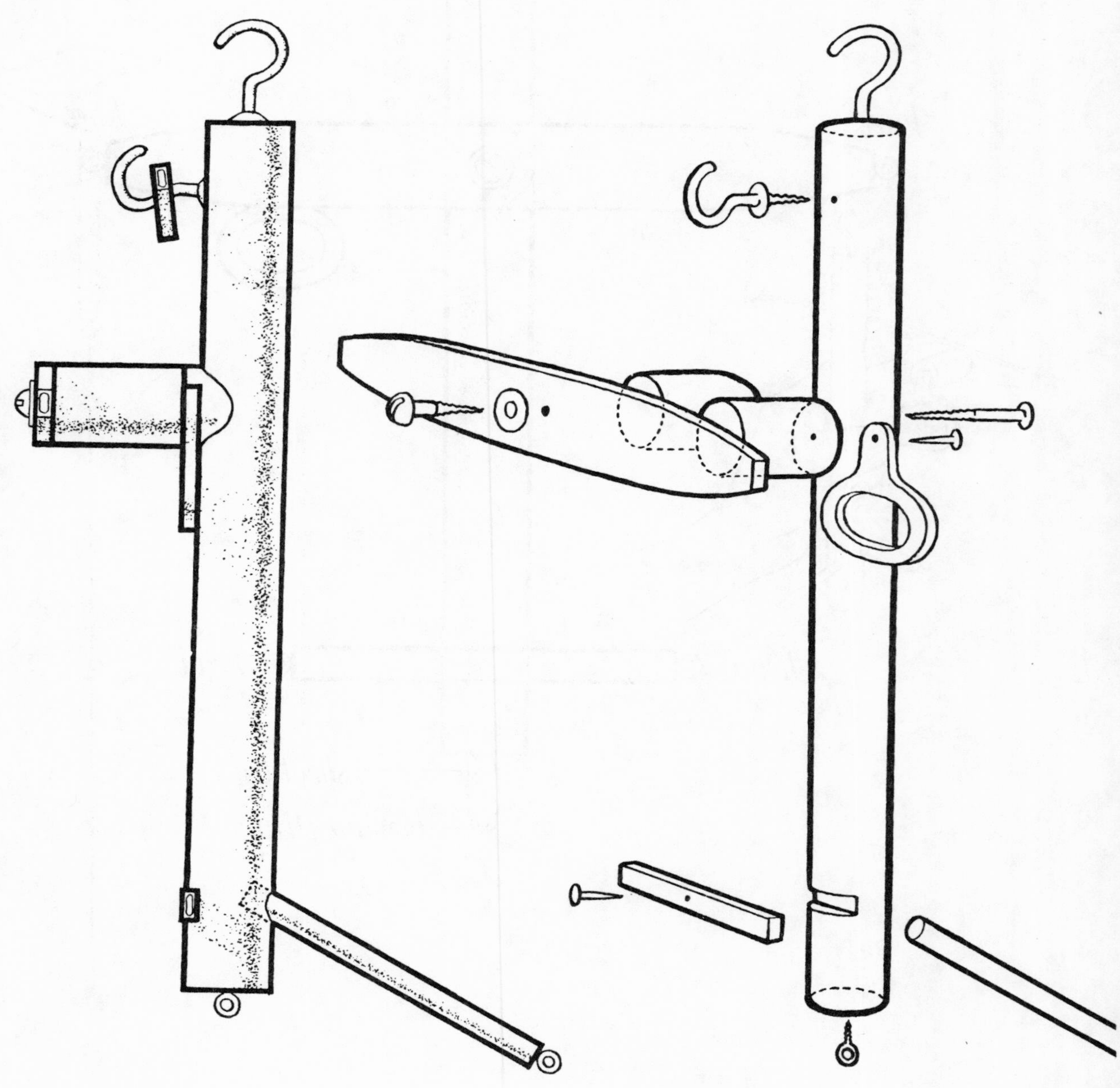

Figure 65 Vertical control bar. Half actual size. Side view

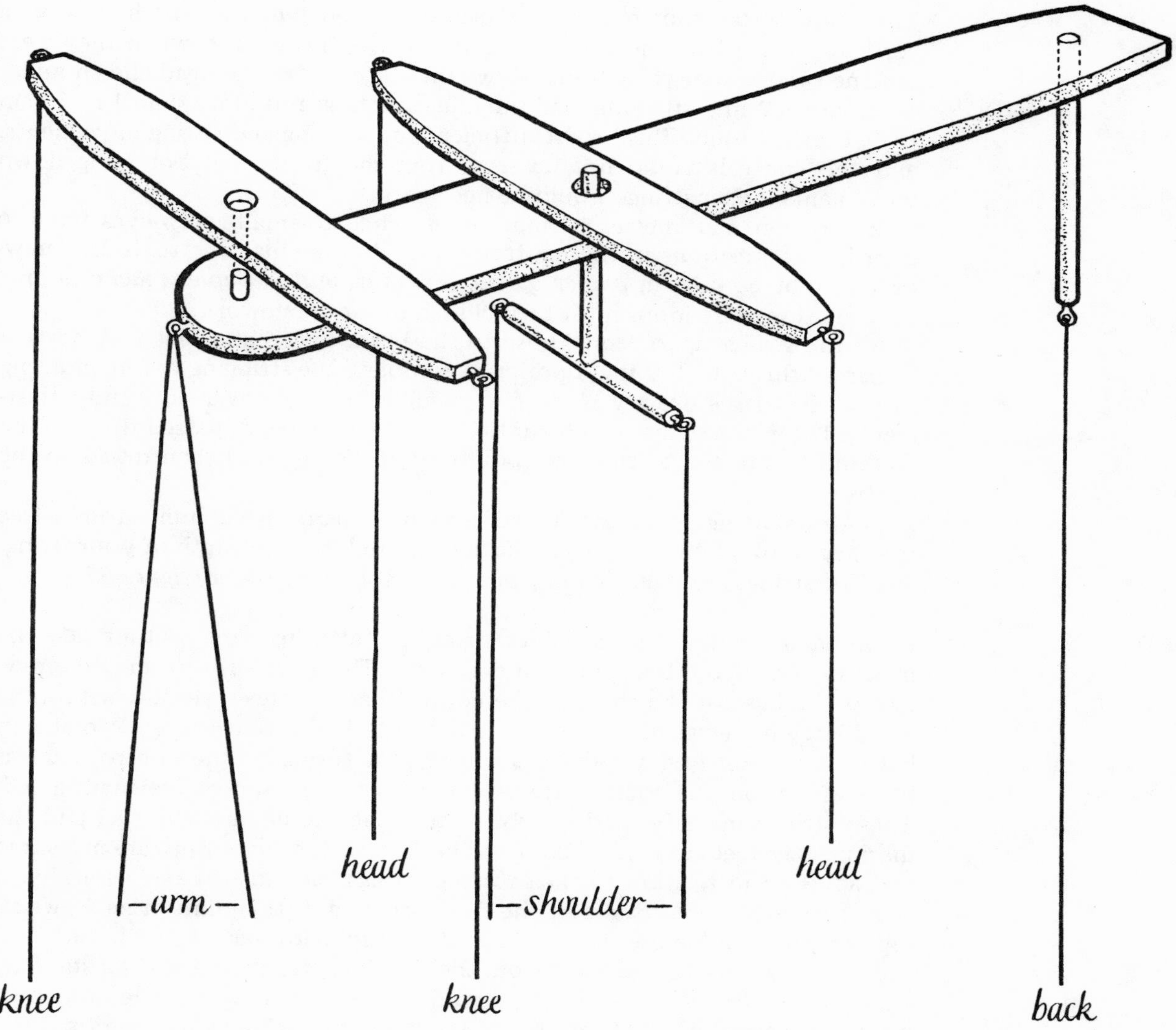

Figure 66 Horizontal control bar. Half actual size

STRINGING

Strings used for marionettes may vary in thickness from *macramé* twine to fine carpet thread. The size and weight of the marionette must guide your choice. I have never felt it to be of great importance that stringing should be invisible, as strings may well be considered an acceptable part of the marionette design. If you do prefer not to see stringing, dark colours show less than light, and fishing twine is very thin, but strong at the same time.

The length of the strings depends on various factors--the height of the marionette, the size and type of control bar, the distance between the leaning rail and stage floor, and the actions that the marionette is to perform. The marionettes shown in these pages are 500 mm (20 in.) high with a vertical control bar, and the leaning rail of the theatre for which they were designed is 1.7 mm (5 ft 6 in.) above the stage floor. The head and shoulder string are 1.2 m (4 ft) long, and the longest strings not more than 1 m 70 cm (5 ft 6 in.). I found this height sufficient for walking and sitting movements, and the controls could not be seen from the front row. For lying down movements longer strings would be necessary.

In wooden marionettes, strings are attached to small screw-eyes fixed in appropriate positions in the control bar, and in the marionette itself. Screw-eyes cannot be used in *papier mâché* however, and in *papier mâché* puppet construction, wire loops must be included in the framework.

All the strings apart from those to the head, hands and feet may have to be passed through clothing. I prefer to complete the stringing before clothing so that I can see exactly what is happening in trial movements and adjustments. Later, the strings can be untied at the control end, passed through the clothing beside the attachment points of the body, and then retied to the control bar.

Before starting to attach the strings, the control bar is hung from a free standing hook at the height you have measured for the length of your stringing. The strings are then tied in place in the following order (*figure 67*):

1 *Shoulder strings* The shoulder strings are attached first, as they take the main weight of the body in all movements. The strings run from one screw-eye at the base of the shaft of the control bar to screw-eyes just within the shoulder joint edge of the upper half of the body. Since these two strings have a common origin, sideways or forward tilting of the control bar has little effect on the marionette and stability and support are maintained. These strings must be tied evenly so that the shoulders hang level and the marionette's feet are just raised from the floor. All other strings are measured and adjusted in relation to the shoulder strings and must be tied carefully so as not to alter the tautness of the first stringing. If the joints at neck, waist, hip, knee and ankle are designed to lie exactly below each other in one line, then the marionette will hang from the shoulder strings in a natural standing pose. A well designed marionette should be able to support a little of its own weight in a standing position, should the manipulator's arm become tired.

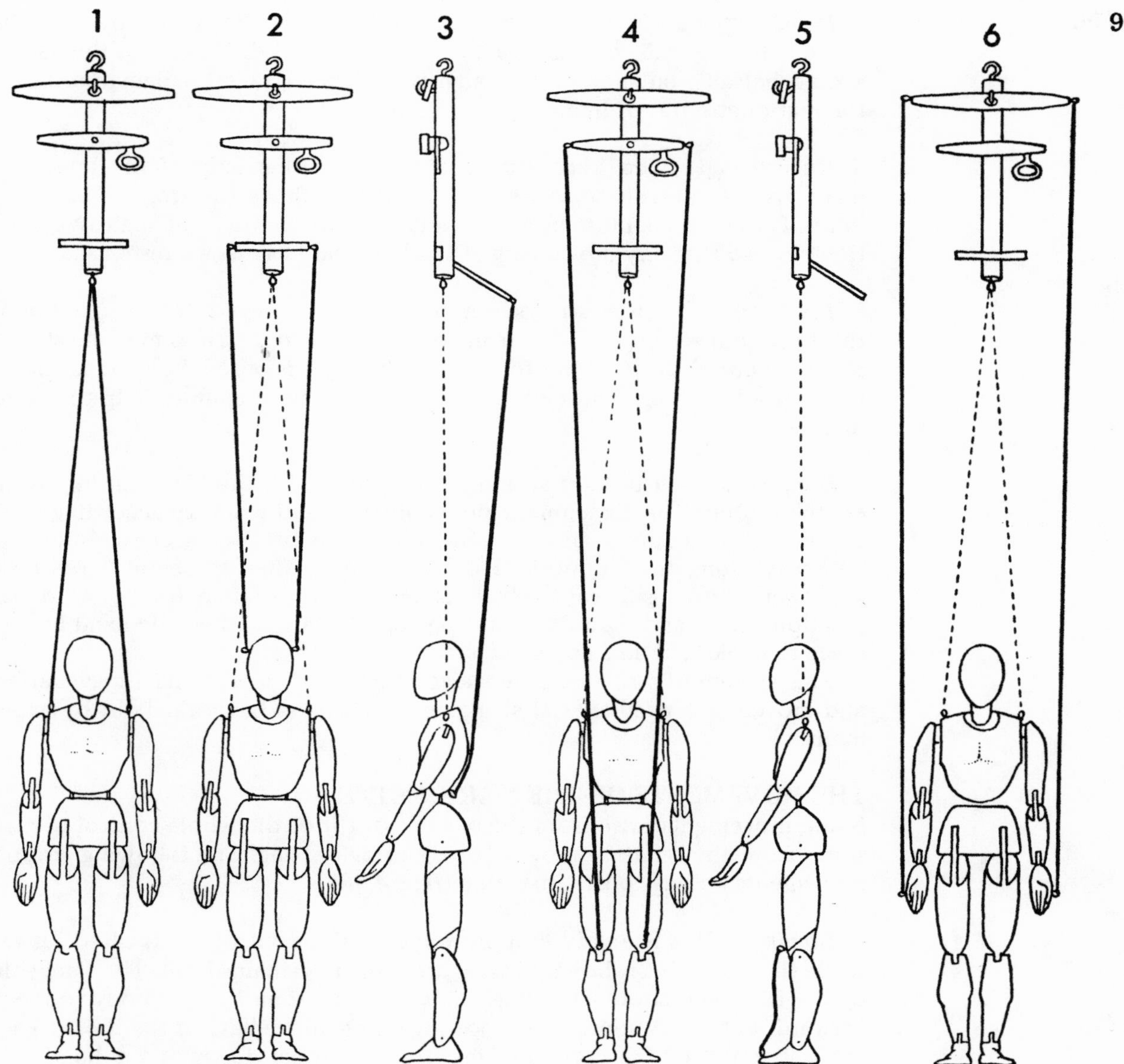

Figure 67

2 *Head strings* The head strings run from either side of the lower cross piece on the control bar to just above the ear on either side of the head. The screw-eyes in the head are placed so that the balance of weight is slightly to the front. When the supporting strings are relaxed the head then falls forward. This is important in nodding and head turning movements.

3 *Bowing string* This string runs from the tip of the backward projecting rod on the controls, and is attached to the base of the thorax at the back. It should be taut, but not taut enough to pull the straight hanging position of the marionette out of line.

4 *Knee strings* The knee strings run from either side of the knee cross piece on the controls to screw-eyes fitted just above the front of each knee joint. These strings must be really taut, even to the point of slightly bending the joint, so that any movement of the knee bar has instant response.

5 *Foot strings* These strings run from the screw-eyes already fixed above the knee joints to the centre front of the feet. Foot strings must be slack to allow a natural drop of the foot when the knee is raised, but not so slack as to let the feet drag. The feet are weighted at the bottom to help this movement.

6 *Hand strings* I usually attach these strings with the hand bar in position on the crutch. The attachment point on the hand can vary according to the action that is required, but for general use it is best to place the screw-eyes half way along the thumb side of each hand. When the hand bar is raised each hand turns sideways which is more natural than the palm forward position. The hands should be strung slightly raised when the hand bar is in place to avoid a lifeless appearance.

This system of stringing covers a good range of movements. Special effects and movements need special stringing which must be worked out by experiment.

THE MOVEMENTS OF THE MARIONETTE

Some movements arise from the balance or tilt of the whole control bar, and some from the separate movement of a single string. The following group of movements belong to the first type (*figure 68*).

1 *Bowing* This is a very easy movement. The control bar is tilted forward while the point of the bowing string attachment remains level. The slackening of the head and shoulder strings allows the upper part of the body to incline forward, but the support of the bowing string at the base of the thorax keeps the lower half of the body straight from the waist down. If the hand bar is left on its hook, the hands hang forward quite naturally with the palms out.

2 *Head turning* This is a more subtle movement and difficult to do at first. If results from a slight forward and sideways tilt of the control bar. The forward tilt allows the head to fall forward. The sideways tilt slackens one head string, and tightens the other, pulling the head to one side.

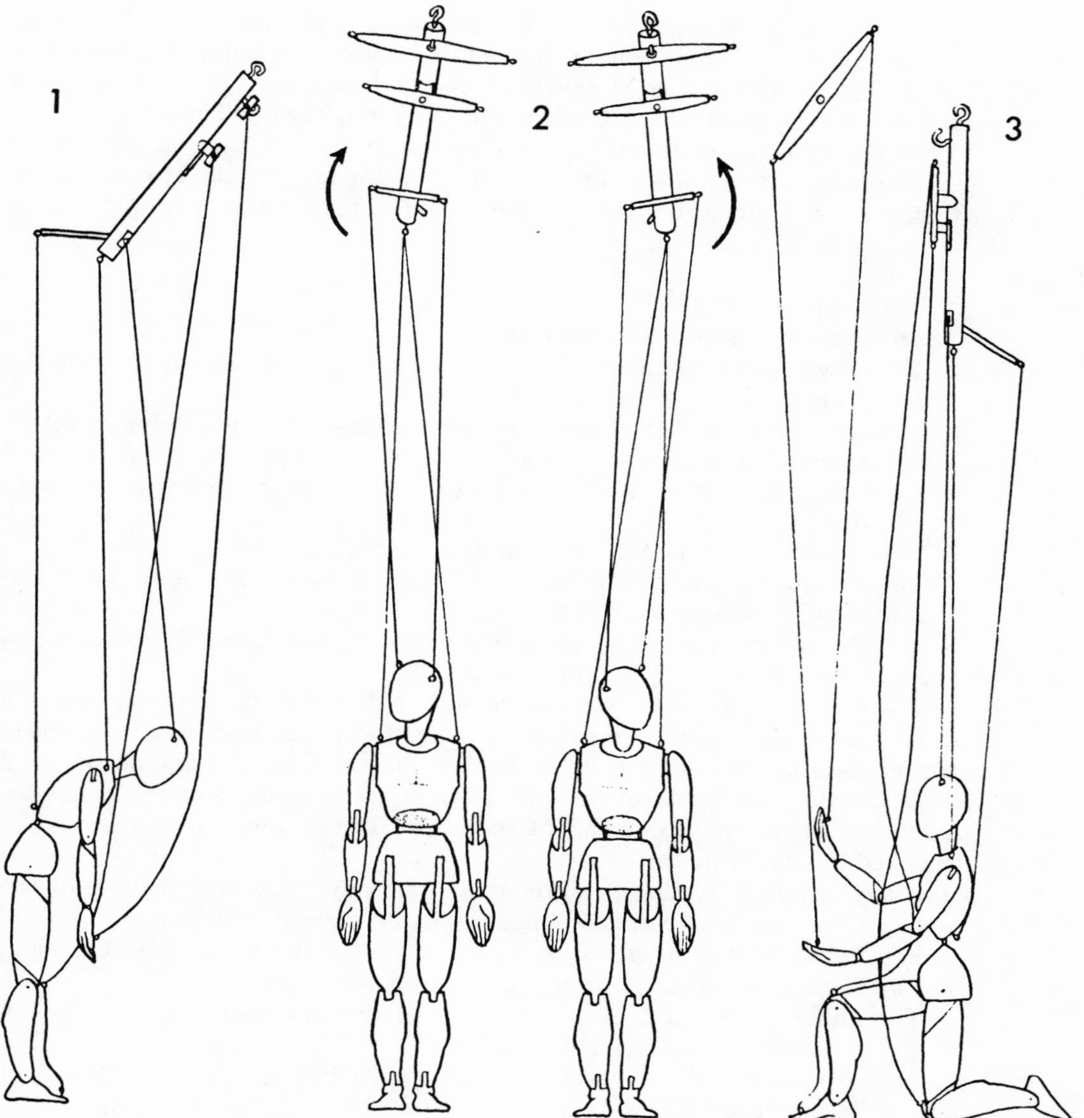

Figure 68 The movements of the marionette

3 *Kneeling on one knee* A downwards movement of the thumb in the knee bar raises and bends the marionette's right leg while the whole crutch is moved forward and lowered. Kneeling on both knees is not so successful, as the forward movement is less controlled and ends with a jerk.

All these movements may be done with one hand only, leaving the other hand free to work the hand bar.

Hand and leg movements belong to the second type of manipulation, where individual strings control the action. Hands are comparatively easy to work. The hand bar may be taken off its hook and used for both hands together, or it may be left in its place and one string for one hand only used at a time. Leg movements are not so easy to control. Not all puppeteers lay equal importance on a walking movement in the marionette. However I feel that a convincing walking movement is important if the marionette is to express itself completely.

4 *Walking (Figure 69)*

1 An evenly balanced starting position.

2 The downward movement of the thumb in the knee bar slackens the left string and raises the right knee.

3 The whole control bar moves forward over the right leg which straightens as the knee bar returns to its horizontal position. The left leg closes beside the right partly from weight and partly from the beginning of the next movement.

4 The upward movement of the thumb raises the left knee.

5 The control bar moves forward over the left leg while the right swings forward to close beside the other.

Although walking has to be described in stages, the forward movement of the control bar is flowing and continuous.

The diagram for the walking movement is drawn as it would be seen in a mirror by a right-handed manipulator, for that is the best way to practise. Early trials in walking a new puppet are nearly always disappointing and adjustments have to be made. Usual faults are dragging feet and a side-to-side swinging of the lower half of the body. The following points should be checked in improving the action.

a Knee strings at resting position must be really taut, so that none of the range of movement is wasted in gathering up slack stringing.

b Feet must be well weighted to keep the lower half of the body stable and to make the toes drop naturally when the knee is raised.

c The ankle joints must be constructed so that the feet turn out slightly, and do not catch in passing each other.

d The marionette must never be raised to a height where neither foot touches the ground in walking, or the lower half will tend to swing.

Tangled strings Through carelessness or bad luck strings can be come tangled. If the tangling is recent and not extensive it may be sufficient to hang up the controls to allow the marionette to untwist, and to work through looped strings without undoing any of the string attachments.

If the tangling is tight and knotted the weight of the hanging marionette will only make things worse. In this case lay out the marionette and controls on a table or floor and undo the hand bar attachments. With these removed you have a better chance of straightening the rest of the stringing. The shoulder strings should never be undone or the balance may be altered.

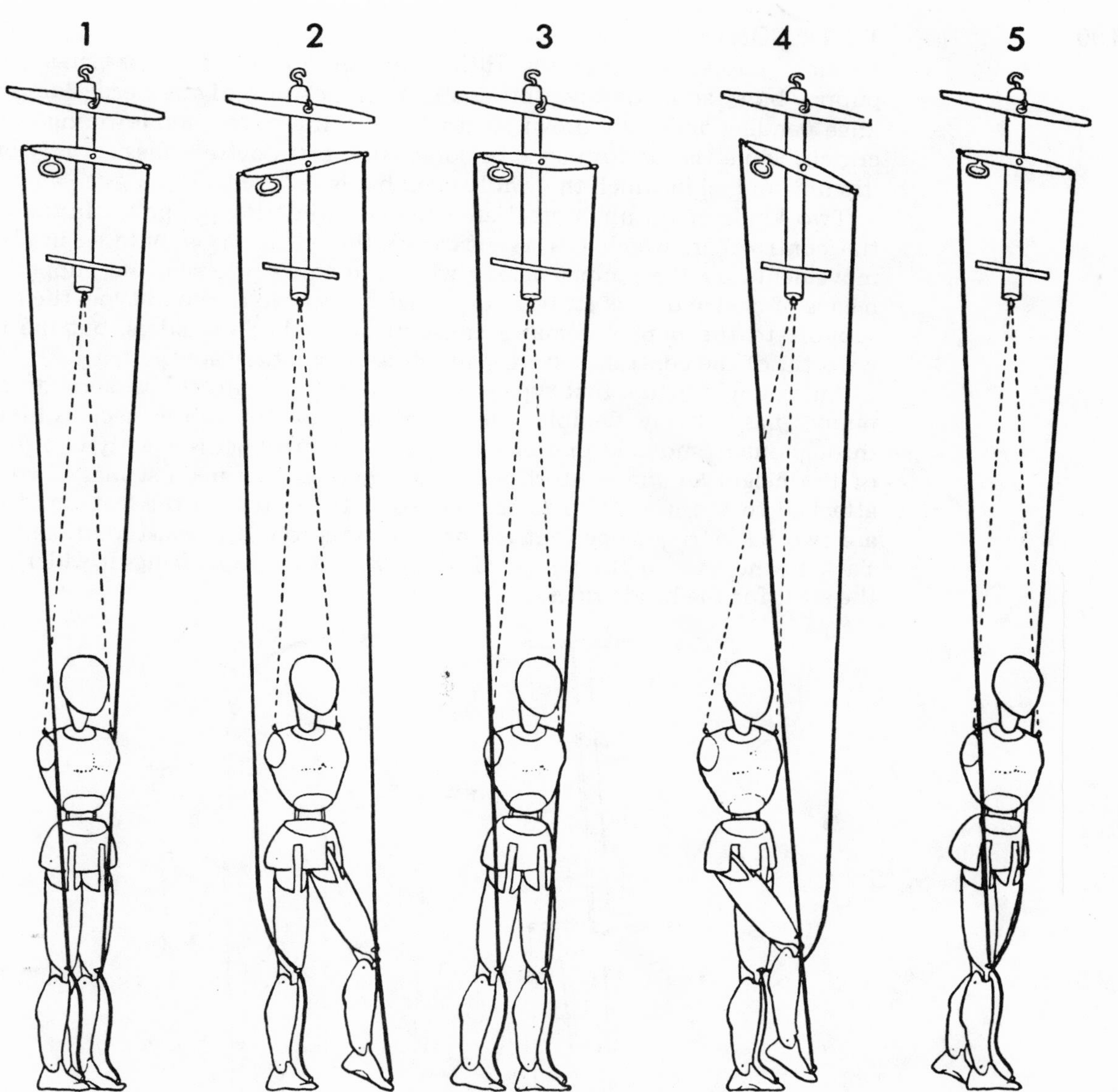

Figure 69 Walking

Handling When lifting or carrying a marionette, hold the controls in one hand, and with the other gather the strings together at mid height. With the hands held well apart the puppet will hang clear of the floor and may be lifted over the bar at the side of the stage quite easily.

TIP UP CONTROLS

In most puppet controls the tilting forward of the main bar makes the puppet bow, and sideways tilting alters the position of the head. Jumping, knee bending and lying down all result from the raising and lowering of the crutch, while the performance of some trick marionettes relies entirely on a 'tip up' control in which the whole main bar is reversed.

Two kinds of tip up control are often seen in trick puppetry. In the first the control bar, which has a vertical starting position, is imitated in all its movements by the puppet below; when the bar is reversed, the puppet, by means of heel and back strings, is reversed as well. In a second type, the main support to the puppet remains constant at head or shoulders, but the forward tilt of the control slackens and releases secondary strings.

An example of the first type can be seen in the contortionist acrobat. The puppet has a freely flexible waist joint, and except at the neck is hinged throughout to move in one plane only. The control bar is exactly two thirds of the height of the contortionist, and there are six main strings. Two are attached to the head, two to screw-eyes in the insteps of the feet, and there are two backstrings, one taut to the centre piece of the waist joint, and one slack to the base of the pelvis. The cross strut for foot strings is wider than the strut for the headstrings.

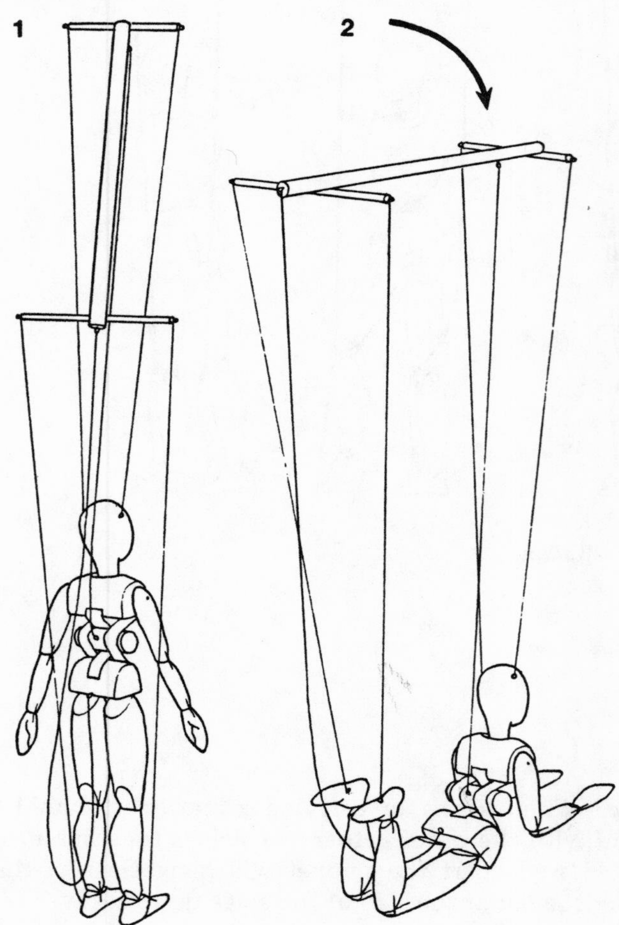

Figure 70a

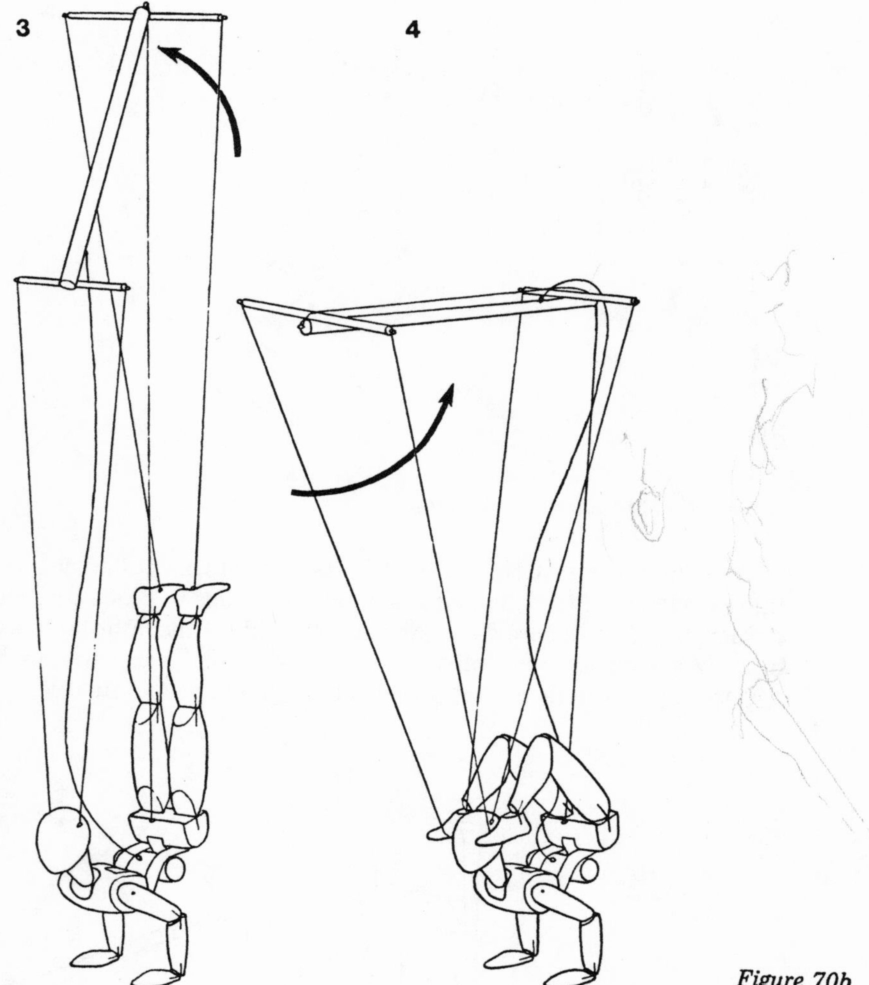

Figure 70b

1 Here the contortionist stands upright supported by the headstrings. One back string is taut, while the other hangs loose.
2 As the control bar is tipped forward the puppet moves onto his knees, and the arms (weighted at the hands) swing forward. When the bar is horizontal, he rests on the ground with raised heels and head.
3 The end of the control bar supporting the head remains in position, while the opposite end is raised vertically drawing the heels upwards. The back string to the pelvis becomes taut (its length is measured for this position) taking over from the waist string which slackens. If the joint angles at wrist and elbow are correctly cut, the contortionist should now balance steadily on his hands.
4 The head string end of the control bar is now pushed backwards between the heel strings, drawing the taut backstring with it. The heel string cross bar moves forward, lowering the puppet's heels to his shoulders.

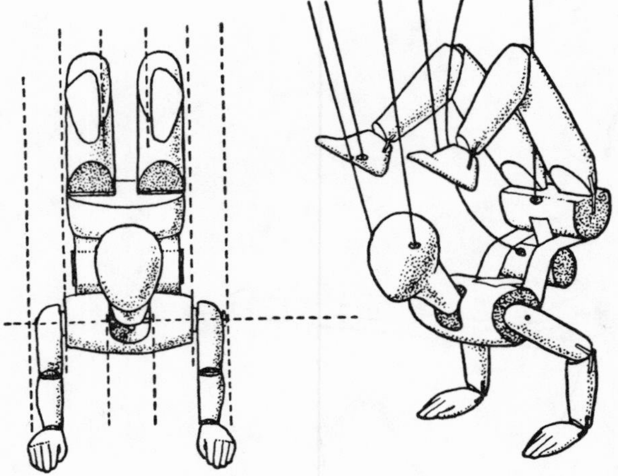

Figure 71 Movement in one plane

A second type of tip up control is seen in this collapsing puppet. The upright position of the bar keeps the arms and legs in place by means of running strings through a screw-eye at each shoulder, and a hole at each side of the hips. Walking is controlled by a detachable bar moving arms and legs together, and the head may be raised and lowered on its own.

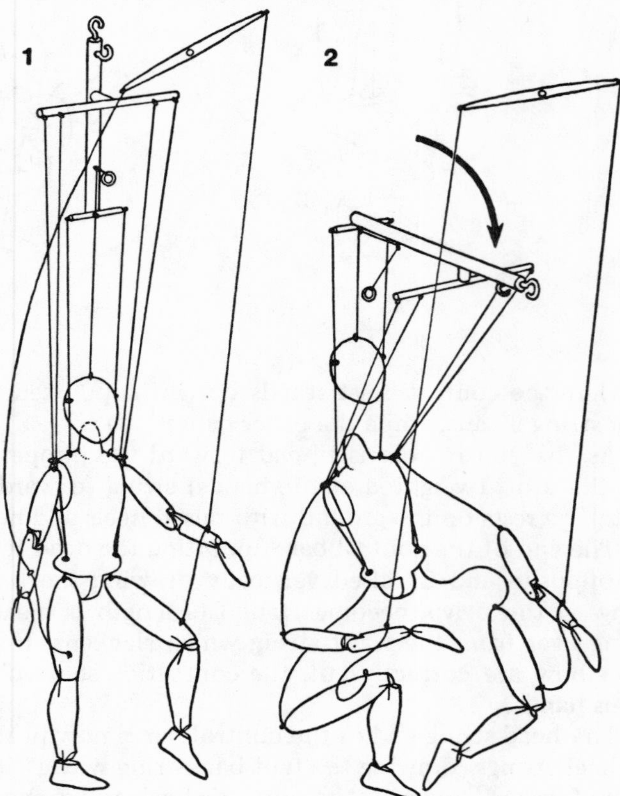

Figure 72 Collapsing puppet

TANDEM CONTROLS

Tandem controls (*figure 73*) are particularly useful when animal (or human) puppets are performing in groups—two or more puppets on one control can be handled by a single manipulator. The control shown below is merely an extension of the standard horizontal control bar which rocks from side to side to cause a walking or trotting movement. The main bar supports the weight of the puppet while the side struts alternately raise and lower the knees. This control may be used for numbers of any type of animal or human puppet arranged in single file.

Figure 73

A second type of tandem control supports animals arranged side by side, and the forward and backward rocking of this control brings about a bounding or galloping movement. In the example shown below two supporting strings are fixed to the back of each performing seal, while an extra detachable bar moves their heads and guides a ball which they throw between them. Seen from above this control appears rectangular but if the struts and supporting bars are jointed flexibly the animals may be turned to face sideways as well as forwards. The ball throwing movement is described later in a section on juggling puppets.

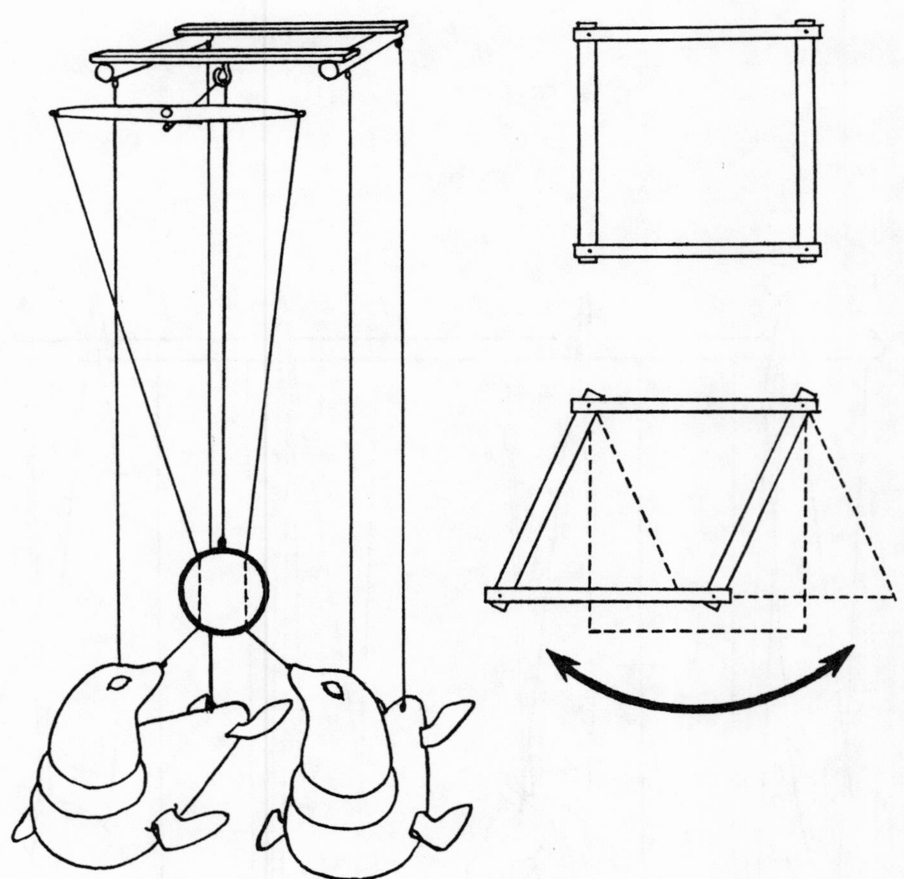

Figure 74

Animal String Puppets

Animal puppets can be made by any of the methods described for human puppets, starting with a drawn plan (see *figure 75* below). Unfortunately when they are made in proportion to human puppets, animal puppets tend to be rather heavy. This can partly be overcome by the use of balsa wood for the main simple body shape, but an animal as large as the elephant must be modelled over a wire frame.

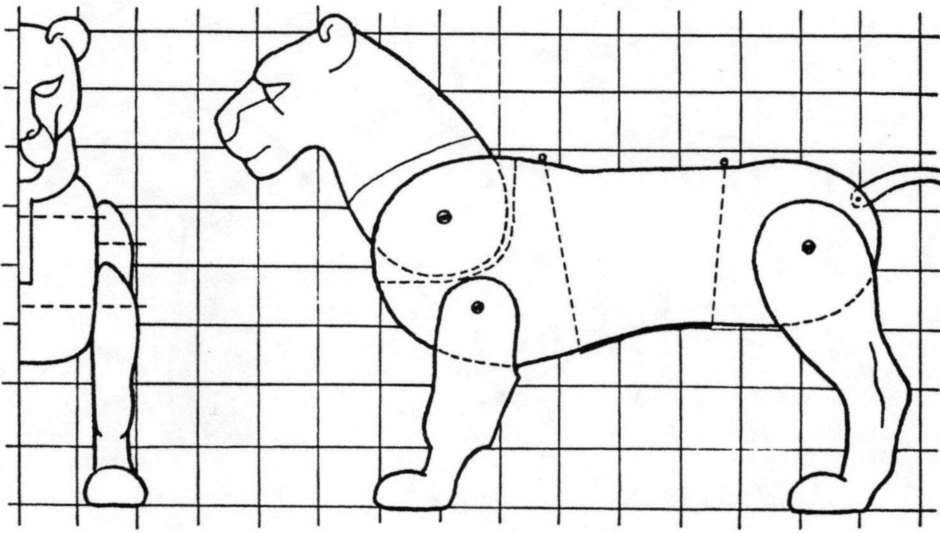

Figure 75

Construction

Although animal heads can be carved, modelled, or cast, the simplest method is to glue two linings from a mould to either side of a cut plywood profile which includes the tongue of the neck joint (1) (*figure 76*).

Legs can be cut in profile from flat sections of hard wood using a spring-saw or fret-saw, then filed or sandpapered to shape. The balsa wood body can be shaped entirely by sanding, and the neck groove cut out with a razor blade and sharp chisel (2).

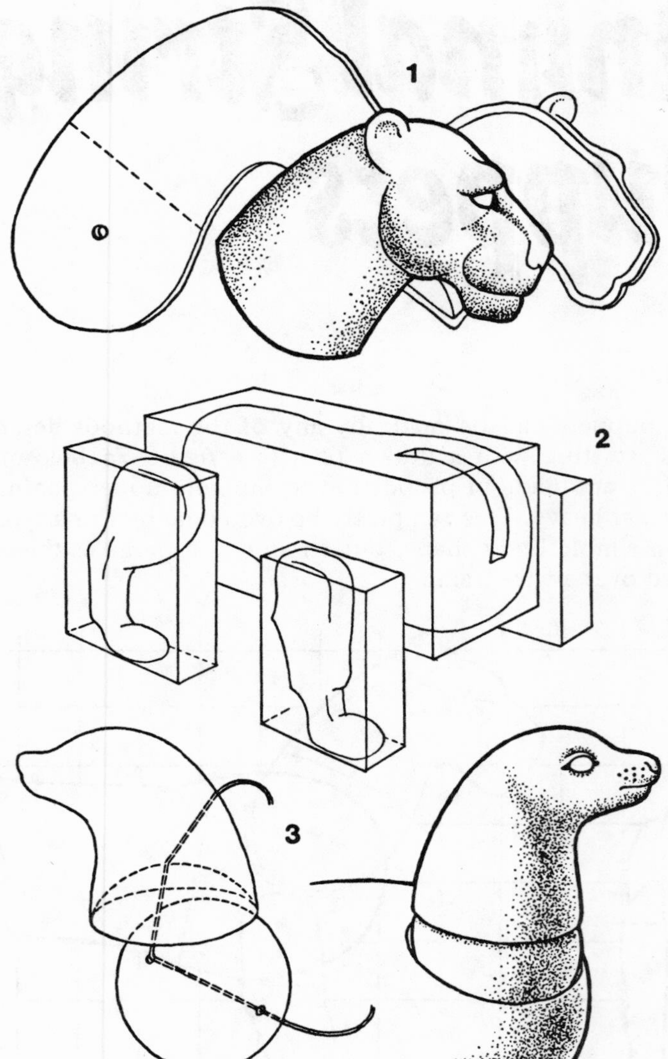

Figure 76

Wire shafts for the leg joints pass through the animal's body and are glued in place. The legs rotate freely on the ends of these shafts, and are fixed with a small washer on each side. Wire loops for the body strings must pass right through the balsa wood and support the weight from underneath. Animal tails can be made of cord, or from felt or leather over a wire stiffening.

The tongue and groove joint, often used for the neck, allows no sideways movement. For some animals a ball and socket string joint is a useful alternative (3).

Figure 77

ANIMAL CONTROLS (*Figure 77*)

1 This control bar has supporting strings only. Forward and backward rocking of the bar causes a bounding or cantering movement. The leather flippers of the seal, hinged on wire staples, move freely with the body.

2 In a second type of control, side to side rocking raises the legs alternately. The cross-over strings to the back legs (described in detail with the circus horse *page 122*) make the leg movement sequence correct for all animals except the elephant where they are not necessary.

The heads of both seal and lion are supported by strings from a wooden knob at the end of a spring or length of elastic attached to the main control.

Figure 78 Juggler

Trick Marionettes

The six trick marionettes described in the following pages are chosen partly because they are particular favourites of mine, and also because they display between them most of the mechanisms found in trick puppetry. Here are seen practical applications of vertical, horizontal, tip up, and irregular controls; puppets with freely moving joints and puppets moving in a restricted plane.

JUGGLING PUPPETS

These are among the easier of circus puppets to make and manipulate, and three varieties are described here. In the first only one ball is used, but although this may not strictly be called juggling, the trick is most effective. As the ball is thrown into the air and caught by each hand in turn, it rises higher and higher and may finally disappear. In a comedy act, the ball can stay out of sight for as long as the operator wishes, and then return unexpectedly. A second juggler uses two balls which are thrown up alternately giving an illusion of juggling although the balls do not actually change hands. In a third trick two balls are again used, but in addition to the movements of the previous trick, they may be bounced on to the puppet's forehead and left foot.

These three tricks are described in stages, but in performance the movements are continuous and flowing. Practice in front of a mirror shows the manipulator what is actually happening; this is not easily seen from above.

Juggling puppets should be made with heads slightly tilted back, and eyes raised as if to follow the movement of the balls. The type of jointing used in body and legs is open to choice, but the arms should be as flexible as possible. I find that a string joint at shoulder and elbow works well here, while leather hinge joints at the wrists stand up best to the wear and tear of jerking hand strings. The balls can be made from table tennis balls, split and weighted inside with plastic wood, and the palms of the juggler's hands should be lined with felt to deaden sound.

The main control bar of the juggler is of standard type, so the puppet may walk, bow, or jump about in addition to doing his tricks. The juggling movements are controlled by a detachable hand bar (or bars) whose strings pass down through the balls to the puppet's hands, forehead or toes.

Figure 79a

1 The hand bar is shown in position on the main control, with the ball resting in the juggler's hands. Strings from each end of the bar run through the ball to the palms, while a third string from the centre of the bar is attached to the ball itself.

2 When the juggler is walking the hand bar should be detached and held forward to allow free movement of the knee strings.

3 The centre string of the hand bar is looped over its hook and the bar sharply tilted to the right, throwing the ball from one hand into the air.

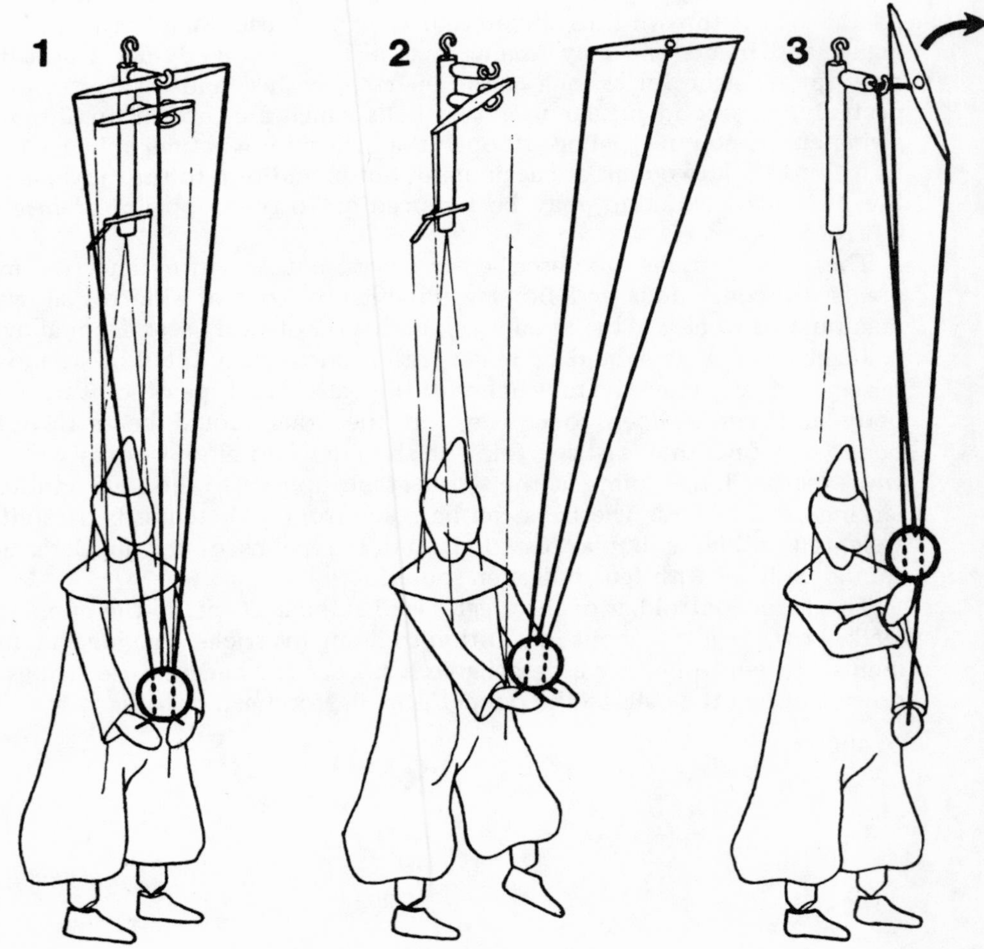

Figure 79b
4 As the hand bar is levelled and moved forward, the centre string draws the ball into the air. The further forward the bar is moved, the higher the ball rises.
5 The hand bar returns close to the main control and is tilted to the left, raising the left hand to catch the ball as it runs down the taut string.
6 The left hand is lowered, and the ball falls back to its first position. The sequence can now be repeated in reverse starting with the left hand, or the ball may be thrown into the air by both hands together.

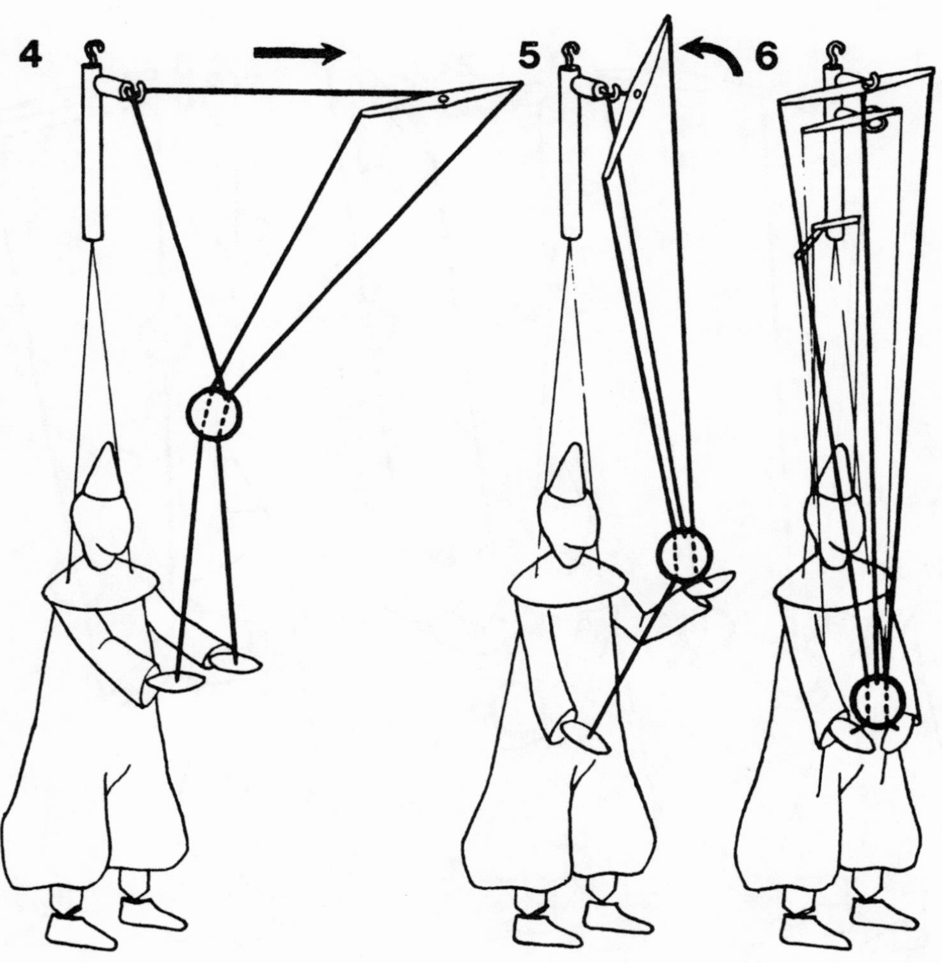

Figure 80

1 In this second trick two balls are used. Strings from the ends of the hand bar are threaded through each ball to the palms of the hands.

2 When the hand bar is jerked sharply from side to side, each ball is thrown into the air in turn, and falls back down its string into place.

3 If the hand bar is turned end-on towards the audience, the balls appear to be thrown from hand to hand.

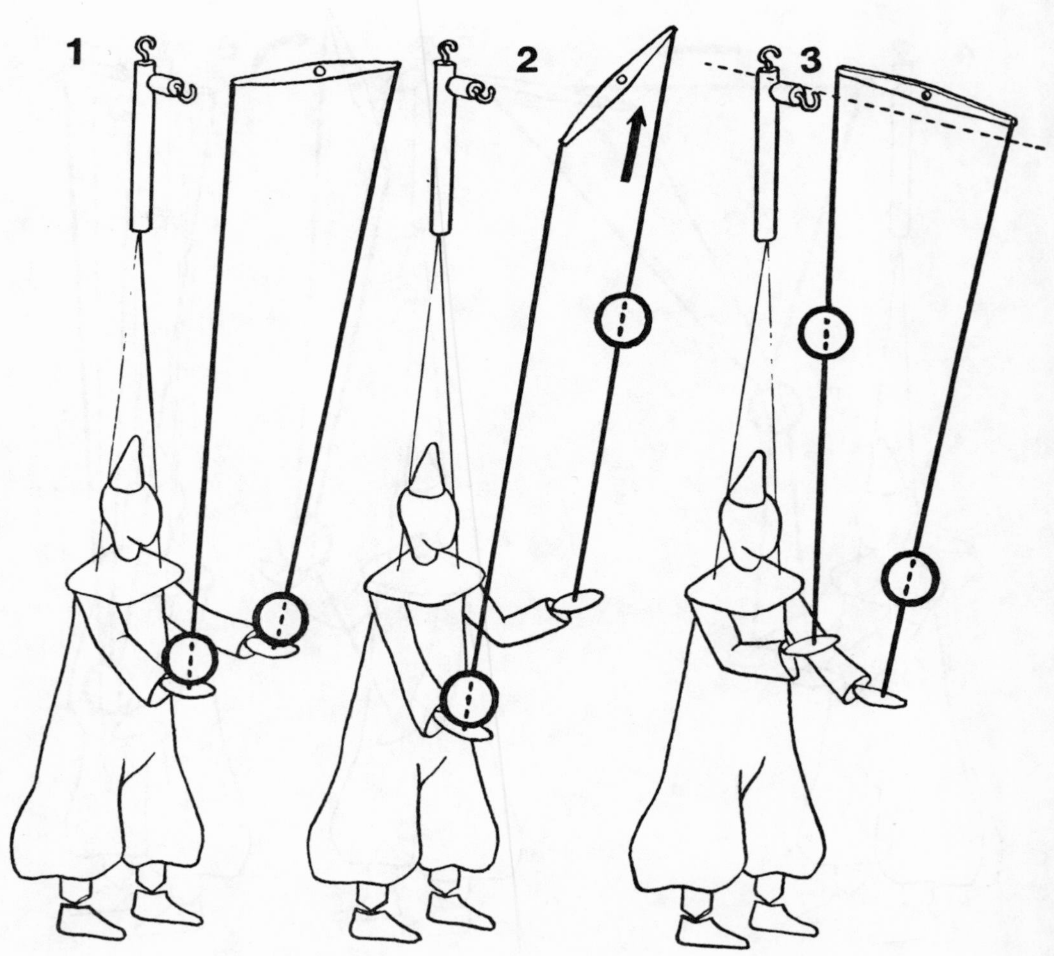

Figure 81

1 A third juggling trick uses an extra bar with strings through each ball to the puppet's forehead and left foot. Since the two bars are held in separate hands, the puppet, after making his entrance, must be supported by a second manipulator or hung from a bracket over the stage.

2 A sharp jerk on the hand bar sends both balls into the air.

3 The hand bar is lowered, the second bar raised, and the balls run back down the taut strings onto the juggler's forehead and left foot. The ball on the foot returns to the left hand by reversing the same movements, while the forehead ball returns by its own weight.

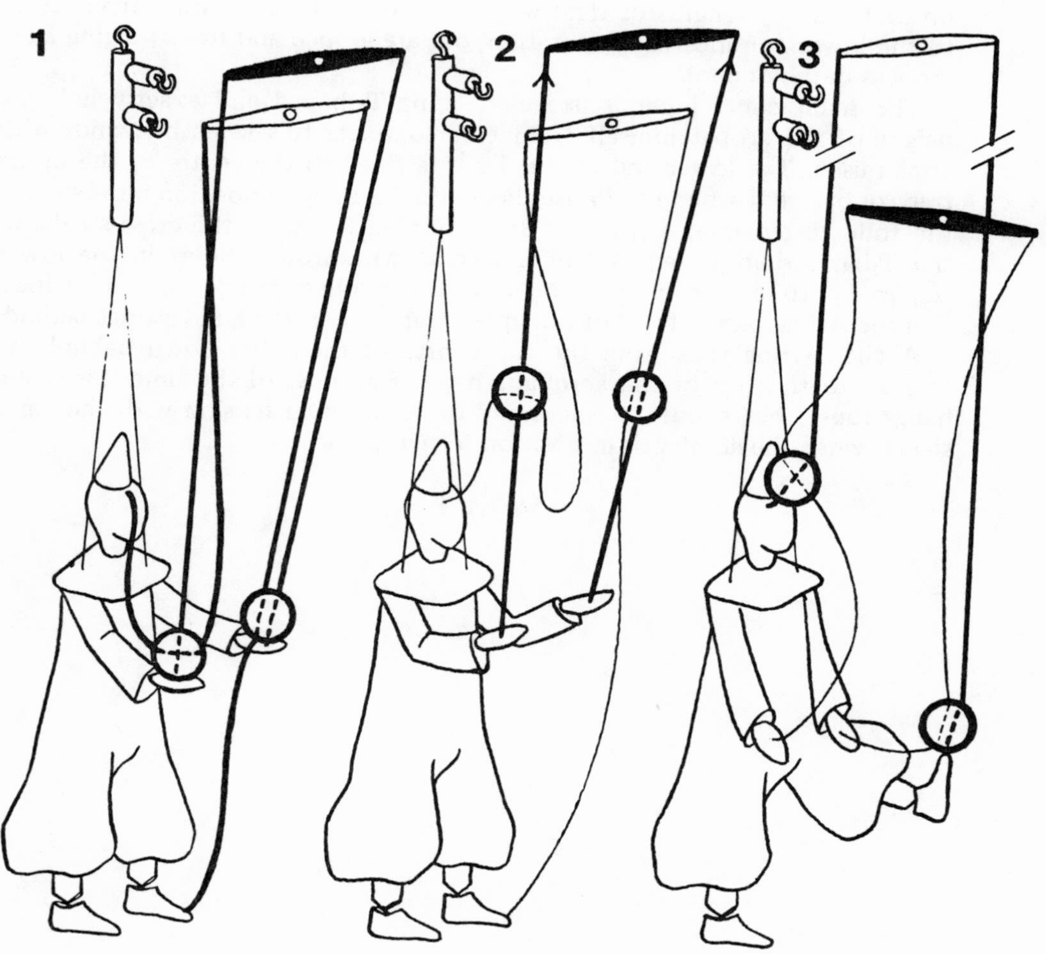

TRAPEZE ACROBAT

The acrobat described here makes his entrance hanging by his hands on a spinning trapeze which is lowered from above. As it reaches the ground he bows to the audience, and rises into the air again as the trapeze begins to swing, raising and lowering his legs to increase the arc of movement. After several swings he raises his feet to the bar, releases his hands, and hangs by the feet alone. Still swinging he returns to the hand hold position and raises himself waist high to the bar, alternately raising and lowering himself by the arms. Finally, from the toe hold position, he rises to stand on the still moving bar.

This puppet is simply constructed and moves in a vertical plane only. From shoulder to finger tip the arms are made in one piece, the palms of the hands being curved to fit round the bar. The shoulders pivot on a wire shaft through the chest, and the head, neck and upper body are made in one. The waist is a leather joint which bends forward only, as backward movement is limited by a canvas strip joining the chest and stomach. The thigh joints should allow no sideways movement, and although the knees may be jointed, the legs can be made in one piece from the thigh joint to the toes which are pointed downwards.

The trapeze is made from an upper and lower wooden dowel bar joined on each side by lengths or rigid wire. The wire ends are turned in and fixed to the lower bar allowing no rotation, but are looped and free swinging from grooves in the upper bar.

The main control bar is irregular, being T-shaped and exactly half the height of the arobat himself from toes to finger tips when he stands with arms raised. The lower end of the T-bar is fixed to the centre of the upper trapeze bar, and when not in use the control is hung in position number 4 of the following diagrams (*figure 83b*). From each side of the cross stroke of the T-bar strings of equal length pass down through holes in the lower trapeze bar to screw-eyes in the palms of the acrobat's hands, and on his toes. The toe strings pass in front of the upper trapeze bar, the hand strings behind.

A fifth string runs from the top centre of the T-bar down behind the trapeze to the top of the acrobat's head. For most of the time this string hangs loose, but should be measured to be of equal tension with the hand strings when the acrobat is in position 5 (*figure 83b*).

Figure 82 Trapeze acrobat

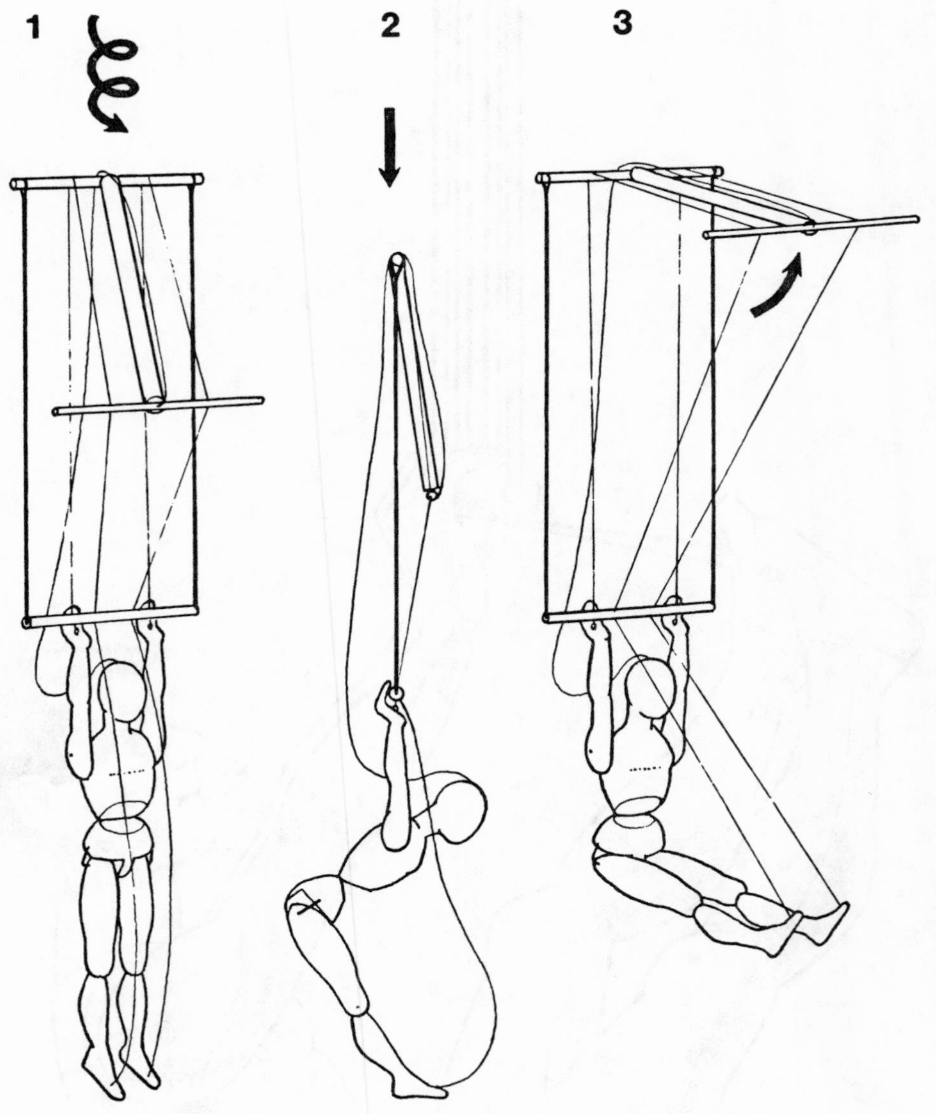

Figure 83a

1 With the T-bar control bent forward to its limit, the acrobat makes his entrance in this position hanging from the trapeze hy his hands. The trapeze is spun round on a string loop, and lowered from above to the centre of the stage as if descending from the top of the circus tent.

2 As the puppet's feet touch the ground, the trapeze stops spinning and the string loop is discarded. The trapeze is lowered still further and the acrobat makes his bow facing the audience. The extended toes push the body backwards at the thigh joint, and the head bends forward between the shoulders.

3 The trapeze is lifted into the air and turned sideways.

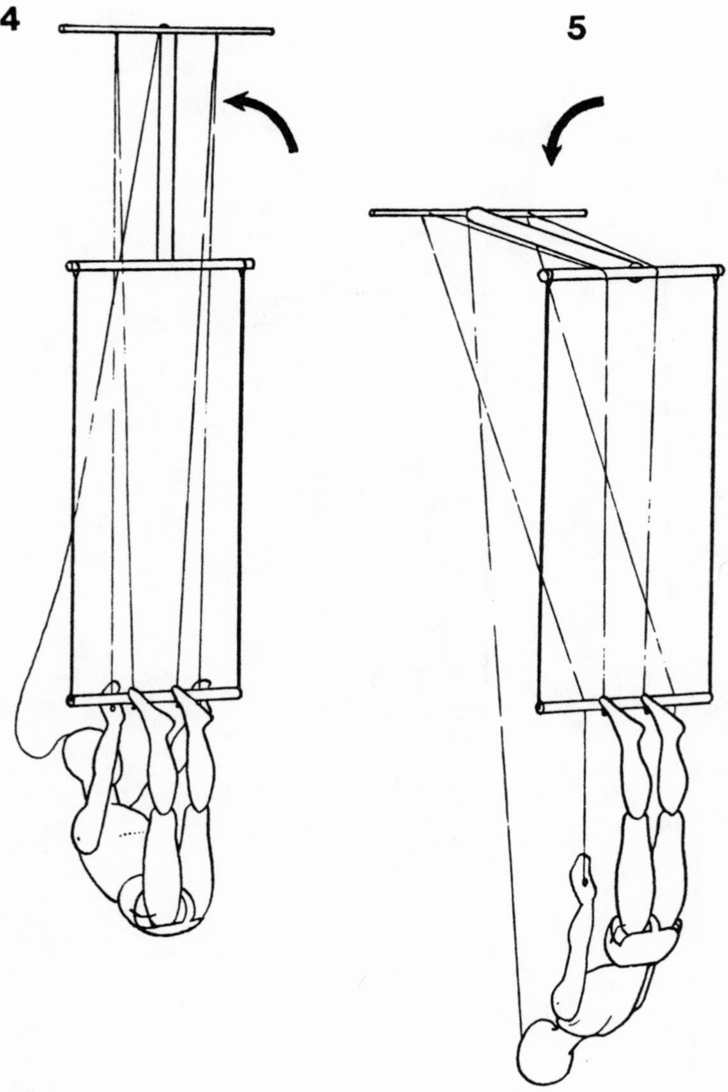

Figure 83b
Alternate raising and lowering of the T-bar to mid position raises and lowers the acrobat's legs, giving momentum to the trapeze as it begins to swing from side to side. From now on the operator continues to support and swing the trapeze with one hand, and move the T-bar control with the other.
4 With the trapeze still swinging, the T-bar is raised upright, bringing the acrobat's feet up to the level of his hands.
5 As the T-bar is bent backward to mid-position, the acrobat's hands drop away from the trapeze, and he is left hanging by the toes alone. This is the only position of the T-bar control in which the head string is stretched taut.

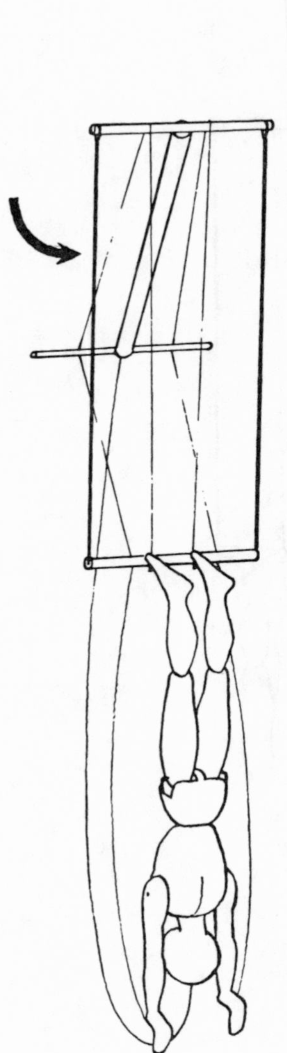

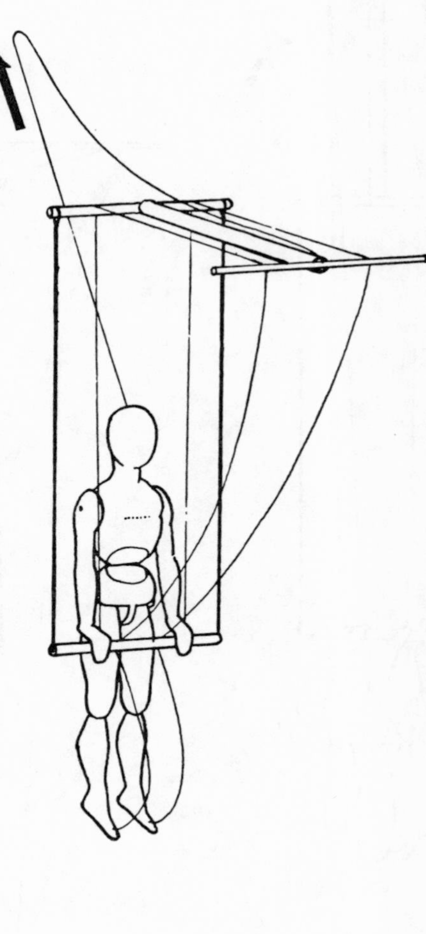

Figure 83c

Figure 83c

6 With the T-bar bent fully backwards, the acrobat's hands stretch down beyond his head. While the trapeze continues to swing, all these movements may be reversed to bring the acrobat back to his original position, hanging from the trapeze by his hands.

7 Here, starting from position 3, the head string is raised until the acrobat balances his weight on the trapeze with his arms. His hands slide round to the top of the trapeze bar pushing the handstrings to one side. While the operator raises the head string his other hand must support and swing the trapeze, keeping the T-bar in position at the same time. The head string may also be used when the acrobat is in position 5 raising him to standing position on the trapeze bar with his hands by his sides! This is not easy to do, as the foot strings must be loosened slightly (by raising the T-bar to a vertical and slightly forward position) before the feet will slide round to the top of the trapeze bar.

Figure 84 Trotting horse

A TROTTING HORSE

In a puppet circus the horse is by far the most effective of animal performers. Lions, tigers and elephants whose tricks are in fact very limited, hold the attention of a real circus audience by the degree of danger to which their trainers are exposed, and this element is lost in the puppet theatre. The horse, however, performs beyond the knowledge of many spectators, and its puppet counterpart carries out many of the classical school movements of *haute école*.

The horse described here can trot, canter, leap over jumps, rear on its hind legs, paw the ground with its hooves, raise and lower its head and tail, and kick with its back legs. Its movements are best shown in a circular track round the centre rostrum described in a later chapter on theatres. However, its individual head, foot and tail control (to which the ears may easily be added) make it a good partner to the ringmaster in the favourite old circus act of the 'talking horse' which answers questions and counts with movements of head and forefeet.

In making the horse, a careful plan should work out front and profiles of various parts with the position of the joints (see *figure 85*). The body, cut from balsa wood to reduce weight, is simple in shape and easily pared and sandpapered. Balsa wood, however, will not hold screw-eyes, so the strings supporting the main weight of the horse are attached to loops at each end of a single wire which passes right through the body, along the belly underneath and up again. The legs, having no weight to bear, may be cut as slender as you like, the upper legs from flat sections of soft-wood and the lower legs from wooden dowelling. Where they join the body the legs pivot on fixed wire shafts running from side to side. All other joints, including the neck, are tongue and groove joints with no sideways movement. Knee action should be limited to one direction only, backwards at the front knees, and forwards at each knee (stifle) of the rear legs.

The trotting horse has a standard horizontal animal control bar, with two projecting leg bars on either side. Because of the narrowness of the shoulder only one string runs to each front leg, passing through it just above the knee joint, and running down behind to join the back of the hoof. This stringing tucks each hoof well under the raised knee in the characteristic trotting movement. Each rear leg bar has one direct and one cross string. The direct string runs to the back of the knee, the cross string to the opposite leg passing through it just above the ankle (hock) and ending in the back of the hoof. The tail is strung through the end of the main control bar and fixed to a movable wooden button. The head is held erect by two strings from behind the ears which join together below the control and finish in a short length of strong elastic or wire spring. Finally, short lengths of round elastic or tiny springs are attached across the front of each hock from just above the joint to the centre of the hoof. This prevents the hooves from dropping to a 'tip-toe' position.

Figure 85

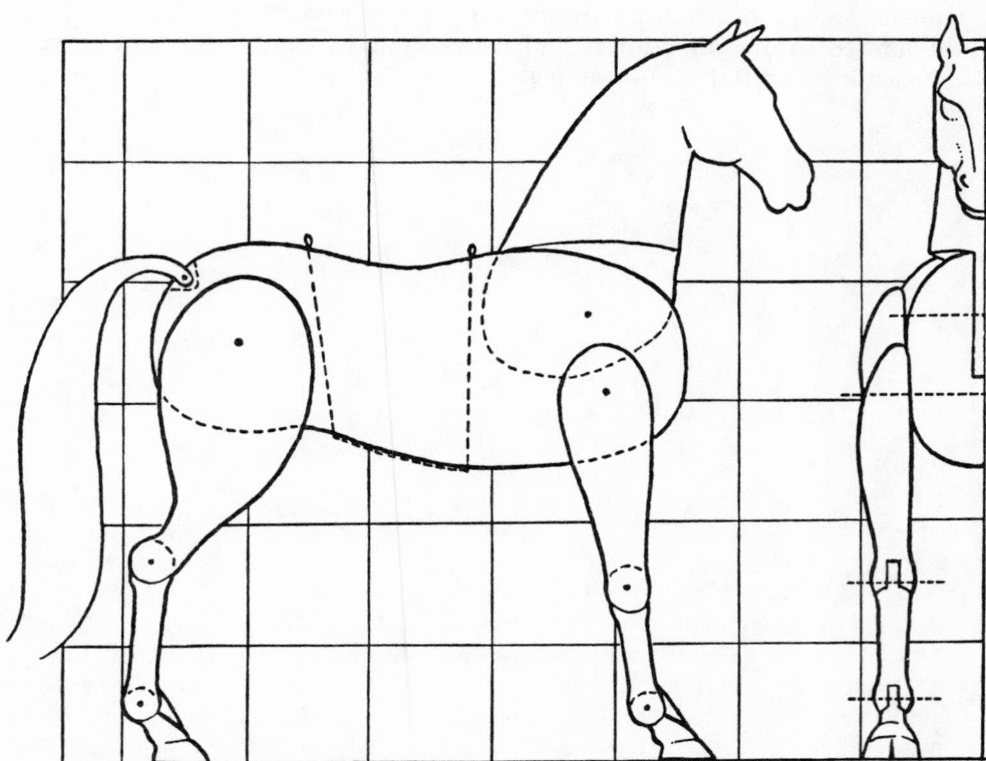

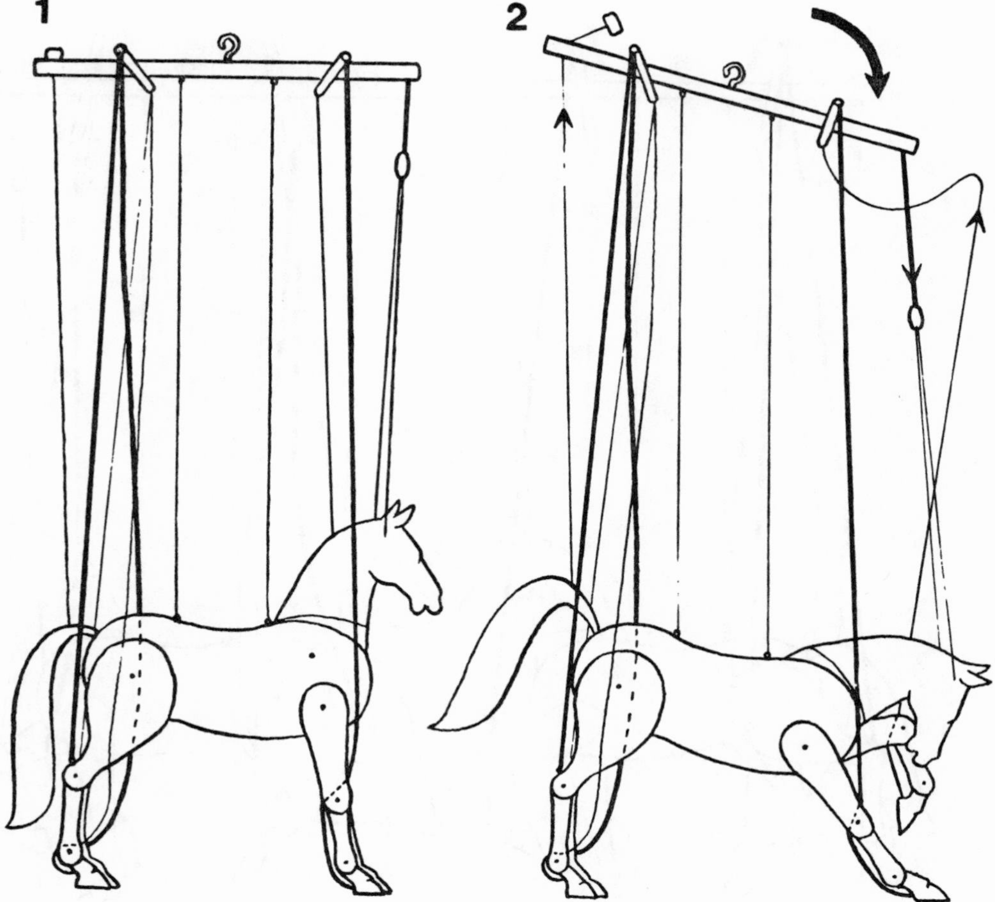

Figure 86a

1 In the standing position the main control bar is held level. All strings are of equal tension except for the cross strings to the hind legs which are loose. For the 'Spanish Trot' (straightforward foreleg raising) the foreleg stringing is altered to pass through the leg just above the hock.

2 When the main control is tilted down at the front, the horse's body alters positon to the same angle. Individual movements show the raising of the tail button to lift the tail; the raising of a foreleg string to bend front knee and ankle, and the stretching of the elastic section of the head string to lower the head.

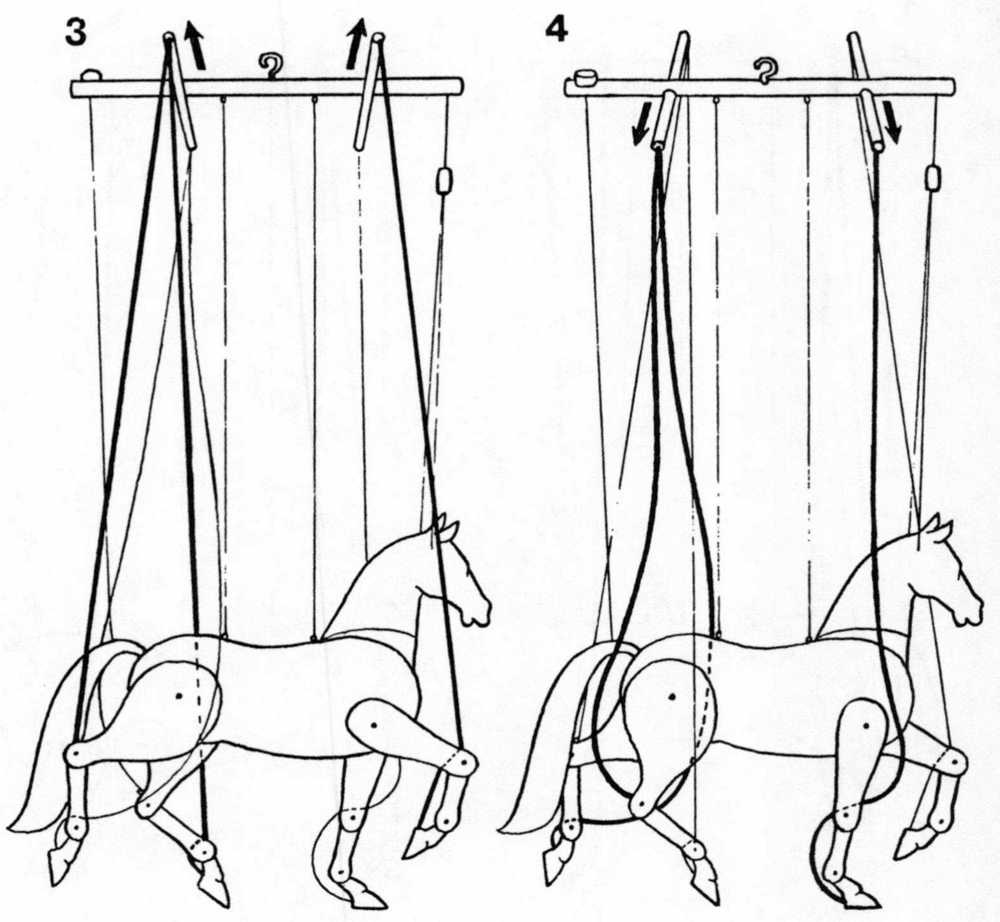

Figure 86b
3 This is stage one of the trotting movement which is carried out by alternate side to side rotation of the main bar. The strings from the raised near side leg bars lift the rear leg backwards and the front leg forwards. The cross string to the far back leg raises it forward.
4 The main control bar is now rotated in the opposite direction, moving the horse into the second position of the trot and continues forward, rising slightly up and down between each change. In the 'passage' (slow trot with bent knees) the rotation dwells for a moment at its limit on each side. This may be done to music.

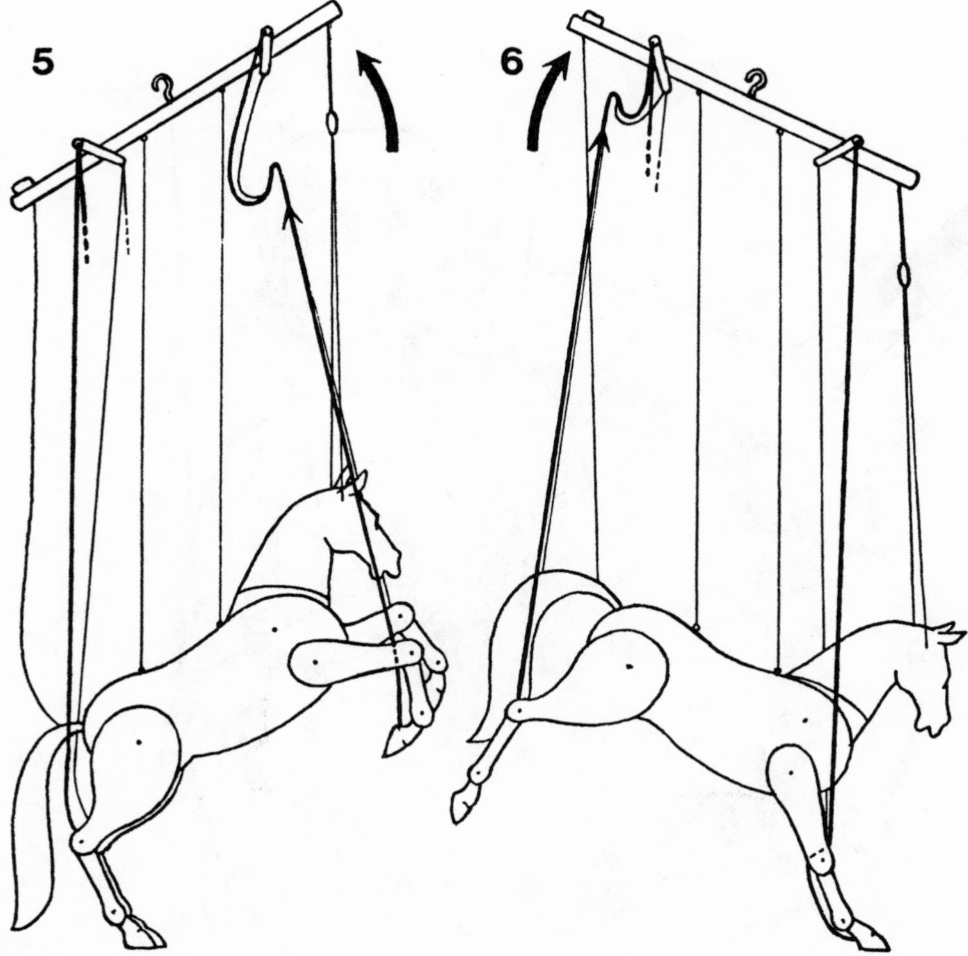

Figure 86c

5 As the foreleg strings are gathered together and raised, an upward tilt of the front of the main control moves the horse into a rearing position or 'levade'. A series of forward jumps on the hind legs alone is known as the 'courbette'. This same position guides the horse to leap over an obstacle following a canter which is carried out by rocking the main control forward and backwards with no sideways movement.

6 For a backward kick the main control bar is raised at the back, and the direct rear leg strings are gathered together and jerked sharply.

Figure 87 Tight rope dancer

TIGHT ROPE DANCER

I have combined in this circus puppet the movements of a ballet dancer and a tight rope walker. The progression of the traditional tight rope walking marionette along his rope is never very convincing as neither foot can pass the other and the result is only a sideways shuffle. The series of hops and turns on one toe by which the dancer moves appear to me much more natural.

The tight rope dancer makes her entrance on a rigid wire previously stretched between two fixed points out of sight of the audience on either side of the stage. With arms undulating before her, and one leg raised sideways she crosses to the centre of the rope in a series of hops on one pointed toe and moves into an arabesque position, bending forward from the hips with one leg raised high behind her. Returning to her entrance position the dancer hops to the far side of the tight rope, lowers her arms and leg and spins round on one toe in a pirouette; as she spins faster and faster, her arms and free leg rise sideways, and her skirt flares round about her. Crossing and re-crossing the tight rope the dancer hops on one toe, pirouettes, and poses in arabesque, until finally returning to the centre of the stage she sinks down with one leg stretched along the rope and the other hanging below, leaning forward from the waist to lay her arms and head towards the outstretched foot. Combinations of these movements carried out to music can make an effective and artistic performance.

The dancer is made with each leg in one piece from thigh to extended toe. The thigh joint of the leg which is attached to the wire is a leather hinge with forward movement only, while the other leg is rounded at the thigh and moves quite freely on a short wire loop between two screw-eyes. The pelvis section on this side is cut away at an angle to allow the leg to move freely upwards, downwards, forwards, backwards and to the one side. The waist joint is hinged to move both forwards and backwards, while the shoulder joint is a loose string joint. The elbow and wrist, being visible, are tongue and groove jointed, the wrist moving both forwards and backwards with the palms of the hands downwards. The toe on one of the dancer's legs is attached to the tight rope by a thin wire loop long enough to allow the hopping movement, and curved backwards so that the leg may be extended along the tight rope. The wire loop is fixed to the toe in a way which allows the dancer to rotate on the rope while the loop stays in position (see *figure 88*).

That part of the main control bar which supports the weight of the dancer is of standard design, but the detachable hand bar has side struts providing strings to the mid forearms as well as to the back of each hand. This bar allows a very fluid movement where wrists may be lowered at the end of raised arms. The single leg bar string to the dancer's free foot is quite irregular, being a loosely hung swinging rod closely related in length and movement to the leg which it controls. This bar is held in position between the fingers of the manipulator's supporting hand, leaving the other hand free to hold the hand bar.

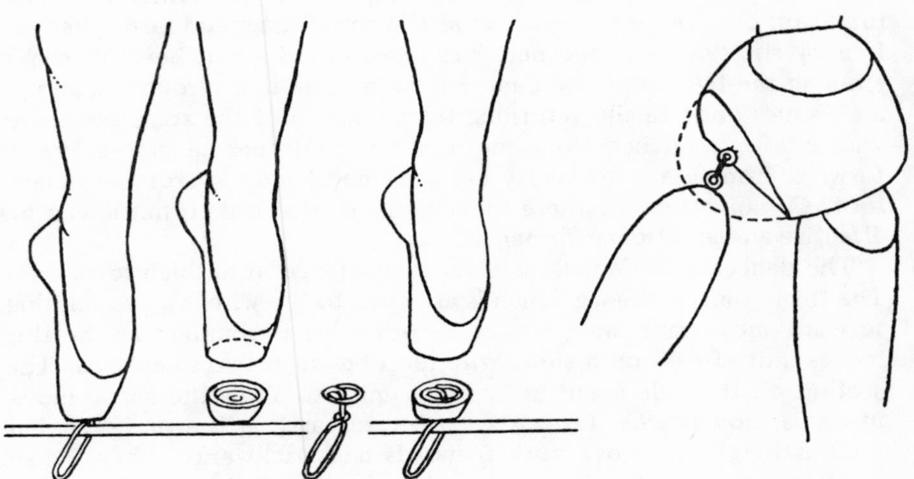

Figure 88 Dancer's toe and hip joint

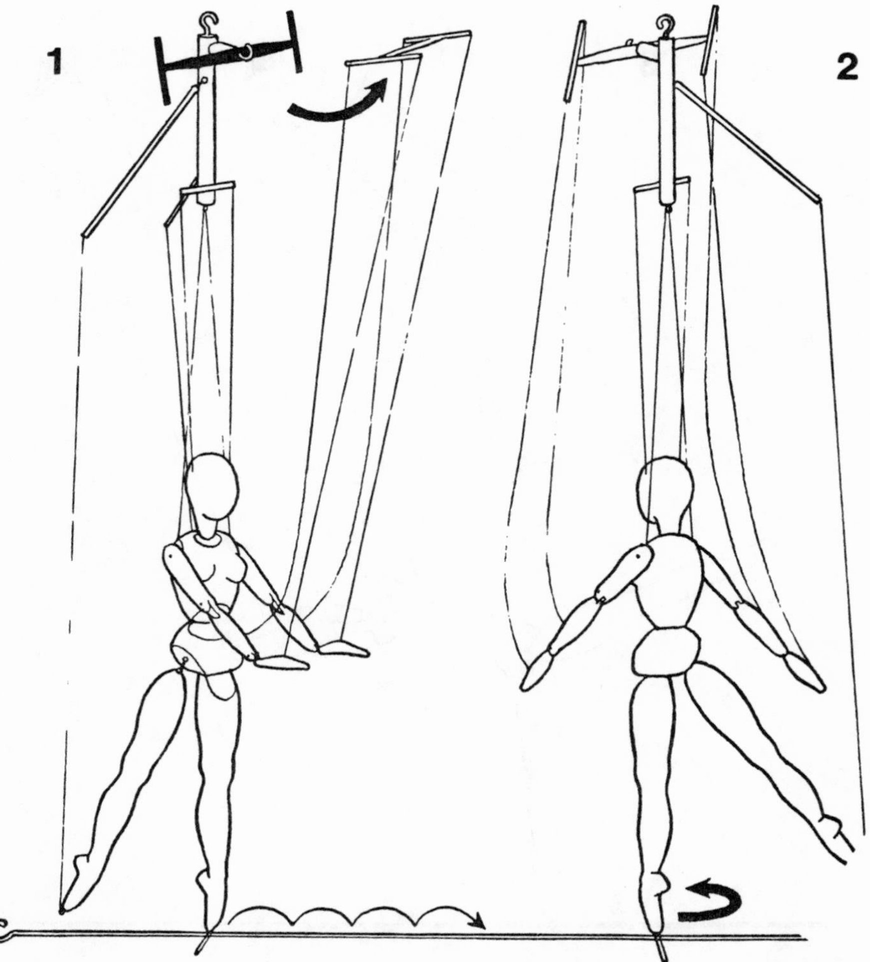

Figure 89a
1 Before the dancer makes her entrance the end of the tight rope wire is passed through the loop at the bottom of the dancer's foot and fixed in place. The hand bar is detached and tilted so that the hands are raised and the wrists dropped. When the hand bar is rocked the arms undulate from the elbow.
2 In the pirouette the hand bar is replaced and the foot bar hangs free. The whole main control bar is spun round by its hanging hook, and the dancer's arms and leg swing outwards with the movement.

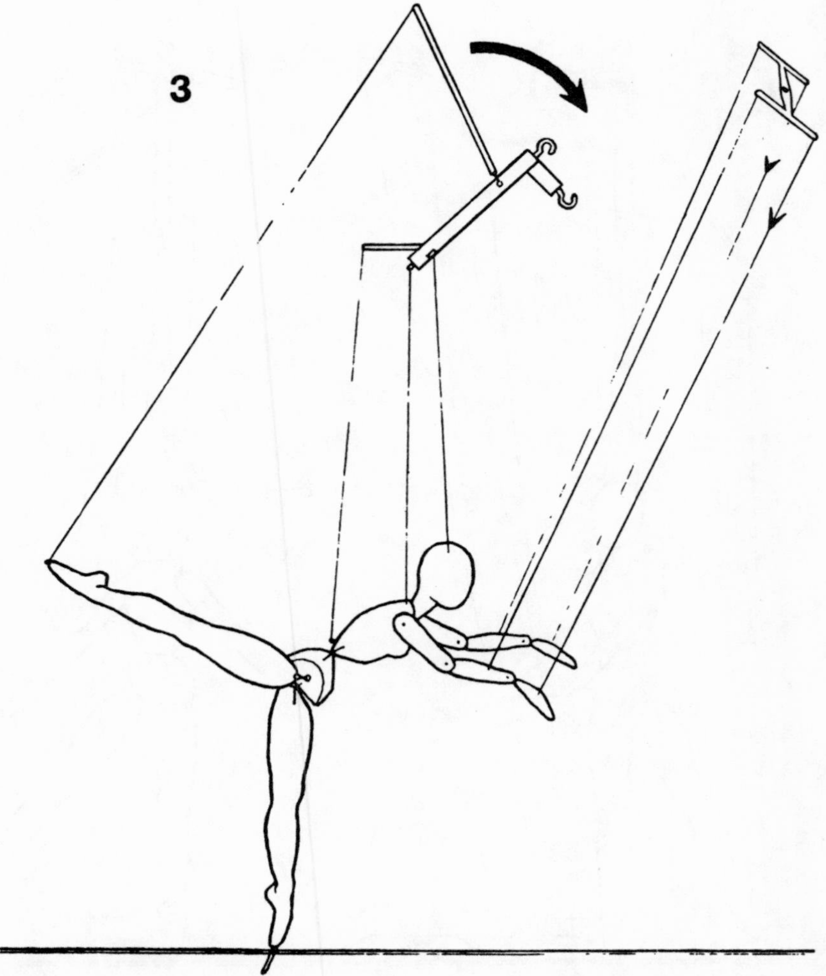

Figure 89b
3 In the arabesque position the main control bar tilts the dancer forward from the waist and the leg bar raises the free leg high behind. The hand bar moves forward to stretch out the arms, and is tilted so that the wrists are raised and the hands hang downwards. In this position a careful manipulator may turn the dancer slowly round on one toe, always remembering that the dancer in arabesque position looks best from the side view. Also, starting from this position, the dancer may be raised erect, and the free leg swung round sideways until it stretches forward in front under raised arms.

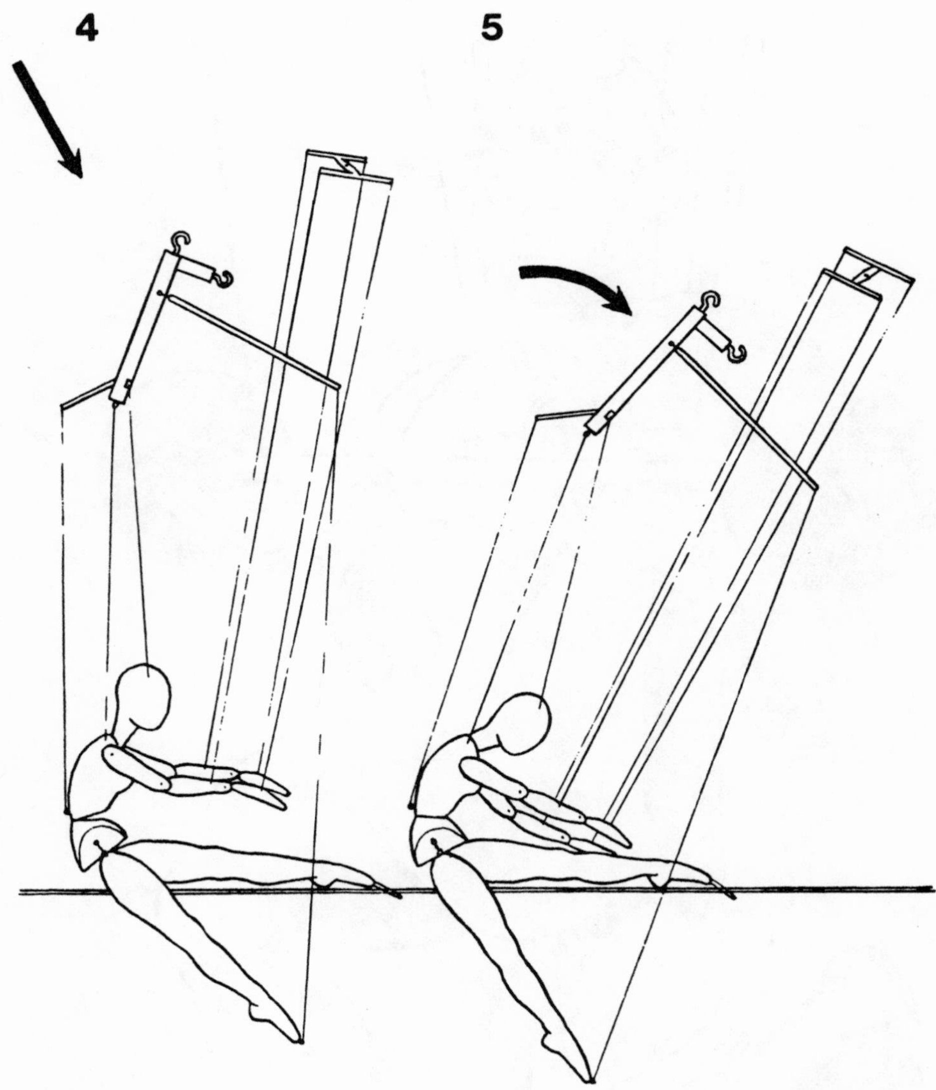

Figure 89c

4 The main control bar is lowered so that the dancer's attached leg lies along the wire and the free leg hangs downward. If the dancer is placed so that the wire passes between the division of the legs, she should stay firmly in place. The hand bar moves forward to stretch out the arms towards the dancer's foot.

5 The main control bar is tilted forward and lowered further until the tight rope wire is supporting most of the dancer's weight.

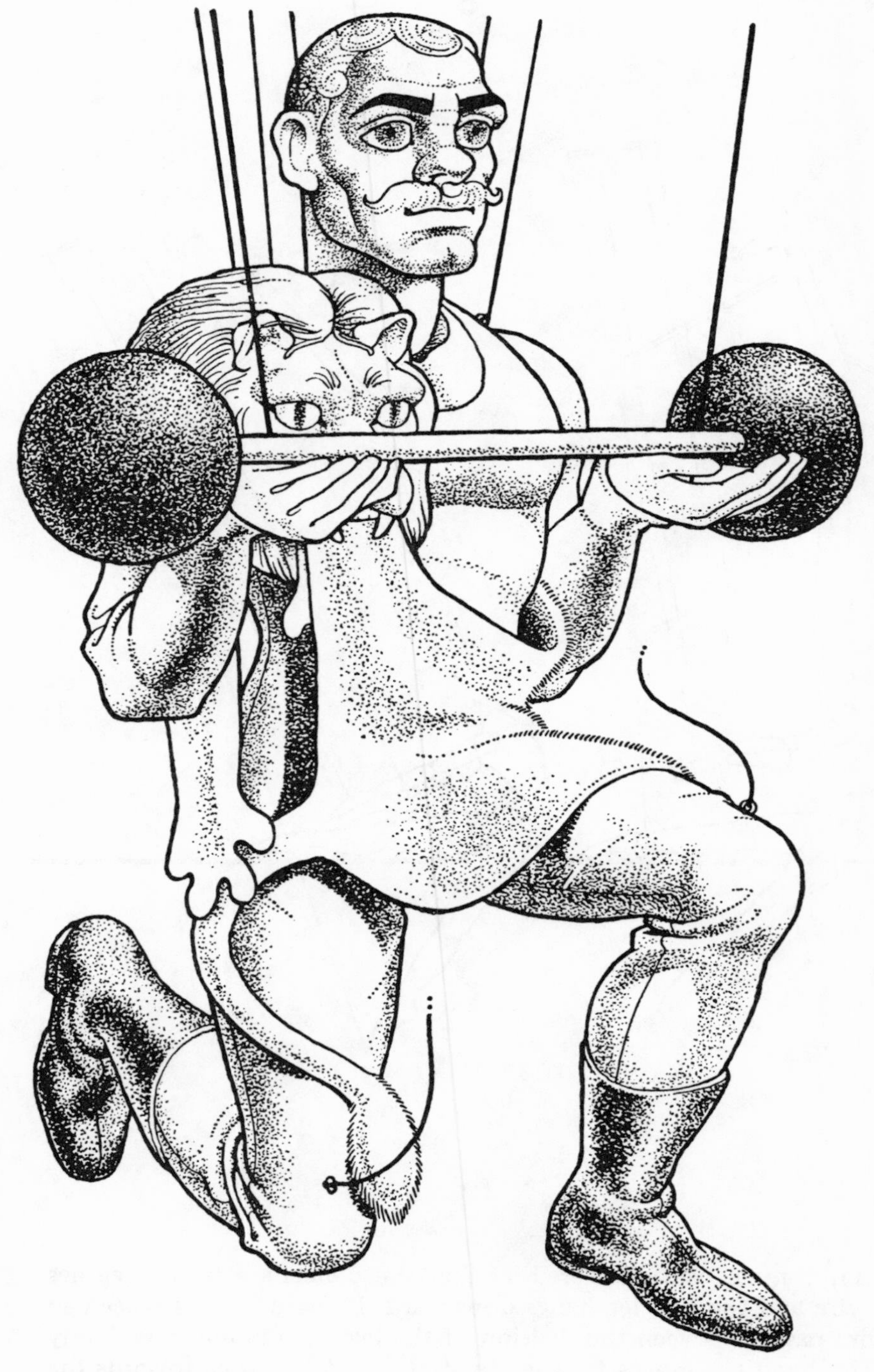

Figure 90   Weight lifter

WEIGHT LIFTER

This is one of the most intricate and entertaining of the circus puppets. The weight-lifter can walk onto the stage, lay his dumb-bells on the floor, and if the hand strings are long enough, rise from a kneeling position and bow to the audience. He can then lift up his weights and, with the appearance of tremendous effort, alternately raise and lower them from a kneeling or standing position. Further stringing makes it possible for this puppet to lie on his back, pass the dumb-bells from his hands to his feet, and raise and lower them with his legs.

The exposed limbs of the weight-lifter demand more careful carving or modelling than is necessary for a puppet in clown's costume. Circus tights of white stockingette cover the joints, but for appearance sake knees and elbows should be made with the concealed hinge described in an earlier chapter. To prevent unnecessary movement all other joints should be firm tongue and groove hinge joints, with a close leather hinge at the waist. The thigh joints, also leather, should be made slightly loose so that the feet move a little apart in raising the dumb-bells. The shoulder joint can be either a close knotted string joint, or it may pivot on a wire shaft passing through the body from side to side.

The main control bar is of standard type with a detachable hand bar and extra foot bar to carry out the weight lifting movements. The wooden dowel shaft of the dumb-bells is pierced vertically for hand and foot strings which pass through it to screw-eyes in the palms of the hands and at the toes. The weights should be heavy enough to remain still on the floor when the hand strings are moving through them.

The presentation of this puppet should be based on the slow and deliberate movements of the real life performance, imitating the stance of the body, and the final quick thrust of the arms as the weights reach the above head position. The feeling of effort can be exaggerated by an accompanying drum roll and final clash of cymbals.

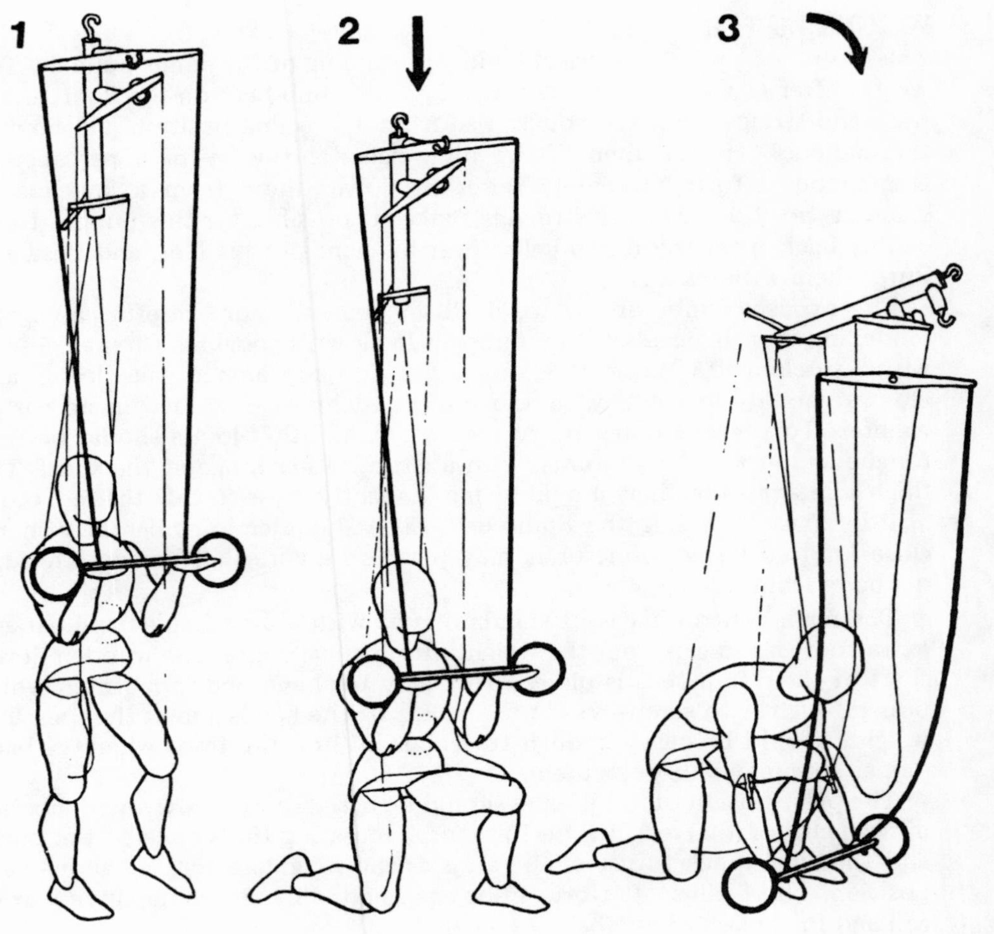

Figure 91a
1 The leg bar is worked by the thumb of the supporting hand as the weight-lifter walks onto the stage to make his bow. With the hand bar in position on the main control, the dumb-bells are held at mid-height.
2 The leg bar is tilted to bring one knee forward, and the whole puppet is advanced and lowered into kneeling position.
3 The main control is tilted so that the puppet leans forward from the waist. The hand bar is detached and lowered so that the hands reach the floor, and the dumb-bells rest on the stage.

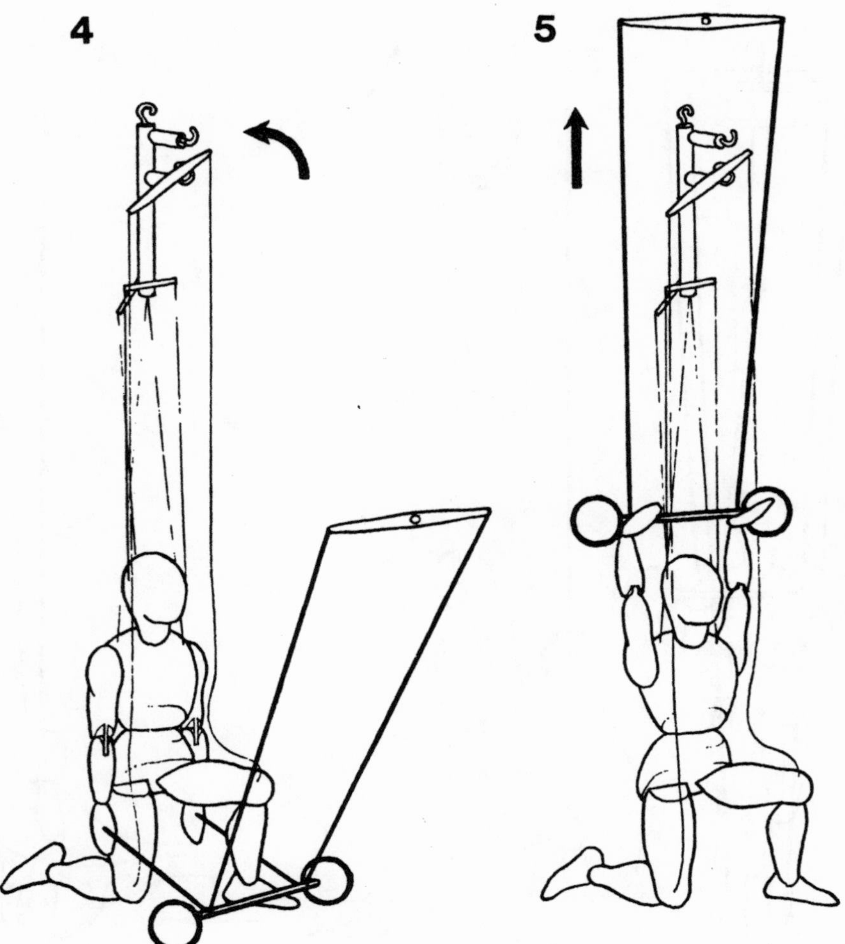

Figure 91b
4 With the hand bar still lowered, the main control is straightened, and the puppet's arms fall back to his sides. The dumb-bells remain in position as the hand strings run through the holes in the shaft.

At this stage the last two movements are repeated as the weight-lifter leans forward to pick up the dumb-bells which return to his hands as the hand bar draws the strings taut once more.

5 The weight-lifter has now returned to kneeling position, and as he kneels or stands the hand bar alternately raises and lowers his weights.

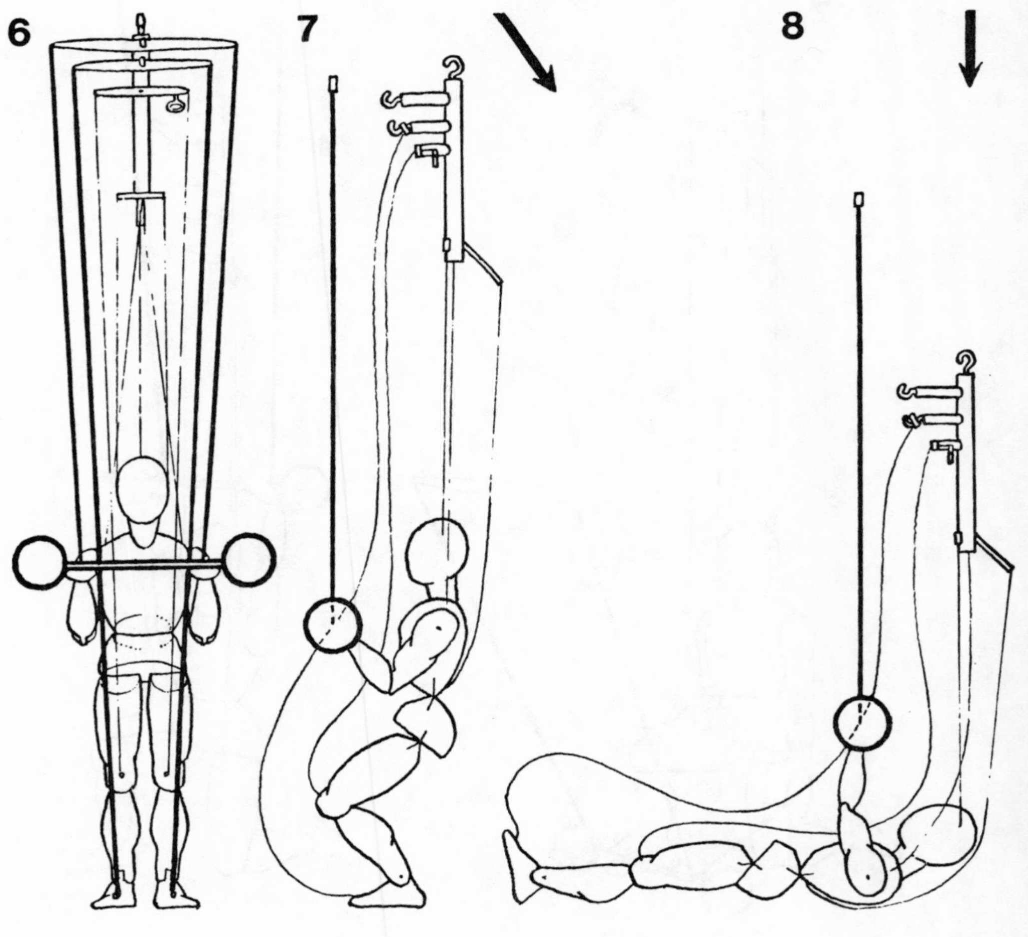

Figure 91c
6 The addition of a foot bar with strings running to the toes through the shaft of the dumb-bells between the handstrings increases the variety of movements which the weight-lifter can do. If the puppet is to be able to perform from a kneeling position, the foot-strings should hang slightly loose when the weight-lifter is standing.
7 The hand bar is detached and held forwards, while the main control bar is lowered and moved backwards.
8 The puppet is now lying on his back, with head slightly raised. The hand bar is used to alternately raise and lower the dumb-bells.

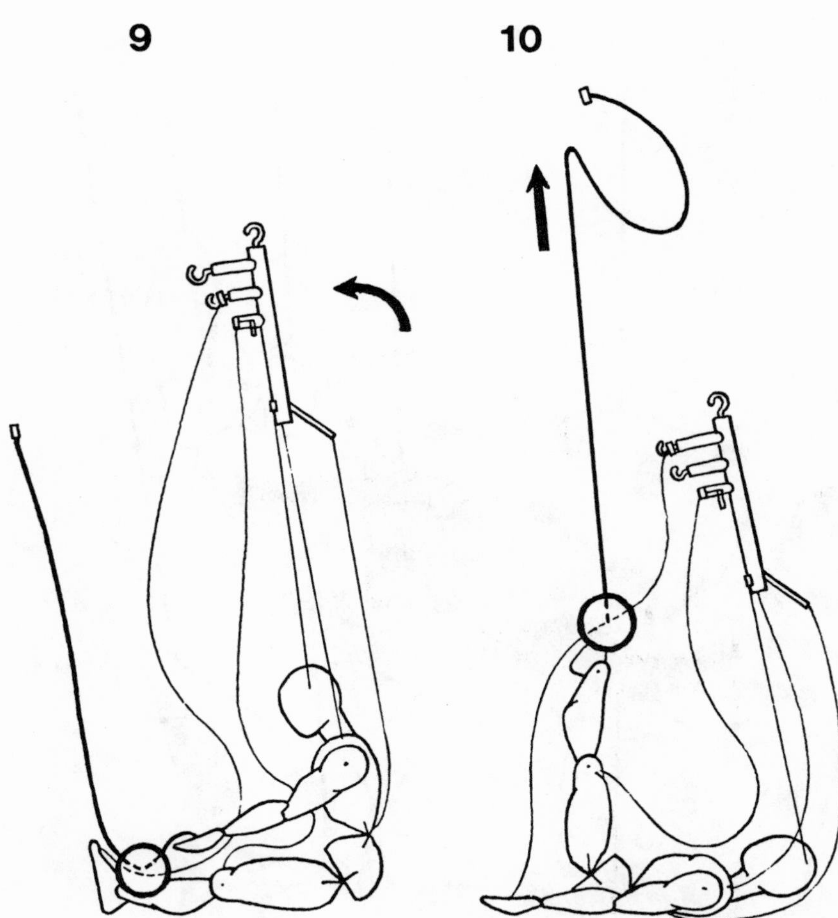

Figure 91d
9 The main control bar now raises the weight-lifter from the waist. The hand bar moves the arms forward, and a slight jerk and loosening of the hand strings tips the dumb-bells on the puppet's toes. This exchange must be carefully done so that no loose strings fall round the ends of the weights.
10 The loosened hand bar is replaced on the main control and the foot bar is detached and raised so that its taut strings hold the dumb-bells in position on the feet. As the weight-lifter lies back, the leg bar alternately raises and lowers the dumb-bells.

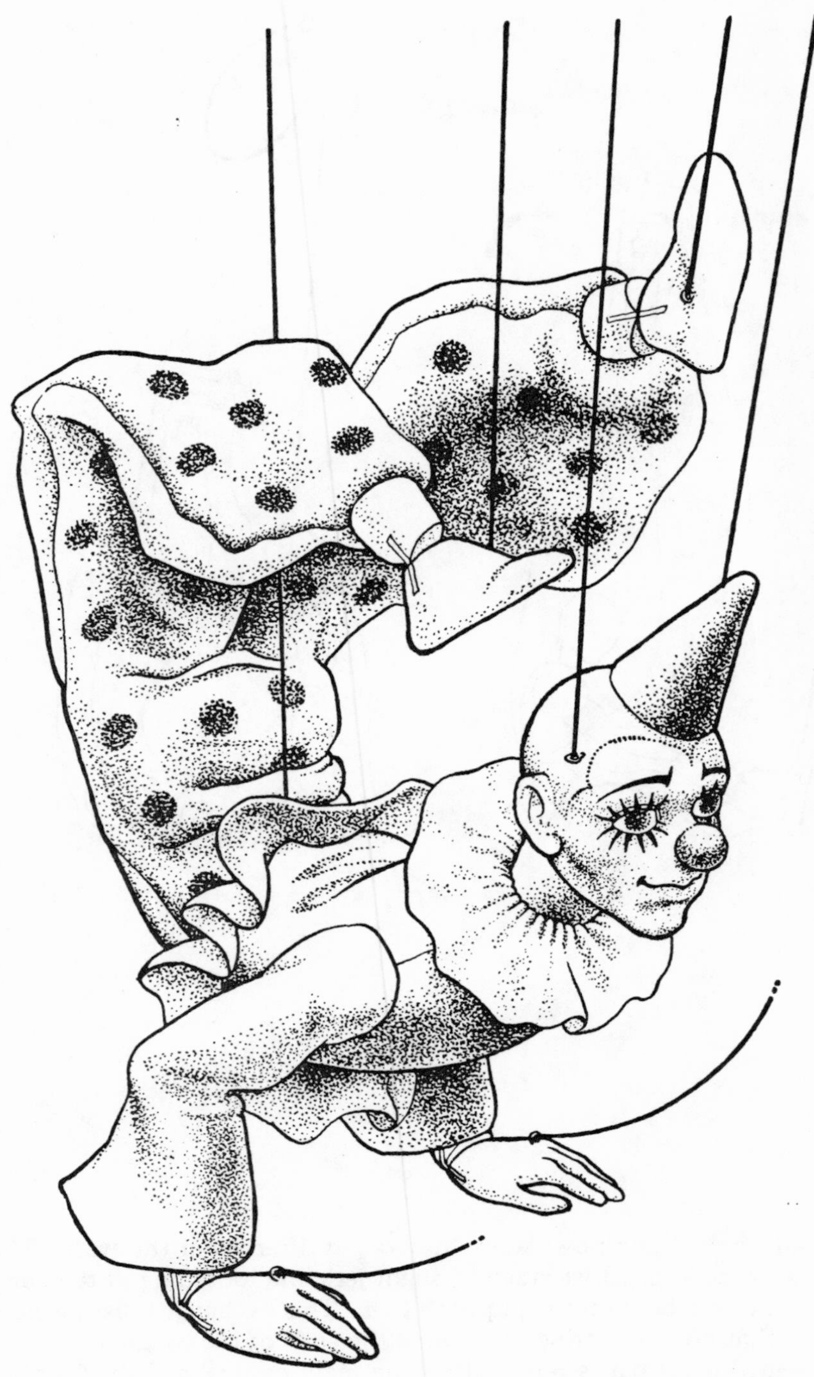

Figure 92 Hand-balancing acrobat

HAND BALANCING ACROBAT

The hand-balancer makes his entrance in a series of jumps, standing upright on his feet. He bows to the audience, bends over from the waist to place his hands on the floor, and balancing on his palms, slowly raises his legs until his feet are straight up above his head. In this position he raises and lowers himself a few times by bending and straightening his elbows, and raises and lowers his feet, or kicks them alternately above his head. Finally, moving one hand at a time he walks round the stage on his hands.

This puppet is designed to move in one plane only with no sideways movement except at the neck. Both hands and feet must be weighted, and if the puppet is clothed in clown's costume, wooden dowel limbs may be used with leather hinge joints throughout. The waist, thigh and ankle joints move freely backwards and forwards, but knee, wrist and elbow bend in one direction only. The shoulder joint rotates on a wire shaft passing through the chest from side to side.

The main control bar is a tip up control. A detachable foot bar with strings to the insteps is placed behind the base of the main bar, and a wire lever with strings to the back of the acrobat's hands is placed in the front centre. Head strings from a fixed bar at the top of the main control support most of the puppet's weight along with a string from the base of the main bar which runs to the acrobat's back. When the main control is tipped forward the index finger of the supporting hand raises the hand string lever forward between the head strings (A). This stringing is irregular but quite simple, and avoids the complication of knee strings for upright walking movement.

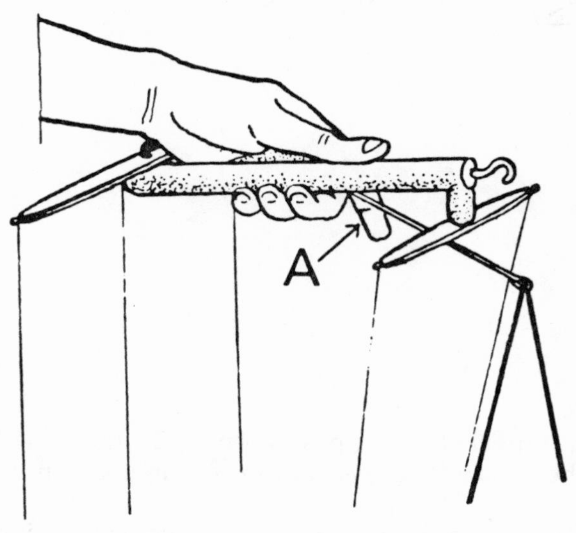

Figure 93

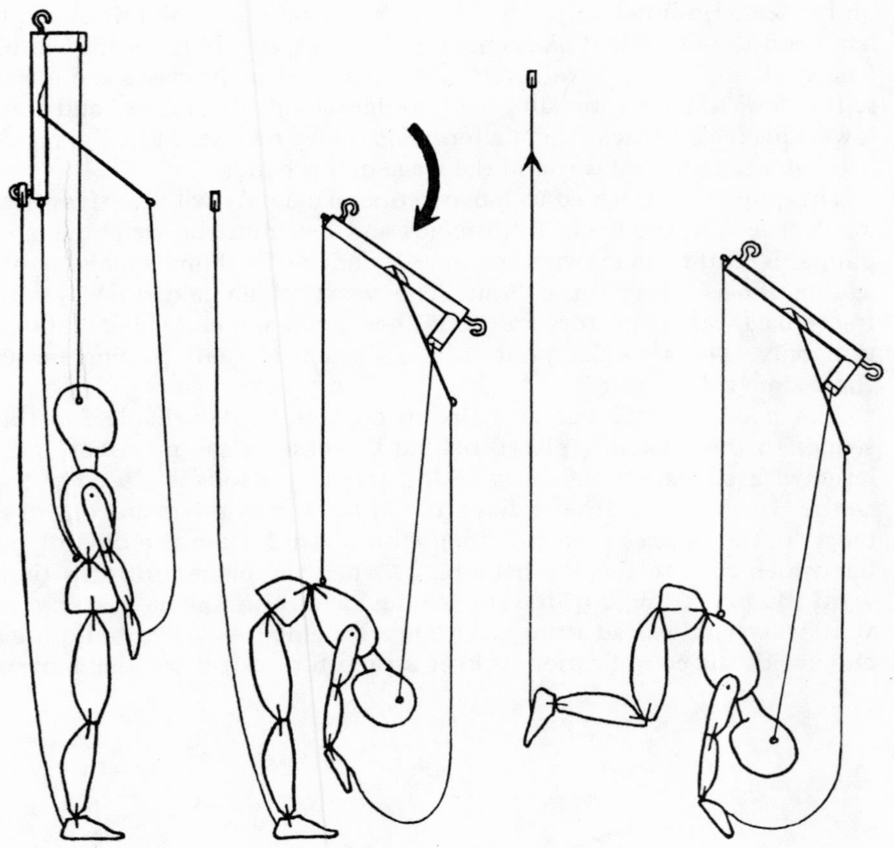

Figure 94a
1 In the normal standing position most of the weight is taken by the head strings. The hand string lever lies in resting position with its strings hanging loose.
2 With the leg bar detached, the main control is tipped over to allow the top half of the puppet to bend down. The hand string lever is moved forward between the head strings by the index finger of the supporting hand.
3 The weighted hands of the acrobat touch the ground and the leg bar is raised, bringing the feet up. The acrobat settles on to the palms of his hands.

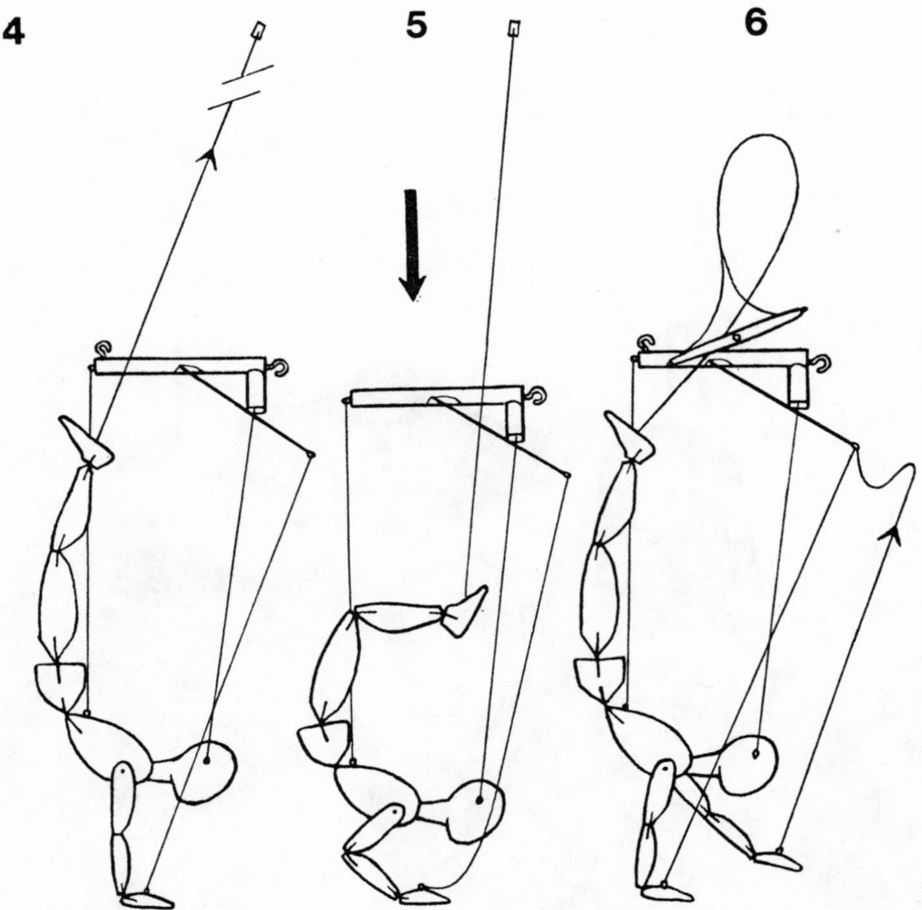

Figure 94b

4 As the leg bar rises further, its strings pass on either side of the main control bar, and the legs on either side of the back string. The main control is levelled, lifting the head and reversing the arch of the back.

5 Movement of the main control makes the acrobat appear to push himself up and down on his hands. The leg bar may be used to raise or lower the legs or to make them kick in turn.

6 The foot bar and its strings, keeping the legs extended, are gathered into the supporting hand, while the free hand moves the hand strings alternately as the acrobat walks forward on his palms.

Figure 95 Eighteenth-century Venetian marionettes

Costume

The marionettes in the opposite picture belong to the eighteenth-century Venetian theatre in the Victoria and Albert Museum. Their clothing provides an example but also a warning.

The silhouette and tone contrast in the costume of each figure is excellent and in this respect they make a good visual effect. However, much of the detail must be lost at a distance, and although these marionettes had a very simple mechanism, the hats at least would get in the way of modern stringing.

There are different opinions on how nearly clothing for puppets should be related to conventional dressmaking.

With loose removable clothing, I feel that proper cutting and sewing are suitable. This sort of clothing can be fastened by hooks and eyes, or press studs, over glove puppets, rod puppets and marionettes. With marionettes, removal for cleaning and pressing is a nuisance as half the strings have to be untied, but I think it is well worth while to be able to give a fresh appearance to a puppet which is used often. With this sort of dressmaking, as with lighting and stage carpentry, some special skill has to be called upon, and there is always at least one girl in the company who can carry out the designs suggested.

Close-fitting clothes are better not to be made by techniques of orthodox dressmaking. Free movements at joints, and particularly at the shoulder joint tend to become restricted. In this case it is better to tack and glue material to give the needed effect, and certain parts can even be included in carving, and be painted. With any type of clothing it is a general rule never to restrict movement at joints, or to push stringing out of line.

In designing clothes for a play, colour and period must be decided upon first. Line and profile are more important than detail, as the visual effect must reach the back row of the audience.

Choice of material will depend on the type of puppet to be clothed. With glove puppets I like to have a basic glove of blanket material to give the body substance. Clothes over this may be as thin as you like, and removable for pressing or cleaning.

With marionettes and rod puppets, thick material can give substance where the puppet is made only of jointed dowelling. Where the body is fully carved or padded, thinner material may be used.

In choosing texture, thickness and pattern for puppets' clothes, great care must be taken to relate the material to a very much reduced scale. Hardly any material woven and patterned for the use of full-sized human beings, hangs or drapes easily on a puppet, but where the draping is close to the body, cloth may be damped with size solution and sculptured into folds while wet. This was done with the clothes of the shepherd and shepherdess marionettes shown earlier in this book.

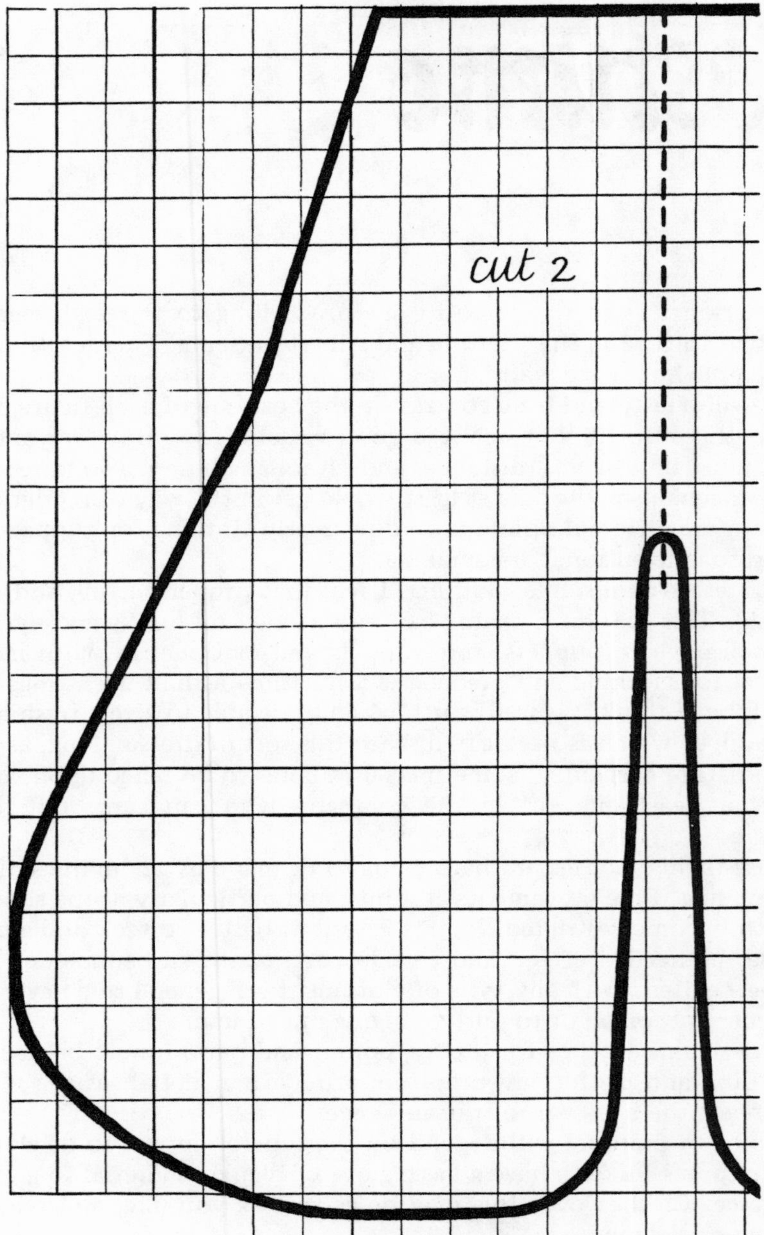

Figure 96 Pattern for clown's trousers

It would be impossible to give patterns for all the clothes which may be met with, so I have drawn a basic shape for the clown's costume alone, which can be drawn on 15 or 20 mm (½ or ¾ in.) squared paper for puppets of 450 or 600 mm (18 or 23 in.) in height. The trousers are attached to the body just below the armpits leaving plenty of room for waist and thigh

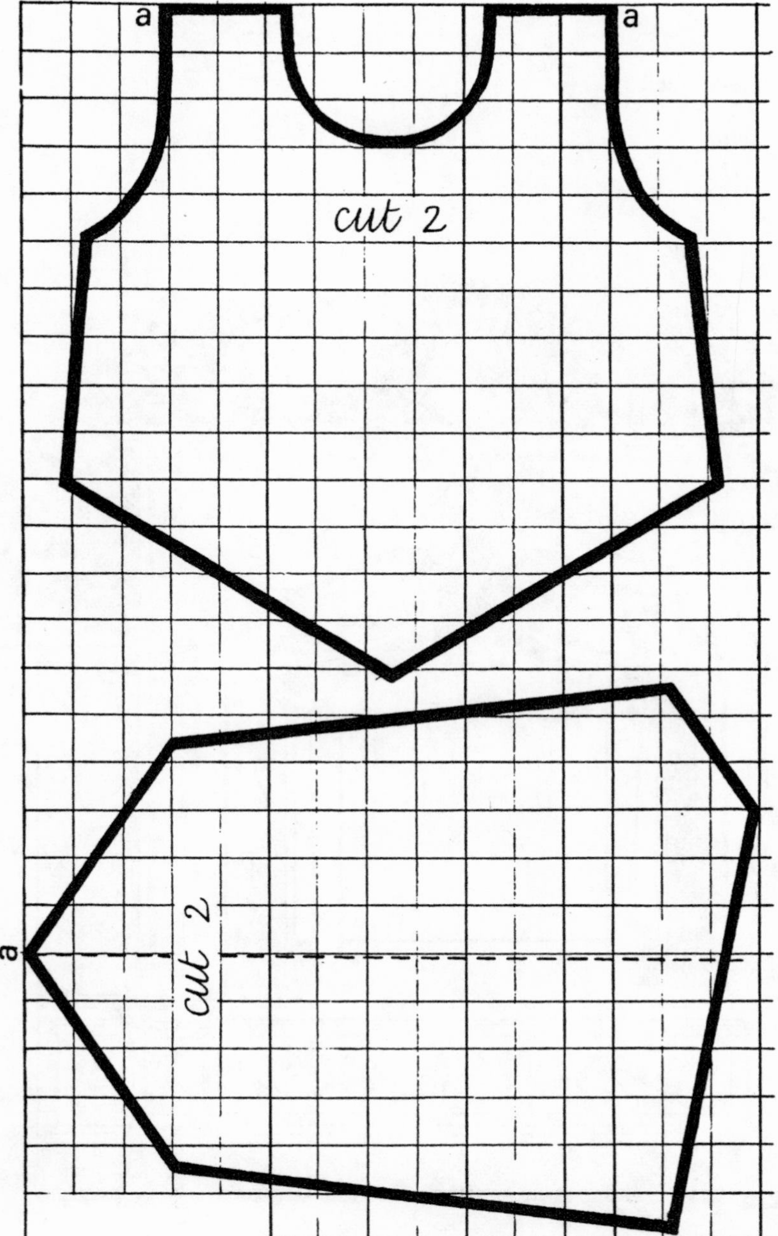

Figure 97 Pattern for clown's tunic and sleeves

movement, while the jacket can be completed by a flounce below, and a ruff at the neck. When clothing acrobatic puppets in tights of stretch stockingette, it is best not to sew the shoulder seams at all where the shoulder has been fully modelled, but to turn the cloth inwards gluing it to the inner joint surfaces.

Figure 98 An eighteenth-century Venetian marionette theatre

Puppet Theatres

A puppet theatre can be improvised from folding screens, chairs and curtain material, or it may be a more permanent theatre involving carpentry work. In either case there are certain features common to all which are described in this chapter. In the past most of the more elaborate theatres have been made of wood framing covered with hardboard or curtain material, but lately I have used a very successful portable folding theatre made from 50 mm (2 in.) thick sheet polystyrene covered, strengthened and hinged with old cotton hospital sheets pasted down with P.V.A. adhesive. The light weight of this type of construction is a great advantage.

The design of a theatre for regular use will depend on the size and type of puppets employed, whether it is to be portable, or permanent, whether it is to be adaptable for different types of puppet, and how many manipulators are likely to be working together at one time. Generally speaking puppet theatres are of two types, – those for puppets worked from above, and those for puppets worked from below. The marionette theatre illustrated later in this chapter can be adapted for glove puppets if the stage floor is removed and the proscenium opening changed from the lower to the higher level.

The main purpose of a puppet theatre is to concentrate attention on a defined acting area, and to screen from the audience those mechanisms of staging and manipulation which the producer wishes to conceal. Both these aims are concerned with illusion and are not always necessary. The manipulators of the puppets of the traditional Japanese Bunraku Theatre are entirely visible as they move the limbs of their jointed fingures by hand, with no lessening of dramatic effect; and in recent years we have seen puppets performing successfully with live actors on open stages and even in the streets. When puppets are well made and dramatic material worthwhile no aids to concentration or illusion appear to be necessary. These types of production, often stylised, ritualistic or symbolic are very suitable for puppets for whom mere imitation is an artistic dead end. But there are many areas of drama where scenery, lighting and properties are helpful, and much of the interest in watching acrobatic and circus puppets lies in trying to guess what mechanism is concealed.

THE PROSCENIUM

The proscenium of the theatre is the screen standing between the spectators and the puppet operators. The drawing opposite (*figure 98*) shows the proscenium of an eighteenth-century Venetian marionette theatre now belonging to the Victoria and Albert Museum. Before a performance, and during the intervals, the proscenium is all that the audience have to look at, so it deserves some consideration in design. Unfortunately many portable theatres have nothing more to offer than an expanse of dark curtaining, but a decorative frame round the proscenium opening could certainly be included in the portable equipment.

THE PROSCENIUM OPENING

The proscenium opening is the area through which the audience sees the stage and is closed by a curtain before, during the intervals and after the performance. The position of this opening is important as it must be visible to the whole audience. Usually the lower rim of the opening (stage level) is at least 1 m 300 mm (4 ft) high, the average head level of a seated audience. This is no problem in the case of a permanent theatre, but in a portable marionette theatre the bulk of units to be carried can become a problem. Luckily, most halls or lecture theatres already have a stage or rostrum which helps to raise the height, but it is best to have a rostrum of one's own available if necessary. In theatres for puppets worked from below, the height of the proscenium opening is not likely to be a problem; the stage level is usually at the height of the operator's head, which is high enough for everyone to see.

After making sure that your audience can see, make sure that they cannot see too much. Particular care should be taken with the front row. The sight lines from the side chairs may lead beyond the edge of the backcloth and wings, and the centre chairs may have a view over the top of the backcloth to the operators at work. These faults can be dealt with either by altering the curtaining, or moving the position of the chairs.

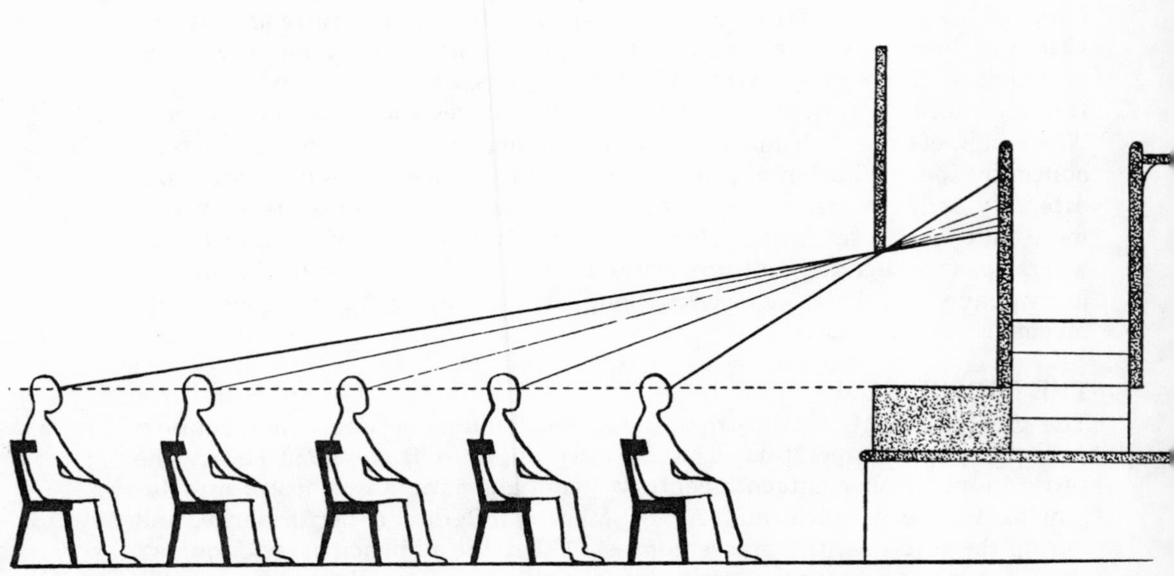

Figure 99 Sight lines to the proscenium opening

A theatre worked from below

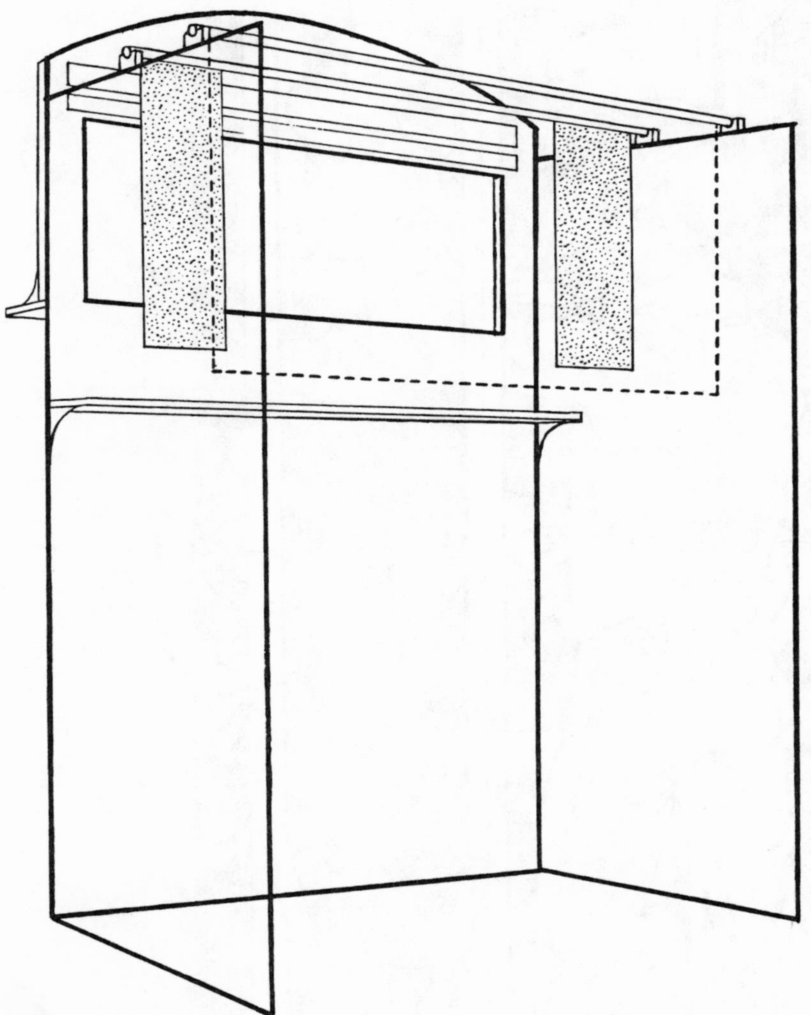

Figure 100 A theatre for puppets worked from below

Any theatre for puppets worked from below follows the principles shown in the above drawing. The front screen may be as wide as you like depending on the number of manipulators taking part at one time, but the height is most conveniently designed where the lower border is 1 m 650 mm (5 ft 5 in.) above the ground at the operator's eye level. The height of the stage opening itself depends on the size of the puppets in use. Glove puppets vary little in size and for them 550 mm (21 in.) may be sufficient. Other types of puppet may well need more height. When shadow puppets are used, the shadow screen is fitted into the stage opening and a light placed behind.

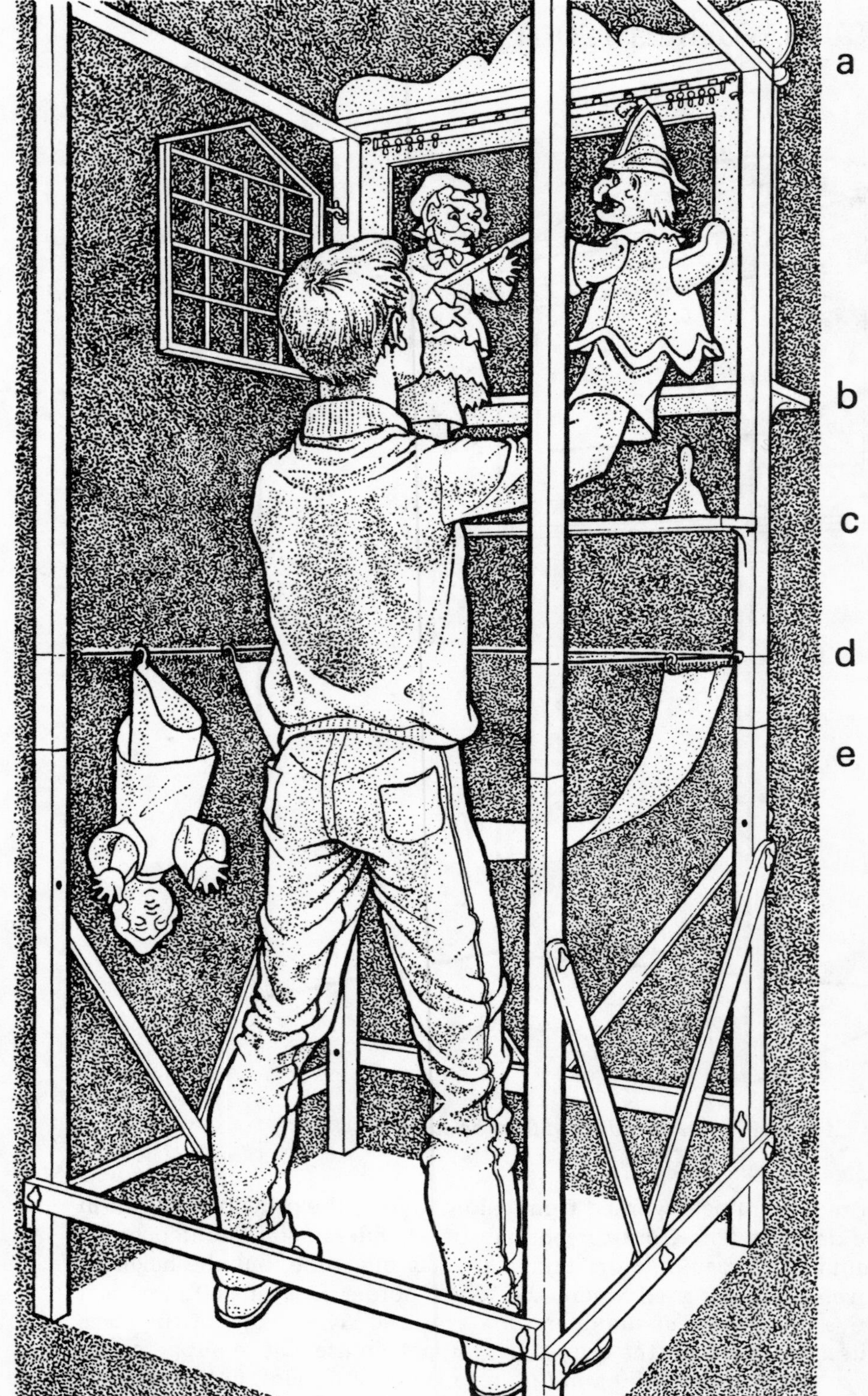

Figure 101 Assembled booth from behind (without curtains)

The traditional Punch and Judy show was presented in a portable booth. I have given here the basic design of such a one-man theatre which can easily be enlarged to the scale of a group production or permanent theatre, and altered for different methods of manipulation.

In the first illustration puppets are held above the head in a stage opening (proscenium) whose lower border is at the performer's eye level. This position presents puppets where they can be seen over the heads of a standing audience. The inside of the booth shows -(*a*) A curtain rail behind the upper border of the proscenium; (*b*) A playboard where much of the action takes place; (*c*) A shelf for properties when not in use, (*d*) A wire round three sides of the booth on which puppets are hung and (*e*) A canvas sling into which puppets are dropped when the have played their part.

Figure 102

In a second less tiring method of manipulation the proscenium is lower, and the operator stands behind a semi-transparent screen resting his elbows on the properties' shelf. Light falls on the front of the screen, but the operator standing in the dark is invisible to the audience.

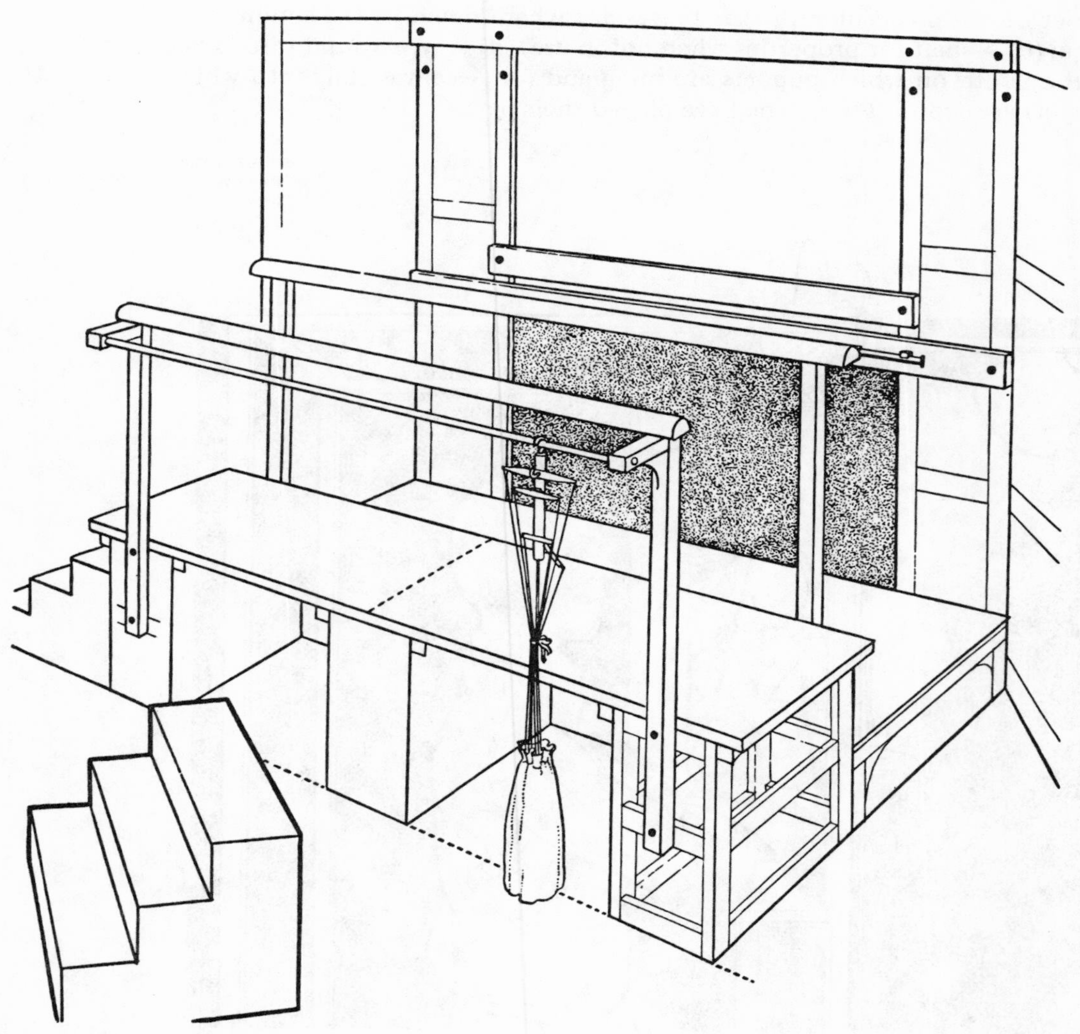

Figure 103 Assembled portable marionette theatre from behind

A theatre worked from above

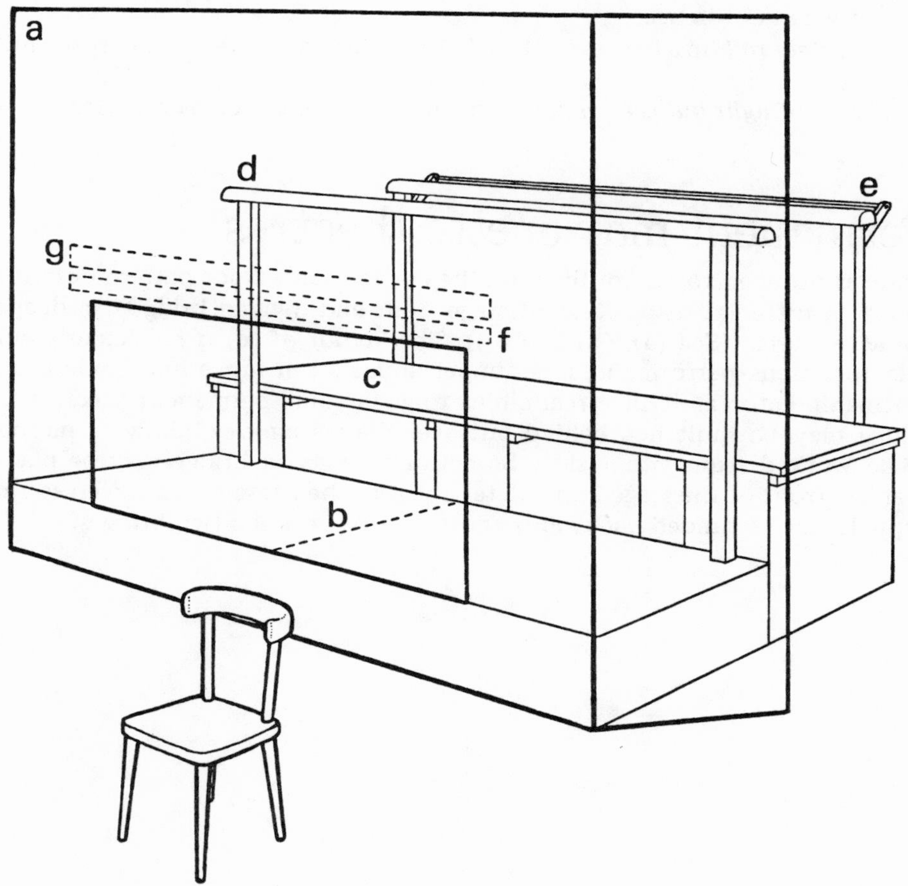

Figure 104 A theatre for puppets worked from above

A theatre for puppets worked from above is more complicated. My drawing shows features common to improvised, portable, or permanent theatres of this type.

(a) *A screen* or *proscenium* must be high enough to conceal manipulators, with a stage opening at a level visible to a seated audience. In your actual structure this may be only 460 mm (18 in.) above the floor, but the whole theatre may be raised on a rostrum, usually available in church, school or public halls.

(b) *A stage floor* is level with the lower border of the stage opening. This floor may be as wide as you like from side to side, but the depth from back to front is seldom more than 915 mm (36 in.) as the operators' arms can reach no further.

(c) *A bridge* is placed behind the stage floor, giving height to the manipulators who stand over their work. The level of the bridge floor is usually 45 cm (18 in.) above the stage but this may vary. The bridge forms the rear limit of the stage, and backcloths can be hung against it.
(d) *A leaning bar* is fixed to the stage side of the bridge. This protects the operators from falling onto the stage, and can be used as an arm rest.
(e) *A perch bar* is fixed to the back of the bridge, and marionettes are hung from it when not in use.
(f) *A curtain rail* on a batten is placed above the stage side of the proscenium opening.
(g) *A row of light bulbs* on a batten is placed above the curtain batten.

Permanent marionette theatres

There is no need to be confined by the conventional floor pattern described above. A different disposition of stage floor and divided bridge can deepen the acting area. (See (a), (b) and (c)). The layout of (c) is particularly suitable for circus performances as puppet animals can move in a circle round the manipulator as if in a real circus ring. In some permanent theatres the bridge may be built not behind but over the acting area, allowing puppets to be worked from either side. Sometimes an extra bridge may be placed over the front of the stage immediately behind the proscenium screen so that puppets can be handed backwards and forwards between two bridges.

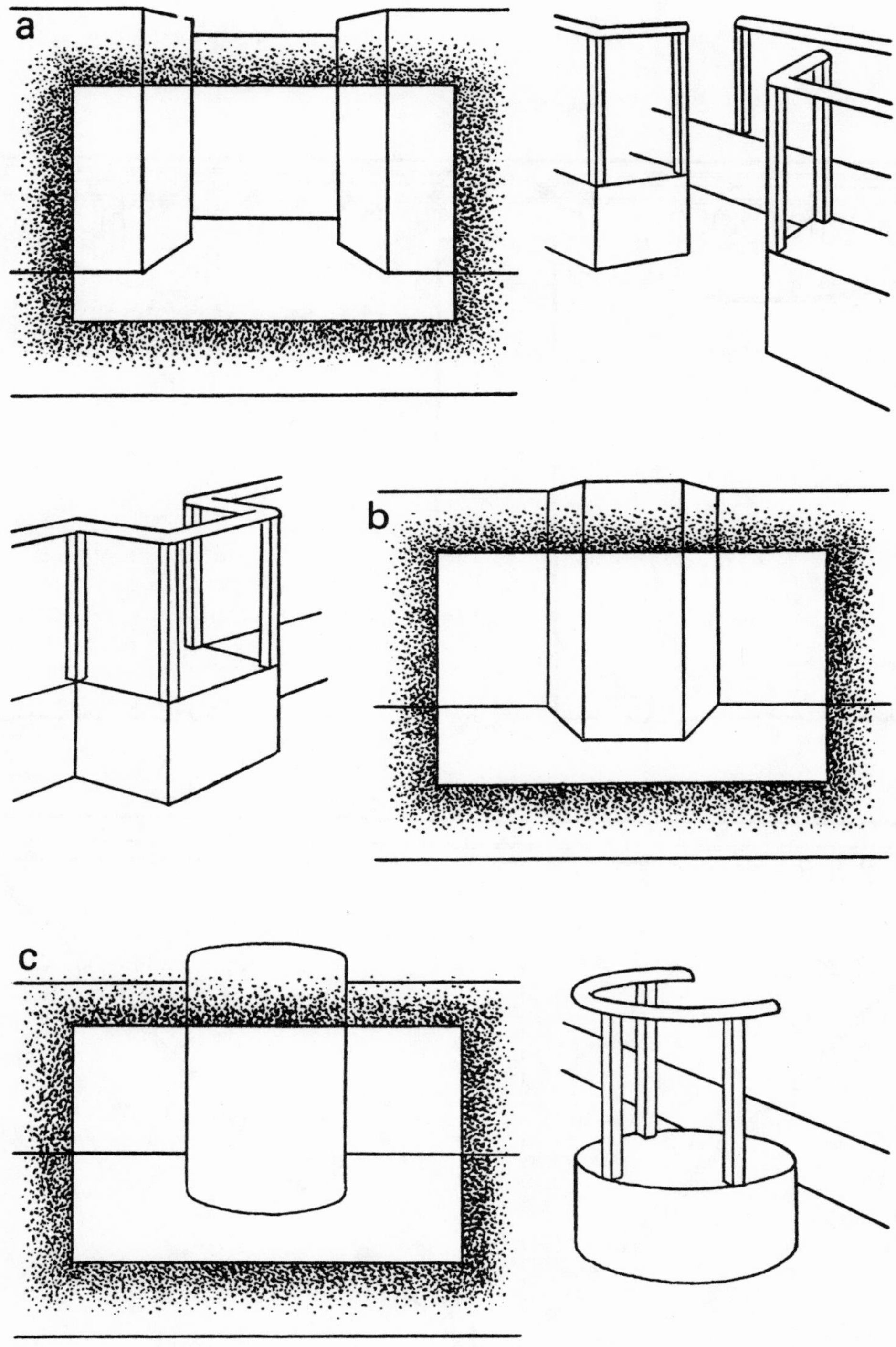

Figure 105

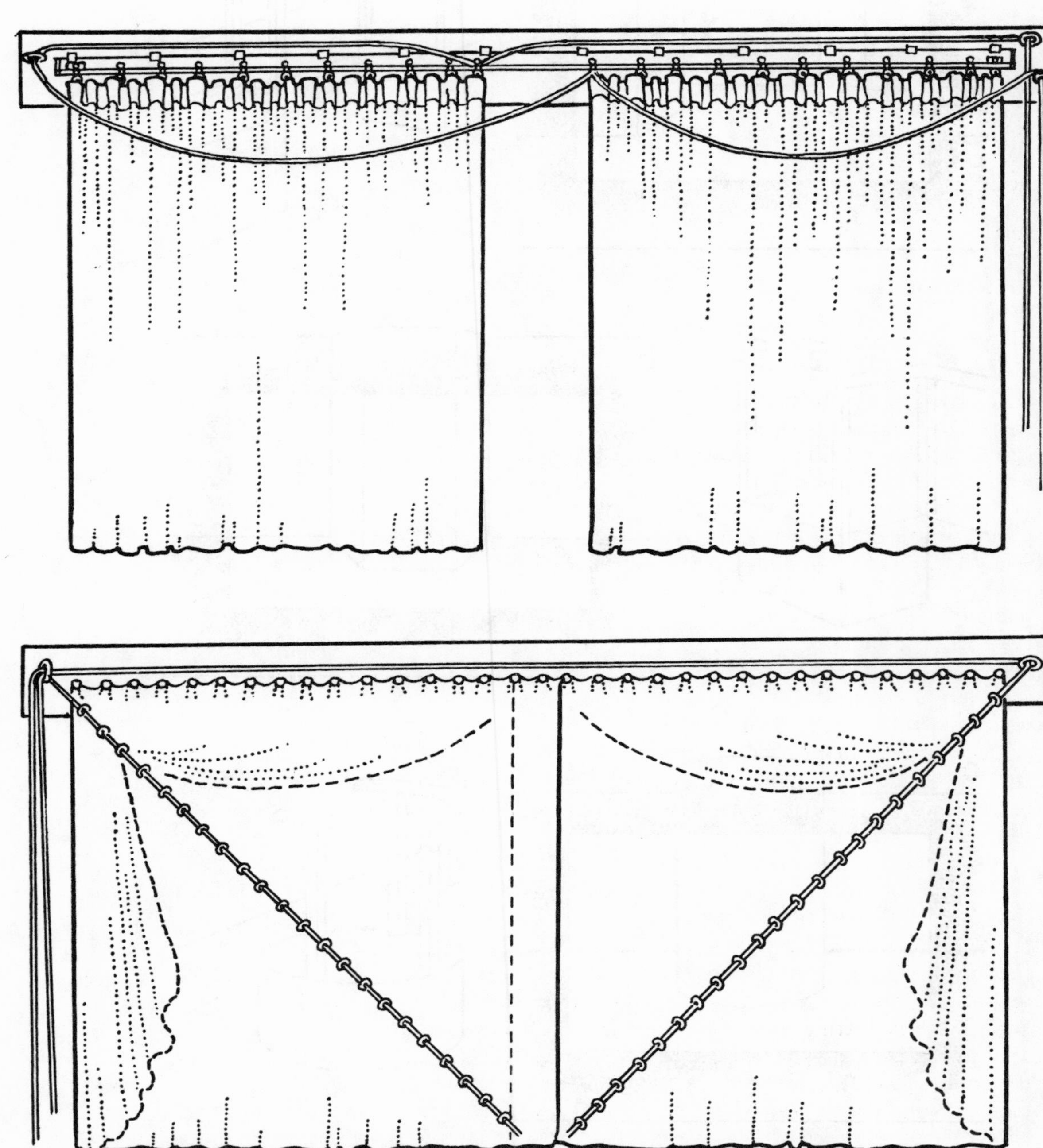

Figure 106 Draw curtains and drape curtains
(Drape curtains must be weighted at the inside lower corners)

Scenery

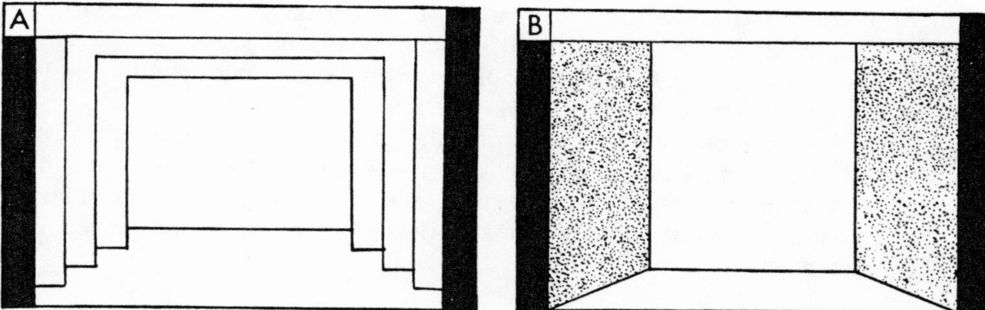

Figure 107

Scenery and properties for puppet productions must naturally be in scale with the puppets performing. Properties can be made of the same materials as the puppets themselves — cardboard, wood, *papier mâché* or any other modelling substance. Scenery can be made of thick card with wood framing where necessary, and backcloths from old sheets. Where large quantities of paint are needed, I find Reeve's Redimix Tempera paint excellent. With one-tenth part of P.V.A. adhesive added it is splash-proof and non-flaking.

The layout of scenery on the puppet stage must be very simple as all possible space is needed for the performers. The diagrams above show the two basic settings of theatre scenery and each has some application in puppetry.

A The wing setting is most conveniently used in the theatre for puppets worked from below. These wings may be cut into profiles, or left quite plain and they hang from a wooden rod which rests on the side walls of the booth. An example of this can be seen in the illustration of a partly assembled glove puppet theatre. Puppets are placed from below behind the wings, and then appear as if entering from the side.

In a theatre for marionettes a wing setting interferes with the strings of the puppets and it is safer to depend mainly on a wide backcloth which extends well beyond the limits of the proscenium opening. Backcloths may be kept on a wooden rod, and hung when in use on hooks fixed to the supports of the leaning rail. An example of this can be seen in the frontispiece illustration.

B The box setting can only be used in the marionette theatre if side rostra are available, and when entrance doorways are cut right to the top to allow the passage of the marionette strings. A type of box setting can be seen in the drawing of the Venetian marionette theatre (*figure 98*). The side walls of the box stop short of the backcloth leaving entrances on either side at the rear of the stage.

With either type of setting the stage floor of the marionette theatre should be covered with a floor cloth to hide carpentry joints, and to deaden the sound of the puppets' movements.

Lighting

To provide safe and effective lighting for a puppet theatre skilled advice is essential. I have included the addresses of stage lighting suppliers at the end of this book. Some of your equipment may be ordered from the their catalogues and some may be made for you locally by a professional electrician. What is really important is that you should know what you aim to achieve by your lighting; the simplest and most direct method of carrying it out will be the best.

In deciding on your aims it may be helpful to remember that the first object of lighting is to enable the audience to see on the stage what is important for them to see at the time and secondly that by changes in strength, contrast and colour, the mood and development of a production can be enhanced.

1 A HANGING BATTEN OF LIGHT BULBS PLACED IN REFLECTORS IMMEDIATELY ABOVE THE CURTAIN RAIL BEHIND THE PROSCENIUM OPENING

This can be made locally, and if 100-watt bulbs are used in reflector compartments of 200 mm (8 in.) long you can have a row of nine to ten bulbs above a 2 m (6 ft.) stage. In some theatres these bulbs are in groups of red, blue and green with a separate control and dimmer for each group. In theory the three colours used together make a white light although it never has the strength of a row of white bulbs. Also dimmers are expensive and it is cheaper to alter colour by using gelatine slides fitted into grooves in front of each bulb. These slides can be changed between scenes.

2 LAMPS EITHER HANGING OR PLACED ON STANDS AT EITHER SIDE OF THE STAGE

These lamps can be floodlamps to give a wide area of light or spotlamps to give a concentrated beam. Where there is little room on a puppet stage one of each will be quite sufficient. Coloured slides can be fitted in front of the floodlamp when needed. These lamps help to counteract the flat effect of lighting from the front only, and can be directed on to the backcloth to eliminate shadow.

3 SWITCHBOARD AND DIMMERS

A 'suitcase' switchboard with dimmers is made by some stage lighting companies and it is very useful for travelling productions. A switchboard has a separate control for each piece of lighting equipment, and ideally a separate dimmer for each circuit. The whole switchboard is fed from a main plug. Each dimmer has the appearance of a lever in a groove, and by raising or lowering the lever the lighting controlled by that circuit is increased or decreased in strength.

As you can see lighting rapidly becomes a complicated and expensive problem. Where the trouble and expense seem unjustified it is perhaps enough to concentrate on the first aim of lighting which is that the performance should be seen.

Production

So much work and ingenuity goes into the making of puppets, that there is sometimes a tendency to neglect the art of production for the skill of the craftsman. From the point of view of an eventual audience, production is of major importance, and planning for the complete performance should begin before the construction of the puppets. Early decisions in production must not only be the choice of play or items for performance, but the size and type of puppet to be used, materials for construction, and plans of colour and period for clothing and scenery. Unless these points are established early there is no chance of unity of style.

Any group of people working together must have a leader in their enterprise and however democratically he may be elected, he must be present to co-ordinate the parts of the whole. Naturally, different responsibilities will be handed to various people, lighting, scenery and costume for instance, but each is aware of the aim of combined work. The director Gordon Craig wrote of his preference for the puppet to the obstructive individuality of the live actor. But even puppets need manipulators, and in amateur shows particularly, personalities and temperament can cause difficulties. Presumably in professional productions the manipulators are more objective and each is paid to perform a defined role. In the end there must be a certain compromise between the personal interpretation of the director, and the individual suggestions of the performers. After all, from the moment it is successfully completed, a puppet develops a life of its own closely linked with its maker or manipulator.

When the puppets have been made, much of the effectiveness of a production rests on a stimulation of the audience by means of various types of contrast, visual and dramatic, in addition to the director's interpretation of the script. The following are some suggestions for visual contrast.

Grouping This is concerned with the visual relationship between puppets at periods of stillness on the stage. This relationship depends mainly on a sense of line and silhouette. The position of an arm or the fall of drapery can help in leading the eye from one puppet to another. In grouping there are contrasts between seated and standing figures, and straight and curved lines.

Floor pattern This is the plan of the position of puppets on a stage as seen from above, both when at rest or in movement. One puppet should never remain immediately behind another where the audience cannot see him, but a variety in the distance of the puppets from the front of the stage gives depth to the scene. Changes in floor pattern should be well defined. The direction of floor pattern can also lead the audience's attention to the centre of importance on the stage.

Tone value This is the intensity of darks and lights on the stage regardless of colour. Extra focus is given to a puppet dressed in pale colours against a dark background, or alternatively dark against pale. As a general rule I prefer that tone contrasts in a backcloth should be less strong than the tone contrasts in the clothing and complexion of the puppets themselves. This is true to nature where distance is muted, and near objects more sharply defined.

Colour There are two types of colour on the stage—atmospheric colour and local colour. Atmospheric colour has very little to do with contrasts, as it is the general colour shed on the whole stage by the lighting. It may of course be altered in intensity by dimming, or in tint by the use of gelatine slides in the floods at the side of the stage. Local colour is the colour belonging to the actual objects on the stage themselves. Here strong contrasts of warm and cool colours are stimulating.

Dramatic contrasts are likely to arise only in longer narrative productions.

Mood This is concerned with the emotional content of drama, and depends to some extent on the script. If you are successful in creating mood in the emotional response of the audience, it is best not to continue too long without change. At its highest level this can be seen in Shakespearean tragedy where periods of comedy lessen the tension.

Climax A gradual increase of pace and interest to a climax is more likely to hold the attention of your audience than an unvaried progression. A Nativity play has a natural climax when all the separate characters eventually meet in the stable scene at Bethlehem. The climax is no less effective for being expected.

Pause An unvaried speed of conversation and action is dull. A pause gives time for the audience to digest what has happened and to prepare for more. Be careful however. Too often in amateur productions the general pace is already too slow, and a pause only makes things worse.

Having spoken of contrasts, it should also be remembered that a certain unity or continuity is essential in good dramatic production. Classical Greek dramatists observed rules of continuity in time, place, and action. Spectacular and violent events did not take place on stage, but were merely described there. Now there is no reason why contemporary drama should necessarily follow these principles, but they are helpful in forming standards. Also in their reduction of technical difficulties they might have been formed specifically for puppets, particularly marionettes. One can avoid constant scene changing, and unconvincing attempts to reproduce violent action, with a clear conscience.

Rehearsing

Rehearsals are most successful when they progress in stages. This allows for adjustment and experiment, and exchange of ideas between the director who sees the production as a whole, and the manipulators who will have their own ideas about the puppets which they have made.

Before meeting together on the stage, each manipulator must practise on his own with his puppet to understand its movements. This is best done in front of a mirror to see the audience's view, and with a marionette the operator can stand on a chair and prop a mirror on the floor in front of him. Although from the beginning each puppet has been constructed to perform certain actions, free play helps to develop the character of the puppet in the performer's mind, and new effective movements may be discovered by accident. With practice the manipulator's thinking and feeling becomes transferred immediately to the puppet's movement.

First rehearsals on the stage are drawn from separate groups of performers. This may be done by practising one scene at a time, only those concerned in each scene being present. These is no need at this stage to combine speech and action. In these rehearsals the director can establish floor pattern and movement and arrange grouping for moments of rest. Difficulties of manipulation such as the passing of one performer behind another at the leaning bar can be practised or eliminated. If it is essential that one puppet be passed in front of another during the action, either the manipulators can exchange puppets or one manipulator can hold both while the other passes behind him on the bridge.

Other separate groups who may rehearse on their own are scene changers, musicians, property managers, lighting technicians and speakers if the speaking parts are performed separately from the manipulation.

Once movement and grouping have been established speaking and movement must be co-ordinated. It is very important here that the puppets should look at one another when speaking, that movement and speech are synchronised and that other puppets remain quite still so that the attention of the audience is not distracted. There may still be a certain amount of further suggestion and alteration in staging as the dramatic sequence becomes more familiar.

Later rehearsals become for the performers largely a matter of remembering and repeating actions and words which should now be established and unchanged. If music be included in a production it should be part of rehearsals from now on, so that the director can see the pace of the complete performance. It will almost certainly be necessary for him to increase the speed of certain sections, and to point out contrasts where they can be effective.

Lighting can be added last and is a final stimulant to the performers. By allowing rehearsals to progress in this way a performance grows as if alive, and does not become a stale repetition. The addition of new elements right up to the end of rehearsals keeps up the interest of the performers and guards against the danger of over-rehearsal.

Sources of suitable material for performance

It would be easy enough at this stage to say, 'Go to your local library and see what plays written for puppets they have to offer.' You can do this, and decide for yourself just what you think of the material available. Unfortunately, in the English and American puppet theatre, plays have been handed down by word of mouth and seldom in written form. Such writing for puppet performance that you will find will be mainly contemporary, and major writers are very seldom represented. Of the material used in the seventeenth and eighteenth centuries, the finest period in the history of the English puppet, there is hardly a trace. This means that you must improvise and adapt for yourself from fantasy, burlesque, biblical stories, folk legend, historical drama and any contemporary work that may be presented in terms of the puppet.

For those who are determined to find plays specifically written for marionettes, some research may bring to light translations of French and Japanese puppet plays.

Effective adaptations can be made from Jacobean drama which has a bravura nature very suitable to glove puppets. There is an added historical interest here for the audience as these plays are seldom performed. The legends and dramas of ancient Greece are also very suitable for puppet performance. The original presentation of Greek drama had a discipline not unlike that of the marionette. Principal actors spoke through masks and movements were highly stylised.

Children will always find a great fund of material in the fantasy of folklore and fairy tales, and are always very happy to improvise. It is not necessary however to have a narrative script for every type of performance. I give below a list of different types of production in order of complexity.

MOVEMENT ONLY WITH MUSIC OR SOUND EFFECTS

This may be effectively presented in dance movements or variety acts using such puppets as the circus marionettes described in this book. The manipulation, however, must be excellent and the action elaborate enough to be interesting. Attention can be reinforced by contrast and competition between the performers, music timed to repeated movement, and imaginative use of sound effects.

MOVEMENT WITH SPOKEN COMMENTARY

This is my own favourite type of performance and it is particularly suited to shadow puppets and to marionettes. The movement of the puppets is a mimed interpretation of the story which is narrated by one person at the same time. The whole production is simple, it may be accompanied by music, and there is none of the trouble of synchronising movement with actual speech. Folk ballads and narrative poetry of all countries and ages may be used.

MOVEMENT WITH WORDS SPOKEN BY THE MANIPULATORS

For this type of performance a specially written play or transcription with parts is necessary. The direct relation between speech and movement is most easily carried out by glove or rod puppets. Either type of puppet may have the addition of lip movement. Plays involving well-defined personalities and rapid action are particularly suitable here and the story of Punch and Judy is an excellent model. Always remember the ability of the glove puppet to hold, to lift and to throw.

MOVEMENT WITH PARTS SPOKEN SEPARATELY FROM MANIPULATION

Quite complicated performances can be carried out by this method, and if marionettes are to be used with spoken parts this is the best arrangement. Problems of space behind stage must be considered as the speakers should be able to see the puppets. Some people tape-record the speaking parts beforehand. I have never liked this method as the puppets must then be moved in time with the recorded sound, which makes no allowance for accidental delays in movement.

AUDIENCE PARTICIPATION IN A PERFORMANCE

This can be done with live performers 'planted' in the audience. I have done this with the Artisans Play from *A Midsummer's Night's Dream*. The parts of the artisans were taken by glove puppets and Theseus and Hippolyta sat among the audience who were very surprised when they joined in the conversation. In a variety act audience participation may be unrehearsed.

COMBINATION OF PUPPETS WITH LIVE PERFORMERS

In some recent European and American productions large rod puppets have been presented in performance with live actors. Here puppets are used not simply to entertain by their imitation of human movement, but in a setting of modern parable where they can personify abstract qualities in a way not always successful with live actors. The puppets themselves must be works of art made by adults for adults. This is a very promising development for the future.

Suppliers of Materials

ARTS AND CRAFTS SHOPS
Cardboard for children's theatre and shadow puppets.
Paper of all thicknesses for plans, tracing and shadow scenery.
Paste, glue and P.V.A. Adhesive for all purposes.
Indian ink for painting shadow puppets.
Craft or mat knives.
Modelling clay for *papier mâché*.
Plasticine for modelling heads and to aid in casting.
Watercolour paint for children's theatre.
Oil, acrylic and tempera paint for wooden and *papier mâché* heads and hands and for properties and scenery.
Cord for string joints.
Picture framer's pins for leather joints.
Paint brushes.
Spirit varnish for sealing *papier mâché* and for water proofing water-based paints.
Leather for leather joints.
DAS Modelling clay substitute.

PAINTERS' AND DECORATORS' SHOPS
Ceiling whiting powder for *papier mâché*.

HARDWARE SHOPS
Wire of all thicknesses for shadow puppet rods, framework for directly modelled marionettes, brackets for toy theatre figures and for tongue and groove joints.
Broom handles for marionette control bars.
Polystyrene sheeting for construction of puppet theatres.

CHEMIST'S SHOPS (DRUG STORES)
Paper handkerchiefs and paper towelling for *papier mâché*.
Plaster of Paris for plaster casts.
Vaseline for lining plaster moulds.
Roller bandaging or adhesive tape for building cores for direct modelling of puppet heads.

CARPENTERS' TOOL SHOPS
All carpenters' tools for cutting and carving wooden puppets.
Table vice and electric sander for holding and shaping wood.
Small screw-eyes for string attachments in wooden marionettes.
Wing nuts and bolts for wood-framed portable theatres.
Nails, screws and washers for marionette control bars.

SPORTS SHOPS
Nylon fishing twine for marionette stringing.
Table tennis balls for juggler puppets.

MODEL KIT SHOPS
Wooden dowelling of all thicknesses for marionette control bars, puppet limbs and centre rods of rod puppets.
Plywood for properties, theatres and animal neck joints.
Plastic wood for fitting special mechanisms inside puppet heads.
Wood glues.

TIMBER MERCHANTS (LUMBER YARDS)
Soft wood for wooden puppet bodies and limbs.
Lime or fruit wood for carved puppet's heads and hands.

WOOLWORTH
Cup hooks for marionette control bars, neck joints and waist joints.
Simple electric fittings and curtain fittings for puppet theatres.

USEFUL WASTE MATERIALS
Remnants of cloth, fur and lambswool for puppets' clothes and hair.
Umbrella ribs for hand rods of rod puppets.
Transparent candy wrappings for coloured insets for shadow puppets.
Used cotton sheets for shadow screens, backcloth scenery and cloth puppets.
Used blankets for glove puppet bodies and substance beneath clothing.

Newspaper for *papier mâché* pulp.
Used leather gloves for leather hinge joints.
Used tennis balls for cores of puppet heads.
Springs from used ball point pens and cigarette lighters for mechanism of special movements.

For the wholesale ordering of materials in England the catalogues of the following suppliers will be found helpful:
DRYAD
P.O. Box 38, Northgates, Leicester LE1 9BU
HOMECRAFT Supplies Ltd,
27 Trinity Road, London SW17 7SF
REEVES,
Lincoln Road, Enfield, Middlesex EN1 1SX
E.J. ARNOLD (Art and Craft),
Butterley Street, Leeds LS10 1AX
NOTTINGHAM HANDICRAFTS Ltd,
17 Ludlow Hill Road, Melton Road, West Bridgford, Nottingham NG2 6HD
MARGROS Ltd,
Monument House, Monument Way West, Woking, Surrey

For ordering materials through the mail in America the following suppliers will be useful:
AMERICAN HANDICRAFTS CO INC
20 West 14 Street, New York
ARTHUR BROWN AND BROTHERS INC,
2 West 24 Street, New York
AL FRIEDMAN,
25 West 45 Street, New York

For stage lighting equipment catalogues can be ordered from:
GREAT BRITAIN
STRAND ELECTRIC AND ENGINEERING CO LTD,
29 King Street, London WC2
W.J. FURSE AND CO LTD,
9 Carteret Street, London SW1

USA
TIMES SQUARE LIGHTING,
318 West 47 Street, New York

Bibliography

GENERAL
The Puppet Theatre Handbook
Marjorie Batchelder, Harpers, New York 1946 Herbert Jenkins, London
Puppets and Plays: A Creative Approach
Marjorie Batchelder, Harpers, New York 1956
The Puppet Theatre
Jan Bussel, Faber, London 1946
Hand Puppets and String Puppets
Waldo Lanchester, Dryad, Leicester 1948
Practical Puppetry
J. Mulholland, Arco Publications, New York 1962
Puppetry
Desmond MacNamara, Arco Publications, New York 1965

Puppetry Today
Helen Binyon, Studio-Vista, London 1966 Watson-Guptill, New York 1966
Introducing Puppetry
Peter Fraser, Batsford, London 1968 Watson-Guptill, New York 1968

MARIONETTES
Puppets Into Actors
Olive Blackham, Rockcliff, London 1948
The Marionette
George Merten, Thomas Nelson and Sons, 1957
Presenting Marionettes
Susan French, Reinhold, New York 1964

HISTORY
History of the English Puppet Threatre
George Speaight, George Harrap and Co, London 1955
Juvenile Drama: The History of the English Toy Theatre
George Speaight, MacDonald, London 1947
History of Java (Vol. 1, chapter 7)
Stamford Raffles, John Murray, London 1817
Punch and Judy
John P. Collier, illustrated by George Cruikshank, Prowett, London 1828

PRINCIPLES OF PUPPET PRODUCTION
The Art of the Puppet Theatre
Bill Baird, The Ridge Press Book & Macmillan, New York 1965
The Marionette
E. Gordon Craig, Florence 1918 Theatre Arts, New York 1925 (The Actor and the Uber-Marionette)
Folk Plays for Puppets you can Make
Tom H. Tichenor, Abingdon, New York 1959

SPECIALISED PUPPETRY
How to do Punch and Judy
Sidney de Hempsey, Max Andrews, London 1939
Specialised Puppetry
H.W. Whanslaw and Victor Hotchkiss, Wells Gardner Darton, Redhill, Surrey 1948
Trick Marionettes
Nicholas Nelson and J.J. Hayes, Puppetry Imprints, Birmingham, Michigan 1935
Animal Marionettes
Paul McPharlin, Puppetry Handbook 10, Puppetry Imprints, Birmingham Michigan 1936
Shadow Theatres and Shadow Films
Lotte Reiniger, Batsford, London 1970 Watson-Guptill, New York 1970
Punch and Judy
Peter Fraser, Batsford, London 1970 Van Nostrand Reinhold Co, New York 1970
Puppet Circus
Peter Fraser, Batsford, London 1971

Reprints of Texts for Early and Mid-Victorian Children's Theatre Plays, (also cut-out prints of actors and theatres), Pollocks Toy Theatres Ltd, London

Index

Numerals in bold type indicate principal references